CONTENTS

Preface
Algoma District
Brant County
Bruce County
Cochrane District
Dufferin County ⌐⌐
Durham Regional Municipality 28
Elgin County 36
Essex County 42
Frontenac County 52
Grey County 61
Haldimand-Norfolk Regional Municipality 69
Haliburton County 76
Halton Regional Municipality 78
Hamilton-Wentworth Regional Municipality 83
Hastings County 93
Huron County 100
Kenora District 108
Kent County 112
Lambton County 117
Lanark County 123
Leeds and Grenville United Counties 130
Lennox and Addington County 143
Manitoulin District 150
Middlesex County 153
Muskoka District 160
Niagara Regional Municipality 166
Nipissing District 185
Northumberland County 190
Ottawa-Carleton Regional Municipality 196
Oxford County 201
Parry Sound District 207
Peel Regional Municipality 211
Perth County 215
Peterborough County 218
Prescott and Russell United Counties 224
Prince Edward County 226

CONTENTS

Rainy River District	229
Renfrew District	232
Simcoe County	238
Stormont, Dundas and Glengarry United Counties	250
Sudbury District	261
Thunder Bay District	263
Timiskaming District	276
Toronto Regional Municipality	279
Victoria County	306
Waterloo Regional Municipality	311
Wellington County	316
York Regional Municipality	325
Index	333
Map of Southern Ontario	
Map of Northern Ontario	

Preface

On September 26, 1956 Premier Leslie Frost participated in the unveiling of a plaque to commemorate the founding of Port Carling. About a month later he unveiled two plaques on the grounds of the Legislature in Toronto: one to Queen's Park, the other to King's College. The erection of these three markers signalled the inauguration of the provincial historical plaquing program.

The objective of the plaquing program is to commemorate people, places, events, sites, and structures of importance to the history of Ontario. What constitutes historical significance? The exploration era, the fur trade, military events, and leading politicians figure prominently in the marking program, to be sure, but other themes also stand out: transportation systems, scientific discoveries, and educational institutions, as well as cultural, social, and economic forces.

Within these themes the range of subjects commemorated is astonishing – from mining rushes in northern Ontario to the invention of the sockethead screw ... from Harold Innis to Stephen Leacock ... from the typhus epidemic of 1847 to the discovery of insulin. Popular culture is also well represented: "Beautiful Joe" commemorates an internationally successful novel about a dog; "When You and I were Young, Maggie" celebrates a famous romantic ballad; "Jumbo" marks the spot where a beloved circus elephant died.

From 1956 to 1975 the plaquing program was the responsibility of the Archaeological and Historic Sites Board of Ontario, in conjunction with various provincial ministries. In 1975 that board was incorporated into the Ontario Heritage Foundation, which itself was restructured and significantly expanded.

PREFACE

As an agency of the Ministry of Culture and Communications the Ontario Heritage Foundation encourages public participation in heritage concerns. To this end it works to preserve and protect sites of archaeological and historical significance, heritage structures, and natural properties. The Foundation also initiates education projects, collects and holds in trust cultural artifacts and real estate for the citizens of Ontario, and it continues to erect historical plaques.

Since 1975 the plaquing system has been broadened to reflect changes in the conception and appreciation of Ontario's history. Markers are now erected in both French and English. As well, the Foundation is working to identify and commemorate subjects in theme areas which have received little attention to date, such as Franco-Ontarian and multicultural history and the active role played by native peoples in shaping the development of the province.

The history of Ontario, like its geography and its people, is vast and varied. Whenever you drive the highways, hike the countryside, or stroll through your own neighbourhood, this book can be a guide. There is much to discover.

ALGOMA DISTRICT

- BATCHAWANA BAY
  ### The Trans-Canada Highway
  Begun in 1949 as a co-operative effort by the provinces and the federal government, the Trans-Canada Highway was officially opened on September 3, 1962. (On a cairn near Chippewa Falls (at the approximate midpoint of the route), Highway 17, about 13 km east of Batchawana Bay)

- BRUCE MINES
  ### The Bruce Mines
  Developed from a claim filed in 1846, the Bruce Mines comprised Bruce, Wellington and Copper Bay mines. They were among the most productive copper mines on the continent until declining profits forced them to close in 1876. (On the grounds of the Bruce Mines Museum, 85 Taylor Street (near the former mine sites), Bruce Mines)

- DESBARATS
  ### "Ripple Rock"
  The prominent ripple marks on this large rockcut were the result of shoreline waves some two billion years ago. Subsequent compression of the earth's crust tilted the sandstone formation to its present 60° angle. (Near the rock outcropping, Highway 17, about 2.5 km west of Desbarats and 4 km east of Highway 548)

- ELLIOT LAKE
  ### The Elliot Lake Mining Camp
  One result of the extensive development of Canada's uranium-mining industry in the 1950s was the establishment of the community of Elliot Lake, which began as a mining camp and model town site. (At the junction of Highway 108 and Hillside Drive South, Elliot Lake)

- GOULAIS BAY
Frederic Baraga 1797-1868
A pioneer missionary in northwestern Ontario, Bishop Baraga was responsible for Jesuit missions from Bruce Mines to present-day Thunder Bay. The Ojibwa grammar and dictionary he produced are still in use today. (On the grounds of Our Lady of Sorrows Roman Catholic Church (a church built by Baraga), Goulais Bay)

- MONTREAL RIVER HARBOUR
Canada's First Uranium Discovery
The discovery in 1948 of uranium-bearing pitch-blende at Theano Point by Robert Campbell was, in all likelihood, the re-discovery of a find indistinctly recorded in the 1840s. (At Alona Bay Scenic Lookout, Theano Point, Highway 17, about 10 km south of Montreal River Harbour and some 100 km north of Sault Ste. Marie)

- POINTE AUX PINS
Superior's First Shipyard
Copper-mining ventures were the impetus behind the construction of the first decked vessels to sail Lake Superior – ships built by Louis Denis, Sieur de la Ronde, in 1735, and by English fur trader Alexander Henry in the 1770s. (At the St. Marys River beach, off Pointe Aux Pins Road (near the early launching site), Pointe Aux Pins – southwest of Sault Ste. Marie)

The Chicora incident dramatically pointed out the need for a canal on Canadian territory at Sault Ste. Marie. The canal (shown here under construction in the 1880s) was open for traffic in 1895. (Archives of Ontario ST 1220)

• SAULT STE MARIE

The American Raid on Sault Ste. Marie 1814

On July 20, 1814 an American force destroyed the strategic, but undefended, North West Company depot on the north shore of the St. Marys River. The Americans were unable to capture Fort Michilimackinac, however, and British forces retained control of the Sault. (Near the eastern end of the Canadian locks, off Huron Street, Sault Ste. Marie)

The Chicora Incident 1870

In 1870 the United States refused to permit the steamer *Chicora*, carrying Colonel Wolseley's Red River expedition, to pass through the locks at Sault Ste. Marie. This incident led to the construction of a Canadian canal, which was completed in 1895. (Near the Canadian locks, off Huron Street, Sault Ste. Marie)

The North West Company Post

Built between 1797 and 1800, the North West Company post at Sault Ste. Marie originally included a sawmill as well as a canal and lock. After it was destroyed by American raiders in 1814, the post was rebuilt and remained in use until 1865. (At the eastern end of the Canadian locks (near the site of the former post), off Huron Street, Sault Ste. Marie)

Colonel John Prince 1796-1870

A colourful, controversial figure, Prince commanded the Essex Militia during the Rebellion of 1837, represented Essex in the legislative assembly for several years, and in 1860 was appointed the first judge of the Algoma District. (Near the duck pond in Bellevue Park (the former Prince estate), off Queen Street East, Sault Ste. Marie)

Anna Jameson 1794-1860

Writer, traveller, and wife of Attorney-General

Robert Jameson, Anna Jameson visited Canada in 1836-37. Her sharp-eyed impressions and lively adventures (which included shooting the rapids at the Sault) were later published in *Winter Studies and Summer Rambles in Canada*. The book is still in print. (St. Marys River Drive, west of the Holiday Inn, Sault Ste. Marie)

Precious Blood Cathedral
Built in 1875 to replace a simple, wooden missionary post, the Church of the Sacred Heart became the cathedral for the newly created diocese of Sault Ste. Marie in 1905. In 1936 it was given its present name. (On the grounds of the cathedral, 778 Queen Street East, Sault Ste. Marie)

The intrepid sightseer Anna Jameson made this sketch of her fellow travellers on Georgian bay in 1837 amid surroundings she later described as "fairy Edens". (Archives of Ontario S 4297)

Shingwauk Hall

Shingwauk Hall, presently the main building of Algoma University College, was erected in 1935 to house a residential school which had been established in 1873 by the Anglican missionary, Reverend E.F. Wilson, and Chief Augustin Shingwauk to provide religious instruction and occupational training for Indian youth. (Outside Bishop Fauquier Chapel, Algoma University College, 1540 Queen Street East, Sault Ste. Marie)

• THESSALON

The Capture of the Tigress and Scorpion

In September 1814 two armed American schooners, *Tigress* and *Scorpion*, were captured by a British contingent from Fort Michilimackinac in the waters between Drummond and St. Joseph islands. (In Lakeside Park, Highway 17B and Stanley Street, Thessalon)

• WAWA

The Michipicoten Canoe Route

This important fur trade route from James Bay to Lake Superior was probably navigated during the French Regime. The first recorded use was in the 1770s when the Hudson's Bay Company began to establish posts along the route. (In the small park beside Highway 17, at the Michipicoten River crossing, Wawa)

BRANT COUNTY

- ## BRANTFORD
The Founding of Brantford
In the 1820s settlers began moving to the Indian lands at Brant's Ford on the Grand River and a community was soon established. Railway construction and agricultural prosperity assured Brantford's continued expansion. (At the city hall, 100 Wellington Square, Brantford)

Brant County Court House
Designed in the Greek Revival style by John Turner and William Sinon, the Brant County Court House was erected in 1852. Subsequent alterations and additions have not obscured the classical dignity of the building, attractively sited facing Victoria Square. (In front of the court house, 80 Wellington Square, Brantford)

Augustus Jones
One of the earliest land surveyors in the province, Jones (c.1763-1836) began his work in the Niagara peninsula in 1787. Subsequent surveys included the north shore of Lake Ontario and the Iroquois lands along the Grand River. In his later years Jones settled in Brant County. (On the grounds of the court house, 80 Wellington Square, Brantford)

The Honourable Arthur Sturgis Hardy 1837-1901
Elected to the Ontario legislature in 1873 as the Liberal member for South Brant, Hardy assumed the portfolios of attorney general and premier following the resignation of Sir Oliver Mowat in 1896, thus becoming Ontario's fourth prime minister. (On the grounds of the Brant County Museum, 57 Charlotte Street, Brantford)

Lawren Harris 1885-1970

A bold use of colour and a clean sense of line distinguish the canvases of this Brantford-born painter. With fellow members of the Group of Seven, Harris did much to encourage public awareness and appreciation of Canadian art. (Opposite the Brant County Museum, 57 Charlotte Street, Brantford)

The Royal Canadian College of Organists

One of the oldest national organizations of musicians in Canada, the college was established in 1909. It is primarily an examining body dedicated to maintaining high standards of excellence in organ playing, choral directing, and musical composition.

At the Ontario School for the Blind in Brantford manual skills such as hammock weaving (shown here in the early 1900s), chair caning, and piano tuning were an important part of the curriculum. (Archives of Ontario S 15528)

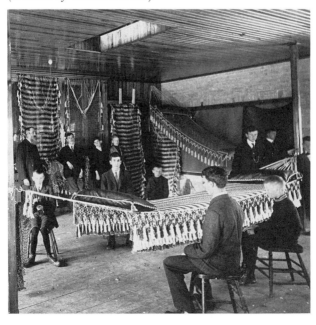

(At the site of the initial organizing meeting, now the Hill and Robinson Funeral Home, 30 Nelson Street, Brantford)

The Ontario School for the Blind

The first provincial school for blind children, this residential institution opened in 1872 with eleven pupils. By 1881 more than 200 students were receiving academic instruction combined with manual and vocational training. (Near "Heritage House", on the grounds of the school, now the W. Ross Macdonald School, St. Paul Avenue, Brantford)

St. Paul's 1785 H.M. Chapel of the Mohawks

Built with funds obtained by Joseph Brant from

On October 1, 1869 Prince Arthur, Duke of Connaught was given an official welcome at St. Paul's Chapel of the Mohawks by Simcoe Kerr, a grandson of Joseph Brant, and by the chiefs of the Six Nations. (Archives of Ontario S 895)

George III, this chapel served the Six Nations Indians who had moved to the Grand River following loss of their lands during the American Revolution. The first Protestant church in present-day Ontario, it was designated a Royal Chapel by Edward VII in 1904. (On the grounds of the chapel, Mohawk Street, Brantford)

"Mohawk Village"
Following the American Revolution some 450 Mohawks led by Joseph Brant settled on the Detroit path, a trail linking the Detroit and Niagara rivers. Of the resulting Indian community, only the chapel remains today. (At St. Paul's H.M. Chapel of the Mohawks, Mohawk Street, Brantford)

The Mohawk Institute 1831
A small day-school set up in 1826 by the New England Company led to the establishment in 1831 of the Mohawk Institute, a residential school offering academic and vocational training to children from the Six Nations Reserve. (In front of the former institute, now the Woodland Indian Cultural Educational Centre, 184 Mohawk Street, Brantford)

Canada's First Telephone Business Office 1877
The first telephone business office in Canada was set up in the home of the Reverend Thomas Henderson in 1877. Henderson, a longtime friend of the Bell family, retired from the Baptist ministry in order to administer the office. (At the Henderson House, part of the Bell Homestead complex, 94 Tutela Heights Road, Brantford)

The Reverend Peter Jones 1802-1856
The son of Augustus Jones and a Mississauga chief's daughter, Peter Jones (Kahkewaquonaby) was a highly regarded Methodist missionary serving communities along the Grand and Credit rivers. He

translated hymns and scriptures into the Ojibwa language, and made several successful fund-raising tours in the United States and Great Britain. (In front of his former home, 743 Colborne Street East, Brantford)

Sara Jeannette Duncan 1861-1922

Journalist and author, Sara Duncan travelled widely and earned international recognition for her writing. Of her many novels only *The Imperialist* is set in Canada. It depicts cultural and political life in a small Ontario town in the 1890s. (On the grounds of First Baptist Church, adjacent to her former home, 70 West Street, Brantford)

This portrait of the Reverend Peter Jones was painted by the English miniaturist Matilda Jones while Jones was on a fund-raising tour in Britain in 1832. (Archives of Ontario S 14230)

William Charles Good 1876-1967

A leading spokesman for agrarian and co-operative movements, Good helped to found the United Farmers of Ontario in 1914, and from 1921 to 1945 served as president of the Co-operative Union of Canada. (On the grounds of his former home, "Myrtleville House", now a public museum, 191 Balmoral Drive, Brantford)

• CAINSVILLE

The Honourable George Brown 1818-1880

An eminent publisher and statesman, Brown was one of the principal architects of Confederation, joining his arch adversary John A. Macdonald to form the "Great Coalition" government of 1864. (On the south side of Highway 2 at Highway 54 in Cainsville, across the river from his former estate)

The Grand River Mission

A chapel erected in 1829 at Salt Springs became the headquarters for Methodism along the Grand River and for a time served both Mississauga Indians and European settlers. (On the grounds of Salt Springs United Church (the present occupant of the former mission site), Salt Springs Road, about 5 km south of Cainsville)

• MOUNT PLEASANT

Dr. Augusta Stowe Gullen 1857-1943

A native of Mount Pleasant, Augusta Stowe Gullen was the first woman to graduate in medicine from a Canadian university. With her mother, Dr. Emily Stowe, she was a forceful leader in the struggle for female suffrage. (On the grounds of the public school on Mount Pleasant Road, Mount Pleasant)

• NEW CREDIT

The New Credit Indian Reserve and Mission

In 1827 Mississauga Indians from the former Credit

River Village relocated on land offered to them by the Six Nations Council. New Credit soon developed into a prosperous farming community. (At the New Credit Council House, Oneida Township First Line Road, west of Highway 6 and north of County Road 20, New Credit)

- OAKLAND
The Battle of Malcolm's Mills 1814
During the War of 1812 settlements in the southwestern portion of Upper Canada were subjected to a series of devastating raids by invading American troops in an attempt to destroy support lines to the British and Canadian forces at Niagara. Such was the fate of the small community of Malcolm's Mills

". . . to sing the stories of my own people" wrote the Mohawk poet and storyteller Pauline Johnson of her career as an author and dramatic reciter. *(Archives of Ontario S 17722)*

on November 6, 1814. (In Pioneer Cemetery, Oakland Street (County Road 4), Oakland)

- OHSWEKEN
Captain John Brant 1794-1832
The youngest son of Captain Joseph Brant, John Brant (Ahyouwaeghs) was a leader respected by his fellow Iroquois and British administrators alike. He was the first Indian appointed superintendent of the Six Nations, and the first Indian elected to the legislative assembly. (In front of the Six Nations Council House, in Council House Park, Ohsweken)

Tom Longboat 1886-1949
An Onondaga from the Grand River Reserve of the Six Nations Iroquois, Longboat won the Boston Marathon in 1907. The following year he represented Canada at the Olympic Games. (Near the Six Nations Council House, in Council House Park, Ohsweken)

- ONONDAGA
E. Pauline Johnson 1861-1913
The author of several volumes of poetry, Pauline Johnson (Tekahionwake) was also much acclaimed for her dramatic readings. She made many tours throughout North America and Great Britain. (At her birthplace, "Chiefswood", now a public museum operated by the Six Nations Band Council, on the Grand River Reserve, Highway 54, Onondaga)

- PARIS
"King" Capron 1796-1872
In 1829 Hiram Capron purchased land at the Forks of the Grand and had it divided into town lots. His leadership in developing the village of Paris earned him the nickname "King". (In front of his former home, 8 Homestead Road, Paris)

The Asa Wolverton House

Built in the 1850s by prosperous lumber dealer and contractor Asa Wolverton, this house, with its adjoining storage wing and carriage-house, exemplifies a style of parallel construction popular in New England and the Maritimes, but rarely seen in Ontario. (In front of the house, 52 Grand River Street South, Paris)

Paris Plains Church 1845

Built by members of the congregation with small stones painstakingly gathered from surrounding fields, this Wesleyan Methodist church is one of the few cobblestone buildings in Canada. (On the grounds of the church, Concession Road 3, east off Highway 24A, north of Paris)

• ST. GEORGE

The Honourable Harry C. Nixon 1891-1961

A supporter of the United Farmers of Ontario, Nixon was elected to the Ontario legislature in 1919. For forty-two years he served in a number of posts, including a brief stint as prime minister in 1943. (In front of the Nixon family farm, Highway 5, about 2 km east of St. George)

Adelaide Hunter Hoodless 1858-1910

An ardent proponent of improved domestic and educational standards for women living in rural areas, Adelaide Hoodless organized the first Women's Institute in Canada at Stoney Creek in 1897. (At her birthplace, now the Adelaide Hunter Hoodless Homestead, a museum operated by the Federated Women's Institutes of Canada, Blue Lake Road, off Highway 24, west of St. George)

• SCOTLAND

Duncombe's Uprising 1837

A strong supporter of the militant reform movement, Dr. Charles Duncombe rallied local "Patriot" troops at the community of Scotland in December 1837. He planned to join forces with William Lyon Mackenzie, but the latter's defeat at Montgomery's Tavern forced Duncombe to flee to the United States. (At the corner of Talbot and Simcoe Streets, Scotland)

BRUCE COUNTY

- ALLENFORD
"The Allenford Pow-wow" 1855
A dispute over the terms of the 1854 Saugeen Treaty was resolved at a "pow-wow" of Ojibwa and government representatives held at Allenford. The boundary line was redefined along a traditional Ojibwa pathway, increasing slightly the acreage of the Saugeen Reserve. (Opposite St. Andrew's Presbyterian Church, Highway 21 near Side Road 10, Allenford)

- CHESLEY
The Founding of Chesley
Following the erection of mills on the Saugeen River in the late 1850s, the community of Chesley began to develop. Prosperity was assured by the completion in 1881 of a branch line of the Grand Trunk Railway. (In Cenotaph Park, opposite the post office at 120 First Avenue, Chesley)

- FORMOSA
The Church of the Immaculate Conception
This monumental, Gothic-style church was built between 1875 and 1883 to serve a thriving Roman Catholic parish of predominantly German settlers. Designed by Joseph Connolly, the church contains fine decorative carving and stained glass executed by skilled craftsmen. (On the grounds of the church, County Road 12, Formosa)

- LION'S HEAD
Sergeant John Pearson, V.C. 1825-1892
Born in England, Pearson served in the Crimean War and was awarded the Victoria Cross for outstanding gallantry during the Indian Mutiny. He later came to Canada and settled on a farm near Lion's Head. (In Memorial Park, John and Main Streets, Lion's Head)

- PAISLEY

The Founding of Paisley

A proposed town site at the confluence of the Teeswater and Saugeen rivers offered an attractive prospect to settlers. Mills were in evidence a few years before the town plot was officially surveyed in 1855. (At the municipal building, 338 Goldie Street, Paisley)

Isabella Valancy Crawford

An important figure in Canadian literary history, Isabella Crawford (c.1846-1887) spent her youth in Paisley after immigrating with her family from Ireland. Her highly romantic stories and poetry vividly evoke the spirit of the Canadian landscape. (At Queen and Goldie Streets, Paisley)

David Brown Milne 1882-1953

An official war artist during the First World War, Milne, who was born near Paisley, devoted his life to painting. Working in both oils and watercolours, he developed a highly distinctive, impression-istic style. (In Willow Creek Park, Queen and Cambridge Streets, Paisley)

- PORT ELGIN

The Founding of Port Elgin

Benjamin Shantz's two mills on Mill Creek provided the nucleus of a community in the 1850s. Other small industries followed and by 1872, with the arrival of the railway, Port Elgin was a busy point of trade. (At Park Place, Park Place Road just off Goderich Street (Highway 21), Port Elgin)

The "Nodwell" Indian Village Site

Archaeological excavations at this Iroquoian village site have uncovered many stone tools, hunting weapons, and pottery vessels used by its fourteenth-century inhabitants. (At the former village site, High and Market Streets, Port Elgin)

- SOUTHAMPTON
The Saugeen Indian Treaty of 1854
The last extensive transfer of Indian lands in southern Ontario took place on October 13, 1854 when most of the Bruce peninsula was surrendered to the Crown by the Saugeen and Newash bands of Ojibwa. (At the Indian Mission Church (successor to the church in which the treaty was signed), Saugeen Reserve, Highway 21, near Southampton)

- TARA
The Founding of Tara
Following the survey of Arran Township in 1851 a small community was established on the banks of the Sauble River. Thirty years later Tara was a thriving commercial and manufacturing centre. (In Centennial Park, Yonge Street near the bridge, Tara)

Sir William H. Hearst 1864-1941
Born near Tara, Hearst was appointed minister of lands, forests and mines in 1911 by Sir James Whitney. He became Ontario's seventh prime minister upon the death of Whitney in 1914, and held that post until his defeat in 1919 by the United Farmers of Ontario. (In Memorial Park, Yonge Street, Tara)

"Cyclone" Taylor 1885-1979
A native of Tara, Frederick the "Whirlwind" Taylor was one of hockey's first superstars. He attracted widespread attention with his exceptional skating and scoring ability, and in 1960 was elected to the Hockey Hall of Fame. (In Memorial Park, Yonge Street, Tara)

- TEESWATER
The Founding of Teeswater
Mills erected on the Teeswater River in the 1850s

promoted the slow but steady growth of a community that by 1875 contained about 700 inhabitants. (At the town hall, 2 Clinton Street East, Teeswater)

• WALKERTON
The Founding of Walkerton
Joseph Walker and his son arrived here in 1850 and began to purchase land. They were responsible for the construction of two mills, an inn, and bridges over the Saugeen River. By the end of the decade a small community had been established. (In front of Walker's former home, 15 Mill Street, Walkerton)

• WIARTON
The Founding of Wiarton
Agricultural prosperity, good harbour facilities, and extensive sawmilling operations ensured the steady growth of Wiarton throughout the latter half of the nineteenth century. (At the town hall, 315 George Street, Wiarton)

COCHRANE DISTRICT

- ## COCHRANE
  ### The Founding of Cochrane
  In 1907 the site of "Little Lakes Camping Ground" was chosen as the junction of two railway lines then under construction, the Temiskaming and Northern Ontario Railway and the National Transcontinental. The town site was renamed in honour of the provincial minister of lands, forests and mines, Francis Cochrane. (On the grounds of the Ministry of Transportation building, 50 Third Avenue, Cochrane)

  ### The Forty-Ninth Parallel
  This line of latitude forms the southern boundary of Canada's western provinces, a subject of bitter dispute between the two neighbouring countries during the first half of the nineteenth century. (Highway 11 (at the point where the 49th crosses the thoroughfare), about 6 km south of Cochrane)

  ### Niven's Meridian
  Surveying a baseline from the CPR tracks due north to the Moose River was the task set Alexander Niven in 1896 by the Ontario government. Two years later an astronomically straight line had been laid down through some 480 kilometres of forests, lakes, swamps and muskeg. (Highway 11 (at the point where the meridian crosses the thoroughfare), about 3 km west of Cochrane)

- ## CONNAUGHT
  ### Frederick House
  In an attempt to counteract the fur-trading activities of its rival, the North West Company, the Hudson's Bay Company established Frederick House in 1785, naming it after the second son of George III. The post was abandoned in 1821. (Near

the site of the former post, Highway 610 at Barbers Bay, near Connaught – east of Timmins)

- ## IROQUOIS FALLS
  ### *The de Troyes Expedition 1686*
  Acting on orders from the governor of New France, the youthful Chevalier de Troyes led an expedition from Montreal in 1686 to attack the English forts on James Bay. Several posts were captured, but were ultimately regained by the English. (Fourth Avenue, Ansonville – within the town of Iroquois Falls)

An experimental farm established by the federal government at the site of Kapuskasing to test the agricultural potential of the Great Clay Belt region was converted to serve as a prisoner-of-war camp from 1914 to 1920. (Archives of Ontario Rev. L.L. Lawrence Collection S 13853)

- ## KAPUSKASING
  ### *The Founding of Kapuskasing*
  A land settlement scheme in this vicinity for veterans of the First World War proved unsuccessful and it was not until the establishment of pulp and paper milling operations in the 1920s that Kapuskasing – the site of a large prisoner-of-war camp between 1914 and 1920 – began to develop as an organized community. (In front of the CNR station, Government Road and McPherson Street, Kapuskasing)

- ## KENOGAMISSI LAKE
  ### *Kenogamissi Post*
  By establishing a post on Kenogamissi Lake in 1794

Strategically situated on Factory Island at the mouth of the Moose River, Moose Factory was the Hudson's Bay Company's main post in the fur-rich territory between James Bay and Lake Superior for 200 years. (Archives of Ontario S 2508)

the Hudson's Bay Company hoped to reduce fur-trading activity in the area by the North West Company. The post operated successfully until it was closed in 1822 following the merger of the two rival companies. (At the public boat access area on Kenogamissi Lake, off Highway 144, southwest of Timmins)

• MATHESON
The Great Fire of 1916
In July 1916 high winds united separate fires burning in the tinder-dry woods along the Temiskaming and Northern Ontario Railway into one vast conflagration that devastated 500,000 acres, destroyed numerous settlements including Matheson, and killed more than 200 people. (Highway 11, about 1 km southeast of Matheson)

• MOOSE FACTORY
Henry Hudson and the Search for the Northwest Passage
In 1610 Hudson navigated the treacherous Hudson Strait and explored the inland waters of Hudson Bay. After a bleak winter in James Bay the intrepid navigator was cast adrift in an open boat by his mutinous crew on their journey back to England. (In Centennial Park, Front Road and Riverside Drive, Moose Factory)

Moose Factory
Built in 1673, captured by the French under the Chevalier de Troyes in 1686, and returned to the British by the Treaty of Utrecht in 1713, Moose Fort served as the Hudson's Bay Company's principal centre on James Bay for two centuries. All inland exploration radiated from the fort. (In front of the Hudson's Bay Staff House, Front Road, Moose Factory)

• MOOSONEE
**Thomas James and the Search for the
Northwest Passage**
In 1631–32 James explored the waters of Hudson and
James bays. He successfully wintered his crew on
Charlton Island, but his vivid account of their
hardships discouraged further exploration for
almost a century. (On River Road, between First
and Cotter Streets, Moosonee)

• PORQUIS JUNCTION
Sergeant Aubrey Cosens, V.C. 1921-1945
Raised near Porquis Junction, Cosens worked briefly
for the railway before enlisting in 1940. The bravery
and personal courage he displayed during the fierce

*Emergency kitchen facilities were quickly set up by the hardy
survivors of the Porcupine Fire in July 1911. (Archives of Ontario
ACC 16959-235)*

fighting in Holland in 1945 earned him, posthumously, the Victoria Cross. (Highway 11, just south of the northern junction with Highway 67, near Porquis Junction)

• TIMMINS
The Porcupine Fire
In July 1911, at the height of the Porcupine gold rush, gale-force winds united scattered bush fires into a massive fire-storm that destroyed several towns and mining camps in the area and claimed many lives. (On the grounds of Northern College, Highway 101, Porcupine, within the city of Timmins)

The Porcupine Mining Area
In the fifty years following Benny Hollinger's 1909 discovery of gold quartz in the Porcupine area, more than 45,000 claims were staked. In 1958 the Porcupine camp produced more gold than any other mining region in the western hemisphere. (At the site of the first mining recorder's office in the Porcupine area, Highway 101 near First Street, Porcupine, within the city of Timmins)

DUFFERIN COUNTY

• HORNINGS MILLS
Horning's Mills
This early community dates from 1830 when Lewis
Horning built a sawmill and grist-mill on the Pine
River. The excellent water power in the region
attracted other pioneer industries, and by the close
of the century a flourishing village was in evidence.
(On the grounds of the Presbyterian Church, River
Road, just off Highway 24, Hornings Mills)

• ORANGEVILLE
Dufferin County Court House
Constructed in 1880-81 to house the judicial and
administrative offices of the newly created County
of Dufferin, the court house building remains today
largely unchanged in both appearance and function.
(At the court house, 51 Zina Street, Orangeville)

The Toronto, Grey and Bruce Railway
Running from Weston to Owen Sound by 1873, the
Toronto, Grey and Bruce line facilitated commerce
between the agricultural and forest resources of
Grey and Bruce counties and the Toronto markets.
The company was absorbed by the CPR in 1884.
(At the CPR station, Mill Street, Orangeville)

• SHELBURNE
The Founding of Shelburne
The business acumen of founder William Jelly and
the economic stimulation provided by the Toronto,
Grey and Bruce Railway assured the development
of Shelburne into a flourishing market town by the
late 1870s. (At the town hall, 302 Main Street East,
Shelburne)

DURHAM REGIONAL MUNICIPALITY

- AJAX

The Founding of Ajax

Named after the British cruiser *H.M.S. Ajax*, this community was founded as a result of the establishment in 1941 of a shell-filling plant. After the Second World War Ajax became a temporary campus of the University of Toronto for thousands of veterans. (At the municipal building, 65 Harwood Avenue South, Ajax)

The Founding of Pickering

A small milling centre was established early in the nineteenth century on the Danforth Road at Duffin's Creek. The construction of a railway line between Oshawa and Toronto in 1856 brought increased prosperity to the small community. (Near the intersection of Kingston Road and St. George Street in the former village of Pickering, now part of the town of Ajax)

- BEAVERTON

St. Andrew's Presbyterian Church 1840

Known affectionately as the "Old Stone Church", St. Andrew's was built from local fieldstone over a period of thirteen years by members of its predominantly Scottish congregation. Services were conducted in both English and Gaelic. (On the grounds of the church, Regional Road 15, east of Beaverton)

- BOWMANVILLE

Lieutenant-Colonel C.R. McCullough 1865-1947

With the intent of encouraging patriotism and national pride among Canadians, Bowmanville native Charles McCullough, along with four youthful companions, founded the Canadian Club movement. The first club was inaugurated in 1893.

(Beside the town hall, 40 Temperance Street, Bowmanville)

- ## CANNINGTON
Robert Holmes 1861-1930
Born and raised in Cannington, Holmes spent his professional life in Toronto as a teacher of design at Upper Canada College and the Ontario College of Art. He was an expert watercolourist and specialized in painting Canadian wildflowers. His works hang in the National Gallery and the Art Gallery of Ontario. (In MacLeod Park, Cannington)

- ## COURTICE
The Bible Christian Church
A small but fervent offshoot of Wesleyan Meth-

Members of the Bible Christian Church gathered for a conference in Bowmanville in June 1865. (Archives of Ontario S 152)

odism, the Bible Christian Church was established in Upper Canada in the 1830s. Membership grew slowly, due in part to the vast size of the preaching circuits. (On the grounds of Ebenezer United Church (formerly a Bible Christian chapel), Regional Road 34, south of Courtice)

• KIRBY
Sir Ambrose Thomas Stanton, M.D., K.C.M.G. 1875-1938
A distinguished authority in tropical medicine, Stanton was born in Clarke Township. He spent most of his professional life working for the British Colonial Office in the Far East. Among his many achievements was the discovery, made in 1907 with Henry Fraser, that beriberi was caused by a dietary deficiency. (On the grounds of the Clarke Museum and Archives, off Highway 35/115, Kirby)

• LEASKDALE
Lucy Maud Montgomery
The noted author of the ever-popular *Anne of Green Gables*, Lucy Maud Montgomery (1874-1942) lived in the Presbyterian manse in Leaskdale from 1911 to 1926, during which time she wrote eleven novels, including two of the *Anne* books and the *Emily* series. (At her former home, Concession Road 7, Leaskdale)

• NEWCASTLE
Joseph E. Atkinson 1865-1948
Born in Clarke Township, Atkinson began his distinguished publishing career as a teenager collecting outstanding debts for the *Port Hope Times*. In 1899 he became editor and manager of the *Toronto Evening Star*, which in time he built into Canada's largest daily newspaper. (On the grounds of the community hall, King and Mill Streets, Newcastle)

Bishop Charles Henry Brent 1862-1929

Born near Newcastle, Brent served as a missionary bishop in the Philippines from 1901 to 1917. He gained considerable respect as a pioneer leader in the international control of narcotics. (On the grounds of St. George's Anglican Church, Mill Street, Newcastle)

The Newcastle Fish Hatchery 1868

Successful experiments by Samuel Wilmot in the artificial breeding of Atlantic salmon led to the establishment of one of the earliest full-scale fish hatcheries in North America on the banks of Wilmot Creek. (At the site of the former hatchery, near the junction of Highways 2 and 115, Newcastle)

The Masseys at Newcastle

Massey-Ferguson, one of the world's largest manufacturers of farm machinery, started as a modest family business in 1848. Under three generations of enterprising Masseys the company prospered and in 1879 was relocated from Newcastle to larger premises in Toronto. (On the grounds of the J. Anderson Smith Company (a former Massey residence), Highway 2, Newcastle)

The Baldwin Homestead

After coming to Upper Canada from Ireland in 1799 Robert Baldwin, Sr. settled in Clarke Township. He is perhaps best known as the father of William Warren Baldwin and the grandfather of Robert Baldwin, Jr., the two leading proponents of responsible government in the province. (At the site of the former homestead, at the mouth of Wilmot Creek, Highway 2, just west of Newcastle)

• OSHAWA

The Honourable Gordon D. Conant 1885-1953

A native of Oshawa, Conant was elected to the

provincial legislature in 1937 and appointed
attorney-general by Mitchell Hepburn. Upon the
latter's resignation in 1942, Conant became the
twelfth prime minister of Ontario, serving until
May 1943. (Near the fountain in Lakeview Park,
Oshawa)

R.S. "Sam" McLaughlin, C.C. 1871-1972

A pioneer in the Canadian automotive industry,
McLaughlin began his career as an apprentice designer
in his father's Oshawa carriage works. In 1907 he
incorporated the McLaughlin Motor Car Company, the
first major automobile manufactory in the country. (At
his former estate, "Parkwood", now a public museum,
270 Simcoe Street North, Oshawa)

*"The most beautiful car I could dream of. . . ." Sam McLaughlin's
dream became a reality in 1907 as his company's McLaughlin-
Buick Model Fs began to appear on Canadian roads. (Archives
of Ontario ACC 16856-1659)*

- SCUGOG ISLAND
James Llewellyn Frise
A self-taught illustrator, Frise (1891-1948), who was born on Scugog Island, created the popular cartoon strip "Life's Little Comedies". The strip was subsequently called "Birdseye Center" and appeared in the *Star Weekly* for more than twenty-five years. (At Scugog Shores Historical Museum, Regional Road 7, Scugog Island)

- TYRONE
Robert McLaughlin 1836-1921
In 1867 McLaughlin, a self-taught craftsman of exceptional skill, built two cutters in the family driving-shed. Two years later he established the

Although Robert McLaughlin's Oshawa company did most of its business in carriages and buggies, Canadian winters demanded the production of high-quality sleighs and cutters as well. (Archives of Ontario S 8052)

McLaughlin Carriage Works, which in time became the largest carriage works in the British Empire. (At the McLaughlin family farm near Tyrone – north of Bowmanville on Regional Road 14)

• UXBRIDGE

The Founding of Uxbridge

Some twelve Quaker families from Pennsylvania settled in the area about 1806. Abundant water power attracted millers, assuring the growth of the community, and by mid-century many small industries were in evidence. (At the public library, 9 Toronto Street South, Uxbridge)

The meeting house at Uxbridge firmly symbolizes the Quaker philosophy of profound simplicity and restraint. The building was furnished with wooden benches, a table, and a lectern. (Archives of Ontario S 12412)

The Uxbridge Quaker Meeting House 1820

Built to replace an earlier log structure, this simple board-and-batten meeting house stands in the heart of the site of the Quaker community established in 1805-06 by twelve families from Pennsylvania. (At the meeting house, Concession Road 6, just west of Uxbridge)

- WHITBY

Ontario Ladies' College

In 1874 the Methodist Conference purchased Trafalgar Castle, an imposing three-storey mansion of somewhat eclectic design, and opened Ontario Ladies' College. For a time the music department was known as the Ontario Conservatory of Music. (In front of the school, now called Trafalgar Castle School, 401 Reynolds Street, Whitby)

ELGIN COUNTY

- AYLMER
The Founding of Aylmer
The water power provided by Catfish Creek encouraged the building of mills, and by 1851 several small industries were operating in Aylmer. Good road connections with ports on Lake Erie ensured the village's prosperity. (At the foot of the walkway, Balmoral Park, John Street, Aylmer)

- PORT BURWELL
Lieutenant-Colonel Mahlon Burwell 1783-1846
A close associate of Colonel Talbot, Burwell officially surveyed vast areas of southwestern Upper Canada, including the revised line of the Talbot Road. The founder of Port Burwell and a prominent office holder in the region, Burwell served some twenty years in the legislative assembly. (At the municipal office, Pitt and Erieus Streets, Port Burwell)

Trinity Anglican Church 1836
A fine example of early Gothic Revival architecture, Trinity Church was constructed on land provided by Mahlon Burwell. Until the arrival of the Reverend Thomas Read in 1843, the congregation was served by travelling missionaries. (On the grounds of the church, Pitt Street, Port Burwell)

- PORT STANLEY
Lieutenant-Colonel John Bostwick 1780-1849
A deputy-surveyor and close friend of Colonel Talbot, Bostwick laid out some of the earliest roads in the Talbot Settlement. Following the War of 1812 he began to develop his land holdings at the mouth of Kettle Creek, which in time became the village of Port Stanley. (On the grounds of Christ Church (where his grave is located), Colborne and Melissa Streets, Port Stanley)

• ST. THOMAS

Dr. Charles Duncombe 1791-1867

Like his friend and colleague John Rolph, with whom he opened the province's first medical school at St. Thomas, Duncombe was both a physician and a political reformer. His fervent support of William Lyon Mackenzie during the Rebellion of 1837 forced Duncombe to seek refuge in the United States after the defeat of Mackenzie at Montgomery's Tavern. (At the Elgin County Pioneer Museum, 32 Talbot Street, St. Thomas)

The Honourable Mitchell F. Hepburn 1896-1953

After he was named leader of the Ontario Liberal party, Hepburn resigned his seat in the federal

The aristocratic colonizer and landowner Colonel Thomas Talbot was, from many reports, an irascible and unsociable man who by his own admission found "... too near Neighbours a great nuisance". (Archives of Ontario S 1362)

parliament to become the prime minister of Ontario in 1934. He held this post until his abrupt resignation in 1942, when he retired to his farm near St. Thomas. (In Mitchell F. Hepburn Park, Talbot Street, St. Thomas)

Captain Daniel Rapelje 1774-1828
Following the War of 1812 Rapelje returned to his Kettle Creek property on the south side of the Talbot Road. He constructed a grist-mill and subdivided a portion of his land into town lots, marking in effect the beginning of present-day St. Thomas. (At the city hall, 545 Talbot Street, St. Thomas)

St. Thomas' Church 1824
One of the earliest churches in the Talbot Settlement, St. Thomas' was constructed on land donated by Captain Daniel Rapelje. The building is considered to be one of the finest remaining examples of Early English Gothic Revival architecture in the province. (On the grounds of the church, 55 Walnut Street, St. Thomas)

Colonel The Honourable Thomas Talbot 1771-1853
The founder of the Talbot Settlement, Colonel Talbot secured an initial grant of 5,000 acres on the shore of Lake Erie in 1803. By 1828 the aristocratic and somewhat eccentric colonizer had established some 30,000 settlers on his extensively developed holdings. (At the Elgin County Court House, Wellington Street, St. Thomas)

Alma College
This Methodist-sponsored ladies' college opened in 1881 with some fifty students, and within two years enrolment had more than tripled. The school offered matriculation for university entrance as well as courses in household science, commerce, and the

fine arts. (At the college, Moore and McIntyre Streets, St. Thomas)

Jumbo
A favourite with children at the London Zoo and with circus audiences throughout North America, Jumbo, a mammoth African elephant, was touring Ontario with Barnum and Bailey Circus in 1885 when he was struck by a train and killed. (Near the site of his death, Woodworth Avenue at the CNR crossing, opposite the Erie Iron Works, St. Thomas)

RCAF Technical Training School
The only facility of its kind in Ontario during the Second World War, this training school was established in 1939 by the RCAF to produce skilled ground crews for active wartime service. (On the grounds of the former school, now the St. Thomas Psychiatric Hospital, Highway 4, St. Thomas)

The Honourable John Rolph, M.D. 1793-1870
A prominent physician, lawyer and legislator, Rolph established, with Dr. Charles Duncombe, the province's first medical school at St. Thomas in 1824. He was elected to the legislature repeatedly and, a tenacious fighter for political reform, was instrumental in founding the Clear Grit party (At the entrance to the former Rolph homestead, Talbot Road, just west of St. Thomas)

The Talbot Road
This pioneer highway was first surveyed in 1804 by John Bostwick under the supervision of Colonel Thomas Talbot. When completed it ran from Waterford to Amherstburg and was an important factor in the successful settlement of the Lake Erie shoreline. (Talbot Road West, 5 km west of St. Thomas)

- SPARTA
The Sparta Settlement
The Quaker community known as the Sparta Settlement was founded on a 3,000-acre land grant
obtained by Jonathan Doan in 1815. Six years later
the prosperous farming centre included mills, a
tannery, and a meeting house and burying ground.
(At the Friends' Cemetery, Sparta-Union Road
(County Road 27), just west of Sparta)

- SPRINGFIELD
The Founding of Springfield
Although a village plot was surveyed in 1857,
growth was slow until the Canadian Southern
Railway built a station at Springfield in the 1870s.
The community subsequently became an important
shipping centre for the county's many agriculture-
based industries. (At the municipal building, 106
Main Street, Springfield)

- TYRCONNELL *see* WALLACETOWN

- VIENNA
The Edison Homestead
A loyalist from New Jersey, Samuel Edison settled
in Upper Canada in 1811 and served as a captain
in the militia during the War of 1812. He is best
known, however, as the grandfather of Thomas
Edison, the renowned inventor. (On the grounds of
the former homestead, near Otter Creek, Highway
19, southwest of Vienna)

- WALLACETOWN
St. Peter's Church 1827
Built by local craftsmen in simple Gothic Revival
style, St. Peter's stands in the midst of the original
Talbot Settlement. The adjacent cemetery contains
the graves of many early settlers, including that of
Colonel Talbot. (On the grounds of the church in

Tyrconnell, southeast of Wallacetown on County
Road 8, near John E. Pearce Provincial Park)

Ellis Wellwood Sifton, V.C. 1891-1917
During the Canadian attack on Vimy Ridge in 1917,
Wallacetown native Ellis Sifton destroyed, single-
handed, an enemy gun post and held the position
against counter-attack until the arrival of his com-
rades. For this act of courage he was awarded,
posthumously, the Victoria Cross. (At St. Peter's
Church in Tyrconnell, southeast of Wallacetown on
County Road 8, near John E. Pearce Provincial Park)

• AMHERSTBURG

Skirmishes at the Canard River

The skirmishes that took place between British and American troops on the Canard River in July 1812 were the first encounters of any consequence on the western front in the War of 1812. (Highway 18, at the bridge over the Canard River, about 8 km north of Amherstburg)

Christ Church 1819

One of the earliest Anglican churches in the province, Christ Church served the garrison at Fort Malden as well as a local civilian congregation

Christ Church in Amherstburg was built in part by the Royal Engineers on land donated by Colonel William Caldwell. Shortly after the time of this 1895 photograph a program of redecoration was begun. (Archives of Ontario S 11985)

which had been in existence prior to the War of 1812. (On the grounds of the church, 317 Ramsay Street, Amherstburg)

Lieutenant-Colonel William Caldwell

After serving with the British during the American Revolution, Caldwell (c.1750-1822) settled in Upper Canada near the mouth of the Detroit River close to present-day Amherstburg. His enormous influence with the Wyandots and Ottawas enabled him to acquire extensive holdings along Lake Erie, where he encouraged former loyalist soldiers to take up land. (On the grounds of Christ Church (where his grave is located), 317 Ramsay Street, Amherstburg)

The Great Sauk Trail

Part of an ancient network of Indian paths, the Great Sauk Trail extended from Rock Island, Illinois, through Michigan to Amherstburg. Until the late 1830s pro-British tribes made annual pilgrimages along the trail to Fort Malden where they participated in gift-giving ceremonies with officials of the British Indian Department. (In King's Navy Yard, Dalhousie Street, Amherstburg)

"Bellevue" 1816

One of the finest remaining examples of domestic Georgian architecture in the province, Bellevue was built by Robert Reynolds, the commissary to the garrison at Fort Malden. (Near the house, 525 Dalhousie Street South and Highway 18, at the southern approach to Amherstburg)

Colonel Matthew Elliott 1739-1814

After serving with the British forces during the American Revolution, Irish-born Elliott took up land in Upper Canada. He served in the Indian Department, and his house on Elliott's Point became the headquarters for Indian affairs on the western frontier. (Near the site of his former home, 849 Front Road South, at Elliott's Point, south of Amherstburg on Highway 18)

The Capture of the Anne 1838
While bombarding the Canadian shoreline near Fort Malden in support of a force of Canadian and American rebel sympathizers on Bois Blanc Island, the schooner *Anne* grounded on Elliott's Point and Canadian forces took her crew prisoner. (At the "Bob-Lo" Island parking lot, Elliott's Point, south of Amherstburg on Highway 18)

• BELLE RIVER
The Founding of Belle River
As a regional shipping point in the 1850s Belle River enjoyed a certain amount of prosperity. Throughout most of the nineteenth century milling remained the major industry in this small community founded by French settlers from the Detroit River area. (In Memorial Park, South Street, Belle River)

• BOIS BLANC ("BOB-LO") ISLAND
Bois Blanc Island Fortifications
With the establishment of Fort Malden in 1796, two blockhouses were built to serve as outposts, one at each end of Bois Blanc Island. In 1838 a third fort was built in the centre of the island. Only the latter building remains. (At the blockhouse, Bois Blanc Island. The island is accessible by ferry from Elliott's Point, just south of Amherstburg on Highway 18)

• KINGSVILLE
Jack Miner 1865-1944
The natural ponds that resulted from clay excavation on Jack Miner's property attracted flocks of migrating ducks and geese. In 1904 the avid naturalist established one of the earliest bird sanctuaries

in Canada. He thereafter devoted his life to the study and conservation of migrating waterfowl. (At the Jack Miner Bird Sanctuary, west of Division Road, north of Kingsville)

- ## LA SALLE
Fighting Island 1838
In February 1838 a large number of poorly armed "Patriots", intent on attacking Sandwich, were ferried to Fighting Island from Detroit. The insurgents were forced to retreat after a short, sharp encounter with British and Canadian militia. (In Youth Centre Park, Highway 18 and Laurier Street, La Salle – opposite Fighting Island)

For his life-long dedication to the conservation of migratory waterfowl Jack Miner was awarded the Order of the British Empire in 1943 by King George VI. (Archives of Ontario s 13345)

- LEAMINGTON
  ### The Founding of Leamington
  Wilkinson's Corners, the fledgling settlement that formed around Alexander Wilkinson's land holdings, was slow to develop until the late 1860s. By then regular stagecoach connections had been established between Windsor and the renamed community of Leamington, and dock facilities were under construction on Lake Erie. (At the Mersea Municipal Building, 38 Erie Street North, Leamington)

- MALDEN CENTRE
  ### The Philo Parsons Incident
  On September 19, 1864 during the second year of the American Civil War, Confederate sympathizers, who had boarded the *Philo Parsons* at Amherstburg and Sandwich, seized control of the American steamer in an unsuccessful attempt to free prisoners held in Sandusky Bay, Ohio. (In Holiday Beach Provincial Park, County Road 50, off Highway 18 south of Malden Centre)

- PELEE ISLAND
  ### The Battle of Pelee Island 1838
  On March 3, 1838 a combined force of infantry, militia and Indians crossed the ice and successfully routed some 300 American supporters of Mackenzie's rebellion from Pelee Island. (At Pelee Island Public School, North Shore and Victoria Roads, Scudder, Pelee Island)

- POINT PELEE NATIONAL PARK
  ### The Sinking of the Kent 1845
  On a clear night in August 1845 two steamships, the *Kent* and the *London*, sighted each other, signaled but failed to alter course, and collided. The *London* attempted to tow the badly damaged *Kent* to Point Pelee but the latter sank with an estimated loss of ten lives. (On the eastern beach, near the point, Point Pelee National Park, County Road 33)

- STONEY POINT
The Founding of Stoney Point
Coincident with increased travel along the Tecumseh Road in the 1830s, small communities of predominantly French-speaking settlers began to form along the south shore of Lake St. Clair. Stoney Point (Pointe aux Roches) flourished briefly in mid-century until depletion of local timber resources reduced the village's mainstay industry. (In front of the municipal building, 6690 Tecumseh Road, Stoney Point)

- TECUMSEH
The Founding of Tecumseh
Originally a way-station on the Tecumseh Road in the 1850s, this predominantly French-speaking community evolved into a significant shipping point for local grain and timber. (At the municipal offices, 917 Lesperance Road, Tecumseh)

- WINDSOR
James Baby 1763-1833
Born to a well-established mercantile family in British Detroit, James Baby was the first member of Upper Canada's French community to gain prominence in government circles. In 1792 he received lifetime appointments to the executive and legislative councils. (On the grounds of the Baby mansion, 221 Mill Street, Windsor)

The Battle of Windsor 1838
American supporters of Mackenzie's rebellion took possession of Windsor on December 4, 1838, but were soundly defeated by the local militia under Colonel John Prince. The Colonel's execution of four of the prisoners did more to increase tension between the two countries than to discourage hostilities. (On the grounds of the Hiram Walker Historical Museum, 254 Pitt Street West, Windsor)

District Court House and Gaol
The first court house to serve the Western District on this site was an abandoned blockhouse which had been moved from Chatham in 1797. The present building is the fourth court house and was constructed by Alexander Mackenzie in 1855 to serve the newly independent County of Essex. (At the former court house, now Mackenzie Hall, Brock and Sandwich Streets, Windsor)

St. John's Church
The present St. John's, built in 1871, incorporates sections of the brick church erected in 1818-19 to replace an earlier structure destroyed in the War of 1812. The Anglican congregation itself was formed shortly after the British withdrawal from Detroit in 1796 and the consequent establishment of the community of Sandwich. (On the grounds of the church, 3305 Sandwich Street, Windsor)

The Honourable Alexander Grant 1734-1813
One of Essex County's most prominent early citizens, Alexander Grant held a number of administrative positions in the Province of Quebec and, after 1791, in Upper Canada. As a naval officer he had full command, for a time, of all vessels on Lakes Erie, Huron and Michigan. (At St. John's Church (where his grave is located), 3305 Sandwich Street, Windsor)

Father Pierre Potier 1708-1781
A Jesuit missionary and scholar, Potier was appointed to the Huron mission at the mouth of the Detroit River in 1744. As the first pastor of Assumption Parish, he ministered to both the Hurons and the French-Canadian settlers in the Windsor area until his death. (At the Church of Our Lady of the Assumption, 350 Huron Church Road, Windsor)

The Huron Church Reserve

The large influx of loyalist settlers following the American Revolution led the Michilimackinac Hurons to disperse and cede much of their land to the Crown. A reserve of some 1,000 acres was retained, most of which was subsequently purchased in 1797-1800 for use as the town plot of Sandwich. (In McKee Marina Park (within the area of the former reserve), Sandwich and Chewett Streets, Windsor)

French Settlement of the South Shore

In 1749 French settlers from parishes along the St. Lawrence were encouraged to relocate along the Detroit River. Joined by discharged soldiers and civilians from Fort Pontchartrain (Detroit), they formed the first permanent agricultural settlement of European origin in what is now Ontario. (In Dieppe Gardens, at the foot of Ouellette Avenue (within the vicinity of the earliest-settled portion of the shore), Windsor)

The Great Western Railway

One of the province's first major railways, the Great Western opened its main line from Niagara Falls to Windsor in 1854. Other lines were added and the railway became an important connecting link to rail lines in Michigan and New York. In 1882 it merged with the Grand Trunk Railway. (Just east of Dieppe Gardens, at the foot of Ouellette Avenue, Windsor)

The Jesuit Mission to the Hurons

The Jesuit mission at Detroit was moved to Bois Blanc Island in 1742 but subsequently re-established in the vicinity of present-day Windsor, closer to the defences at Detroit. With the arrival of French settlers in the area, the Huron mission served both native and European residents, and in 1767 became the Parish of Assumption, the earliest Roman Catholic parish in present-day Ontario. (In Ambassador Park, Riverside Drive near the bridge (within the area of the former Huron Church Reserve), Windsor)

The Siege of Detroit 1763
Displeased with the rigid policies of the British administrators who had taken control of the area in 1760, the great Ottawa chief Pontiac raised a strong Indian confederacy and attacked several British posts. His unsuccessful attempt to capture Detroit effectively ended the uprising and by 1765 general peace had been re-established in the region. (In Reaume Park, Riverside Drive and Pillette Road, Windsor)

Colonel Arthur Rankin 1816-1893
Soldier, showman, businessman and politician, Rankin was one of the county's most colourful personalities. He commanded the Ninth Military District 1855-61 and served three brief terms as the federal member for Essex, although his quick temper and lack of tact ultimately cost him his political career. (In Ernest Atkinson Park, Riverside Drive, Windsor)

Hull's Landing 1812
In the first American invasion of the western frontier in the War of 1812 Brigadier-General William Hull crossed the Detroit River with some 2,000 troops on July 12. Several skirmishes were fought on the Canard River, but by mid-August Hull and his men had retired to Detroit. (On the grounds of the Hiram Walker Company, Riverside Drive East (the approximate site of the landing), Windsor)

The University of Windsor
This university had its origin in Assumption College, a primarily theological institution founded by

the Jesuits in 1857. The college grew steadily, expanding its curriculum and affiliating with numerous other colleges over the years. It was granted university status in 1953. (At Windsor Hall, 401 Sunset Avenue, Windsor)

FRONTENAC COUNTY

- BARRIEFIELD
St. Mark's Church 1843
A fine example of Gothic Revival architecture, St. Mark's was built with financial assistance from the British Admiralty and local settlers, many of whom were employed at the Navy Bay dockyards. (On the grounds of the church, Barriefield – east of Kingston on Highway 2)

- BEDFORD MILLS
Bedford Mills
Stimulated by the construction of the Rideau Canal and the consequent growth of small industries, the community of Bedford Mills, situated at Buttermilk Falls, flourished for a time until, by 1890, depletion of the area's forests had severely reduced the local timber trade. (On the grounds of St. Stephen's Anglican Church, just off County Road 10, Bedford Mills – about 48 km north of Kingston near the Frontenac-Leeds county line)

- HARTINGTON
The Holleford Crater
Discovered in 1955 by geologists studying aerial photographs of the Canadian Shield, the Holleford crater is generally believed to be the result of a giant meteorite hitting the earth some 500 million years ago. The crater is approximately 2.5 kilometres in diameter and 240 metres deep. (At the site of the crater, Babcock farm, Holleford Road, about 5 km northwest of Hartington – north of Kingston on Highway 38)

- KINGSTON
"Heathfield"
Professor James Williamson purchased Heathfield in 1865 and rented a large portion of the capacious

house to his brother-in-law, Sir John A. Macdonald. The latter used it during frequent visits to Kingston between 1865 and 1878. The house has been demolished. (Near the site of the former house, Princess Street (Highway 2), at the western approach to Kingston)

"Hillcroft" 1853
Built by a mayor of Kingston, Hillcroft later became the residence of Sir Alexander Campbell, a member of the legislative council and a life-long associate of Sir John A. Macdonald. (At the house, Hillcroft Drive, off Union Street, Kingston)

Louis de Buade, Comte de Frontenac et de Palluau 1622-1698
One of the most controversial and influential figures in Canadian history, Frontenac, as governor-general of New France, established a series of fortified fur-trading posts, including Fort Frontenac at the site of present-day Kingston. (In the northeast corner of Confederation Park, opposite the city hall, Ontario Street, Kingston)

The King's Royal Regiment of New York
Raised in 1775 under the command of Sir John Johnson, the "Royal Yorkers" was the largest loyalist corps in the Northern Department (the old Province of Quebec) during the American Revolution. When the regiment was disbanded many of the men settled in townships bordering the St. Lawrence River. (In Confederation Park, opposite the city hall, Ontario Street, Kingston)

The Reverend John Stuart 1740-1811
The first resident Anglican priest in Upper Canada, Stuart settled at Cataraqui (Kingston) in 1785. He ministered to native and loyalist settlers in the Bay of Quinte area and travelled as far west as the Grand

River. (On the grounds of St. George's Anglican Cathedral, King Street East at Johnson Street, Kingston)

Bishop Alexander Macdonell 1762-1840

Patriot, colonizer, and religious leader, Macdonell served as chaplain of the hard-fighting Glengarry Light Infantry during the War of 1812. In 1826 he became the first bishop of the newly established diocese of Kingston. (In front of his former residence, Bagot and Johnson Streets, Kingston)

Molly Brant

Highly respected by her fellow Mohawks as well as by governing officials, Molly Brant (Degonwadonti), who was born about 1736 allegedly in the Ohio Valley, played a leading role in persuading the Iroquois Confederacy to support Britain during the American Revolution. She fled to Canada in 1777, living first at Niagara and later on land granted to her at Cataraqui (Kingston), where she died in 1796. (On the grounds of St. Paul's Church, Queen and Montreal Streets, Kingston)

Sir Oliver Mowat 1820-1903

During a long life of public service, Kingston native Oliver Mowat held many responsible positions, ranging from postmaster-general of the Province of Canada to lieutenant-governor of Ontario. He succeeded Edward Blake as the province's third prime minister in 1872 and retained that post for almost twenty-four years. (On the grounds of the Frontenac County Court House, Court Street, Kingston)

Charles Sangster 1822-1893

A major poet of the pre-Confederation period, Sangster wrote much of his poetry while working as a journalist in Kingston. His writings reveal a deep, patriotic love for his country, its scenery and history. (At the Cricket Field (near his former home), Barrie Street near Court Street, Kingston)

The Typhus Epidemic 1847
The potato famine in Ireland in the 1840s brought a wave of immigration to North America, and with it a major outbreak of typhus. In Kingston, despite heroic ministrations by charitable and religious organizations, some 1,400 people died. (At St. Mary's Cemetery, Kirkpatrick and Kingscourt Streets, Kingston)

"Rockwood" 1842
Originally the country villa of prominent Kingston lawyer and politician John Cartwright, Rockwood was acquired by the government in 1856 and with another nearby building formed the nucleus of the present psychiatric hospital. (At the house, on the grounds of Kingston Psychiatric Hospital, off Front Road west of Portsmouth Avenue, Kingston)

Regiopolis College
Established by the energetic Bishop Alexander Macdonell, Regiopolis College opened in 1846 offering academic and theological training to Roman Catholic youth. The original building is now part of the Hôtel Dieu Hospital. (On the grounds of the hospital, 123 Sydenham Street, Kingston)

Government House 1832
Built by the fifth baron of Longueuil, Alwington House served as the vice-regal residence from 1841 to 1844 when Kingston was the capital of the Province of Canada. The building was demolished in 1959 following a fire. (At the site of the former building, King Street near the penitentiary, Kingston)

The Honourable René-Amable Boucher 1735-1812
The descendant of a noted French-Canadian family, Boucher was born at Cataraqui (Kingston) and

served in the French forces until the British capture of Canada. He settled at Boucherville, Quebec and was later a member of the legislative council of Lower Canada. (In James Roe Park, Clarence Street near King Street, Kingston)

René-Robert Cavelier de La Salle at Cataracoui
A major figure in the expansion of the French fur trade into the Lake Ontario region, La Salle (1643-1687) was placed in command of Fort Frontenac in 1673. Using the fort as a base, he undertook expeditions to the west and southwest in the interest of developing a vast fur-trading empire. (In the northeast corner of City Park, on the West Street side, Kingston)

Militia Garrison 1837-38
When regular forces were dispatched to Lower Canada in 1837-38, supporters of Mackenzie's rebellion congregated on Hickory Island, intending to attack the undefended city of Kingston. Their plan was thwarted by Richard Bonnycastle who quickly assembled a number of militia regiments to defend the city. (In the northeast corner of City Park, on the West Street side, Kingston)

The Kingston Observatory
The first optical astronomical observatory in Ontario was established in Kingston in 1855 after a solar eclipse aroused public interest in astronomical study. The observatory produced barometric readings, fixed meridians for surveying purposes, and provided a time service as well as recording astronomical observations. (At the site of the former observatory, City Park, Stuart and Barrie Streets, Kingston)

The Founding of Queen's University 1841
Chartered in 1841, Queen's University opened the

following year in rented premises with twelve students. Early financial difficulties were eventually overcome and in 1853 the institution purchased Summerhill, its first building on the present campus. (At the footpath leading from the campus entrance on University Avenue, Kingston)

"Summerhill" 1839
Originally the home of a prominent Kingston citizen, Summerhill was leased for a time as government offices. In 1853 it was purchased by the fledgling Queen's University and for several years was that institution's only building. (In front of the building, on the university campus, University Avenue, Kingston)

The Loyalist Landing at Cataraqui 1784
In 1783 official surveying of the countryside around Cataraqui was begun in anticipation of an influx of loyalist settlers following the end of the American Revolution. The next year some 300 loyalists led by Michael Grass established a temporary camp at Mississauga Point while awaiting township allotments. (At Mississauga Point, Kingston)

The Royal Military College of Canada
The first officer-training college in Canada, the Royal Military College opened in 1876 with eighteen cadets receiving military and academic instruction. In 1959 it was granted university status. (Near the entrance to the college grounds, Highway 2, Kingston)

Point Frederick
A naturally defensible site, Point Frederick was reserved as early as 1788 for construction of a battery. Various fortifications were built on the point over the next fifty years. The martello tower still in existence was one of four erected to fortify

Kingston during the Oregon Crisis in 1846. (At the tower, on the grounds of the Royal Military College of Canada, Highway 2, Kingston)

The Stone Frigate
This large stone building, completed in 1820, was designed to hold gear and rigging from British warships dismantled in compliance with the Rush-Bagot Agreement. It served as a barracks briefly in 1837-38, and by 1876 had been refitted to house the Royal Military College of Canada. (At the building, on the grounds of the military college, Highway 2, Kingston)

The Rush-Bagot Agreement
Under the terms of this 1817 arms-limitation agreement the United States and Great Britain agreed to dismantle most of their armed vessels on the Great Lakes and Lake Champlain, and to construct no new warships. The agreement, technically, is still in force. (In front of the Stone Frigate building, on the grounds of the Royal Military College of Canada, Highway 2, Kingston)

Fort Henry
Built between 1832 and 1836 as part of a large-scale system of defence to protect the naval dockyards at Kingston and the Rideau Canal, the present fortifications replaced an earlier fort dating from the War of 1812. Fort Henry is now a historical museum. (At the main gate to the fort, just east of Kingston at the junction of Highways 2 and 15)

In 1834 Thomas Burrowes sketched the locks at the northern entrance to the Rideau Canal at Ottawa (top) and at the southern entrance at Kingston Mills. (Archives of Ontario. Thomas Burrowes Sketch #13; Sketch #73)

Sir Richard Bonnycastle 1791-1847

A distinguished officer of the Royal Engineers, Bonnycastle played a prominent role in the construction of Fort Henry and the defence of Kingston during the Rebellion of 1837. He travelled widely in British Nor nfth America and wrote several books dealing with contemporary Canadian life as well as works of history. (In the parade square at Fort Henry, just east of Kingston at the junction of Highways 2 and 15)

The Rideau Canal 1826-1832

Constructed to provide a secure military route between Upper and Lower Canada, the Rideau Canal was a major engineering feat traversing more than 100 kilometres of unsettled country and requiring the construction of forty-seven locks. (At the lock-keeper's house at Kingston Mills, Kingston Mills Road between Montreal Road (County Road 11) and Highway 15, north of Highway 401)

• MOUNTAIN GROVE

The Frontenac Road

Surveyed in 1852-53, this route was opened as part of a network of colonization roads intended to encourage settlement in the southern region of the Precambrian Shield. Portions of the original road have been incorporated into the present county and township road systems. (In the municipal park, Mountain Grove (near a section of the former road) – about 3 km south of Highway 7)

- CHATSWORTH

The Toronto-Sydenham Road

Surveyed by Charles Rankin, this colonization road was constructed mainly between 1848 and 1851. It served to open up portions of Grey and Dufferin for settlement and provided a more direct route between Owen Sound and Toronto. Highway 10 now follows much of the old roadway. (Near the northern terminus of the route, in Memorial Park, Highway 6/10, Chatsworth)

Nellie L. McClung

The franchise, improved health-care and fairer property rights for women, temperance, and better conditions for factory workers were just some of the causes to which the indomitable Nellie McClung devoted her life. Born near Chatsworth in 1873, she moved to Manitoba when still a child and lived in western Canada until her death in 1951. (At the Chatsworth United Church, Highway 10 near Crawford Street, Chatsworth)

- CRAIGLEITH

The Craigleith Shale Oil Works 1859

The distillation of bituminous shales to obtain crude oil was an early attempt to meet the growing demand for oil. William Pollard's shale works at Craigleith, the only such enterprise in Ontario, operated for four years until the discovery of more accessible oil at Petrolia and Oil Springs rendered the cumbersome shale process obsolete. (Near the site of the former oil works, at the east end of Craigleith Provincial Park, Highway 26)

The Sinking of the Mary Ward 1872

Heroic action by a local rescue party in small fishing boats during a violent storm saved the lives of many of the people on board the *Mary Ward* after the steamship had grounded on a nearby reef. (Near the site of the wreck, Craigleith Provincial Park, Highway 26)

• DURHAM
The Founding of Durham
Situated on the old Garafraxa colonization road on the banks of the Saugeen River, the town of Durham was founded in the mid-1840s by a small band of hardy settlers led by Archibald Hunter. (On the grounds of the town hall, 137 Garafraxa Street North, Durham)

The Durham Road
Surveyed in 1848-49, the Durham Road was one of several colonization roads opened in Grey and Bruce counties to provide access to previously unsettled areas. It ran from the Grey County line in the east to present-day Kincardine on Lake Huron. (At the entrance to the Durham Conservation Area, Durham Road, 1.5 km east of Highway 6)

The Garafraxa Road
One of the earliest colonization roads in the province, the Garafraxa Road was begun at present-day Arthur in 1840 and completed to Sydenham (Owen Sound) eight years later. Today, Highway 6 follows, more or less, the route of this pioneer road. (In Rocky Saugeen Park, off Highway 6, about 9.5 km north of Durham)

• HANOVER
"Tommy Burns"
A natural athlete with exceptional muscle coordination, Noah Brusso was born near Hanover in 1881. He became a professional boxer under the ring name "Tommy Burns", and in 1906 became the first Canadian to win the heavyweight cham-

pionship of the world. He died in 1955. (At Seventh Avenue and Second Street, Hanover)

- ## HEATHCOTE
The Old Mail Road
Running northwesterly from Duntroon to Griersville, the Old Mail Road was in use possibly as early as 1835, although it was not established as a public highway until 1846. It was travelled regularly, despite its chronic state of disrepair, by settlers taking up land in the new townships. Only the eight-kilometre section between Heathcote and Griersville remains in use. (Beside the old road, overlooking the village of Heathcote, County Road 13)

- ## HOPEVILLE
Agnes Campbell MacPhail 1890-1954
The first woman elected to the Canadian parliament, Agnes MacPhail, who was born near Hopeville, championed many causes during her years in federal and provincial politics, particularly prison reform, improved health-care, and rural co-operative movements. (At the entrance to the park on Concession Road 12, Hopeville – approximately 12 km north of Highway 89 in Proton Township)

- ## LEITH
Tom Thomson 1877-1917
One of Canada's best-known painters, Thomson grew up in Leith and worked as a commercial artist before he started to paint in oils. His canvases of the forests of northern Ontario reveal a distinctive style of painting and were a strong influence on the Group of Seven. (In Leith Cemetery (where his grave is located), off County Road 20, Leith)

- ## MEAFORD
The Founding of Meaford
By the time the Northern Railway reached Col-

lingwood in 1855, Meaford was a good-sized settlement with several small industries and craftsmen. Steamboat connections with nearby ports stimulated the town's economic growth. (On the grounds of the town hall, 12 Nelson Street East, Meaford)

The Right Honourable Sir Lyman Poore Duff 1865-1955

A native of Meaford, Duff was one of Canada's most eminent jurists. An expert in constitutional law, particularly as applied to provincial and federal rights, he held many appointments during his career, including chief justice of Canada. (In Willow Park, Bayfield Street near Sykes Street, Meaford)

Frederick Stanley Haines 1879-1960

Painter, etcher, and printmaker, Meaford native Fred Haines usually took the Ontario landscape as his subject, which he rendered in a realistic, uncluttered style. As principal of the Ontario College of Art from 1933 to 1953 he introduced new and refreshing ideas into established teaching methods. (On the grounds of Georgian Bay Secondary School, 125 Eliza Street, Meaford)

Beautiful Joe

During a visit to Meaford in the 1890s Margaret Marshall Saunders heard from William Moore how he had rescued a much-abused dog from its cruel owner. She decided to tell the story, and the resulting novel, *Beautiful Joe*, was an immediate success. By 1939 it had been translated into ten languages. (In Beautiful Joe Park, Victoria Crescent, Meaford)

Shown here in the wilderness he loved to paint, Tom Thomson supplemented his income by working as a guide and fire ranger in Algonquin Park. (Archives of Ontario S 2793)

• OWEN SOUND

The Founding of Owen Sound

At the northern terminus of the Garafraxa Road on the shores of Owen Sound, a town plot was laid out in 1840 to encourage settlement in that part of the county. Originally called Sydenham, the settlement took the name of its adjacent body of water in 1857 when, with 2,000 residents, it was incorporated as the Town of Owen Sound. (On the grounds of the city hall, 808 Second Avenue East, Owen Sound)

The Newash Indian Village 1842

Following the signing of the Saugeen Treaty the government rebuilt a former Indian village adjacent to the settlement at Owen Sound for a band of Ojibwa led by Chief Newash. In 1857 the residents ceded their land and moved to the reserve at Cape Croker. (In front of First United Church (the site of the former Indian chapel), 4th Avenue West at 21st Street, Owen Sound)

The Toronto, Grey and Bruce Railway

Running from Weston to Owen Sound by 1873, the Toronto, Grey and Bruce line facilitated commerce between the agricultural and forest resources of Grey and Bruce counties and the Toronto markets. The company was absorbed by the CPR in 1884. (At the CPR station, 198 First Street, Owen Sound)

William Avery Bishop, V.C. 1894-1956

Courage and marksmanship made Owen Sound native Billy Bishop one of the leading fighter pilots of the First World War. He was officially credited with the destruction of seventy-two enemy aircraft and was awarded several military decorations for his actions. (In Queen's Park, First Avenue West and Eighth Street, Owen Sound)

Thomas William Holmes, V.C. 1898-1950

For his courageous initiative in the fighting at Passchendale in the First World War, Holmes was awarded the Victoria Cross. After the war he returned to his home town of Owen Sound, and later worked for the harbour commission in Toronto. (In Queen's Park, First Avenue West and Eighth Street, Owen Sound)

• THORNBURY

Charles Rankin 1797-1886

A provincial land surveyor, Rankin began surveying the Nottawasaga Bay area in 1833, settling west of present-day Thornbury. His surveys included several townships in Grey County and a number of colonization roads which were intended to attract settlers to newly opened territory. (In Bayview Park, Bay Street, Thornbury)

Major Charles Stuart 1783-1865

A moving force behind the establishment of the Anti-Slavery Society of Canada, Stuart, who settled near Thornbury in 1851, devoted much of his life to humanitarian causes, strongly influencing the anti-slavery movement in England and the United States, and speaking fervently in support of temperance. (In Bayview Park, Bay Street, Thornbury)

John Muir 1838-1914

On one of his many walking trips John Muir travelled much of the present-day Bruce Trail, and for a few years lived in the Meaford area. The dedicated American naturalist played a significant role in the development of the United States National Parks Service. (At Beaver Valley Lookout, off Highway 26 on the Fourth Line, south of Thornbury)

- WIARTON

  The Loss of the Jane Miller

  In November 1881 the heavily-laden freight and passenger vessel *Jane Miller* capsized in Georgian Bay en route to ports along the peninsula and Manitoulin Island. Driving snow and gale-force winds made rescue of the thirty passengers and crew members impossible and all lives were lost. (In Colpoy Range Conservation Area, Island View Road, about 11 km northeast of Wiarton)

HALDIMAND-NORFOLK REGIONAL MUNICIPALITY

- CAYUGA
The Haldimand Grant 1784
In recognition of their loyalty to the British during the American Revolution and in recompense for the loss of their land in New York State, the Six Nations Iroquois were granted a tract of land extending for six miles on either side of the Grand River from its source to the Lake Erie shore. (At the Haldimand County Court House, Highway 54 and Echo Street (within the area of the former land grant), Cayuga)

- CHEAPSIDE
Wilson Pugsley MacDonald 1880-1967
A lyric poet of fine sensitivity and musical expression, MacDonald, who was born in Cheapside, wrote many poems and ballads celebrating the beauty of the natural world and condemning urbanization. He published several anthologies during the 1920s when his popularity was at its peak. (At the Wilson MacDonald Memorial School Museum, Rainham Road near Cheapside Road, Cheapside)

- LONG POINT
The Long Point Portage
The portage across the isthmus joining Long Point to the mainland was an important link in the canoe route along the north shore of Lake Erie. First recorded in 1670 by two Sulpician missionaries, the portage was used steadily until 1833 when a storm broke a navigable passage through the neck of land. (Just inside the entrance to Long Point Provincial Park (in the vicinity of the former portage) – at the foot of Highway 59)

The Long Point Settlement
Surveyed in 1795, the Long Point settlement orig-

inally comprised five townships along the Lake Erie shore from west of Long Point to the Six Nations' land on the Grand River. The area, rich in timber and water power, was an important source of supplies during the War of 1812. (Within the area of the original settlement, on the grounds of the O.P.P. office, Highway 59, north of Long Point and south of Walsingham)

• PORT DOVER
The Founding of Port Dover
Efforts by the government in 1842 to build up the harbour facilities at the mouth of the Lynn River stimulated the development of the small community of Port Dover. Shipyards, tanneries, mills and a foundry soon formed the industrial core of this significant Lake Erie port. (At the Harbour Museum, 8 Harbour Street, Port Dover)

Campbell's Raid 1814
Lieutenant-Colonel John Campbell led some 800 American regulars and militia in a raid which destroyed the communities of Dover and Ryerse's Mills, and much of the surrounding countryside including farms and livestock. Official protests were lodged and the raid was subsequently condemned by a U.S. Army court of inquiry. (In Heritage Park, Main Street and Mill Road, Port Dover)

• PORT MAITLAND
The Grand River Naval Depot 1815
Plans were begun in 1815 for the construction of an elaborate naval depot at the mouth of the Grand River, but with the Rush-Bagot Agreement severely restricting armed vessels on the Great Lakes two years later, the depot never really flourished. Gradually it fell to ruin and was abandoned in 1834. (In Esplanade Park, Regional Road 11, Port Maitland)

• PORT ROWAN
The Heroine of Long Point
In November 1854 Abigail Becker single-handedly rescued eight sailors from the icy waters of Lake Erie when their schooner was wrecked in a fierce storm near Long Point. She received several awards, and a personal letter from Queen Victoria for her action which she steadfastly insisted was merely her "duty". (In the park next to the cenotaph, Port Rowan)

The John Backhouse Mill
Reputedly built in 1798, the Backhouse mill fortunately escaped destruction by American raiders during the War of 1812 and was operated by the Backhouse family for more than 150 years. In 1955 the mill was purchased by the Big Creek Region Conservation Authority and today is a restored heritage site open to visitors. (At the mill, in the Backus Conservation Area, off Regional Road 42, north of Port Rowan)

• PORT RYERSE
William Pope 1811-1902
After three exploratory trips in Upper Canada, the British-trained artist William Pope settled near Port Ryerse in 1859. His finely executed watercolours and detailed journals provide an excellent record of the natural history of this part of Ontario during the nineteenth century. (Adjacent to Norfolk Park, Front Road, just west of Port Ryerse)

Lieutenant-Colonel Samuel Ryerse 1752-1812
A loyalist refugee following the American Revolution, Ryerse settled on land granted to him at the mouth of Young's Creek in 1795. An astute businessman as well as a military and civil administrator, he erected a grist-mill around which the community of Port Ryerse subsequently developed. (On the

grounds of Port Ryerse Memorial Church (where his grave is located), King and William Streets, Port Ryerse)

• ST. WILLIAMS
The First Forestry Station 1908
On 100 acres of wind-eroded, sandy soil the first provincial forest nursery in Canada was established largely through the efforts of Edmund Zavitz. Today the station covers 4,000 acres and produces millions of seedlings annually for reforestation projects across Ontario. (At the station's head office, Highway 24 near Regional Road 16, north of St. Williams)

• SIMCOE
The Founding of Simcoe
The small hamlet surrounding Aaron Culver's mills was burned and looted by American troops during the War of 1812. Undaunted, Culver laid out a village plot a few years later, and the resulting community of Simcoe eventually became the seat of the Talbot District. (In Lynnwood Park, Norfolk Street North (Highway 24), Simcoe)

The "Alligator" Tug
A boon to the flagging lumber industry in the late nineteenth century, the amphibious Alligator scow was able to tow large log booms cheaply and efficiently from areas which previously had been inaccessible. A modified version of the original vessel produced by West & Peachey of Simcoe is still in use today. (In Lynnwood Park, Norfolk Street North at Alligator Lane, Simcoe)

Norfolk County Court House and Gaol
Diverse in both function and architectural style, the buildings comprising this court house complex were constructed variously between 1837 and 1893. None-

theless, the jail, registry offices and court house form a pleasing, cohesive unit unique among public buildings in the province. (On the grounds of the court house, Colborne Street, Simcoe)

• VITTORIA
The District Capital 1815-1825
For a ten-year period Tisdale's Mills was the judicial seat of the London District. After the court house and jail were completed about 1817, the community was renamed Vittoria in honour of an important British victory over Napoleon during the Peninsular Campaign. (On the grounds of Christ Church (which rests on the foundations of the former court house and jail), Township Road 46, Vittoria)

The Madawaska was one of many ''Alligator'' tugs plying the waters of Ontario's lakes and rivers. (Archives of Ontario. Charles Macnamara Collection S 4856)

The Reverend Adolphus Egerton Ryerson
1803-1882

Clergyman, journalist, and educator, Ryerson, who was born near Vittoria, was head of the department of education for thirty years. He established Ontario's present system of public education making free elementary and secondary schooling available to all children in the province. (On the grounds of Woodhouse United Church, Highway 24, near Vittoria)

• WATERFORD
The Founding of Waterford

Located in a rich agricultural and lumbering region, Waterford developed into a thriving market centre and by the middle of the nineteenth century contained many small industries and trade shops. (At the old town hall, 76 Main Street South, Waterford)

• YORK
The Nelles Settlement 1785

Captain Hendrick Nelles was one of several loyalists invited by the Six Nations Indians, on the advice of Joseph Brant, to settle on the Indian tract bordering the Grand River. Nelles and his family took up land in Seneca Township and by 1828 about thirty families were established on his land. (On the grounds of St. John's Church, Highway 54 and Nelles Road (within the area of the former settlement), York)

Retirement in 1876 did not curtail the energetic output of the Reverend Egerton Ryerson's ready pen. He published a two-volume work on the loyalists and a comprehensive study of Canadian Methodism; his autobiography appeared posthumously. (Archives of Ontario S 623)

HALIBURTON COUNTY

- ## DORSET
The Bobcaygeon Road
Designed to open the interior of Haliburton for permanent agricultural settlement, this colonization road was completed from Bobcaygeon to the Oxtongue River by 1863. The southern section of the road, between Bobcaygeon and Minden, is still in use. (In the Ministry of Transportation Park, Highway 35, Dorset)

- ## HALIBURTON
The Founding of Haliburton
Development of this part of Ontario began in the 1860s when the Canadian Land and Emigration Company of London, England purchased some 360,000 acres for settlement purposes. The area and the community which developed were named after company chairman Judge Thomas Haliburton, a politician and the author of the *Sam Slick* stories. (In Sam Slick Park, in front of Haliburton Highland Secondary School, Highway 121, Haliburton)

The Victoria Railway
Begun at Lindsay in 1874, the Victoria Railway reached Haliburton four years later. As a link with other rail lines at Lindsay it became an important carrier for timber and mining interests in the region. (At the railway station in Head Lake Park, York Street, Haliburton)

- ## MAPLE LAKE
B. Napier Simpson, Jr. 1925-1978
A highly respected restoration architect in Ontario, Simpson devoted his professional life to raising public awareness of the importance of heritage conservation. Black Creek Pioneer Village in Toronto, Century Village near Peterborough, and

the Historic Naval and Military Establishments at Penetanguishene are but three of the many projects in which Simpson was involved. (On the grounds of St. Peter's Anglican Church (where his grave is located), Maple Lake)

• MINDEN
Gull River and the Clergy House
The Gull River watershed was a traditional camping ground for Indian bands hunting in the Lake Simcoe region. The Clergy House, built about 1870 and reputedly the oldest remaining log structure in Haliburton, served as headquarters for itinerant Anglican missionaries at the turn of the century. (In front of the Clergy House, South Water Street, Minden)

St. Paul's Church
Construction of this simple frame church was begun in the late 1860s to accommodate the Minden congregation of the Reverend Frederick Burt who had been ministering throughout Haliburton since 1865. Except for the addition of a parish hall and tower in 1947, the church remains virtually unaltered. (On the grounds of the church, North Water Street, Minden)

HALTON REGIONAL MUNICIPALITY

• ACTON
The Founding of Acton
Although the community of Acton got its initial impetus from business generated by saw- and grist-mills, it was the tanning industry that became the town's mainstay. By the mid-1870s the Nelles tannery was producing up to 20,000 sides of leather annually. (In front of the public library, 17 River Street, Acton)

• BURLINGTON
La Salle at the Head of the Lake
In 1669 La Salle (1643-1687) set out from Montreal on the first of several voyages of exploration seeking, ultimately, a passage to the Far East. On this particular trip, accompanied by the Sulpician missionaries Dollier and Galinée, he reached Burlington Bay, travelled inland for a time, and then returned to Montreal. (In La Salle Park, North Shore Boulevard East, Burlington)

The Brant House
About 1800 the renowned Mohawk leader Joseph Brant (Thayendanegea) built a large house on Brant's Tract (later Wellington Square) for himself and his family. The house stood until 1932. In 1937-38 a replica was constructed incorporating the staircase and various other pieces of the original structure. (On the grounds of the house, now the Joseph Brant Museum, 1240 North Shore Boulevard East, Burlington)

The Founding of Burlington
The small milling community of Wellington Square grew slowly until the construction of the Great Western Railway in the 1850s. Transportation facilities stimulated economic development and in 1873

Wellington Square and neighbouring Port Nelson were incorporated as the village of Burlington. (On the grounds of the civic building, 426 Brant Street, Burlington)

The Reverend Thomas Greene at St. Luke's, Wellington Square

Constructed in 1834 on land originally patented by Joseph Brant, St. Luke's was served by itinerant Anglican missionaries for four years before the arrival of the Reverend Thomas Greene. The extensive landscaping carried out during Greene's tenure is still in evidence, but the church itself has been

This sketch of Captain Joseph Brant's house at Wellington Square was made in 1806, a year before Brant's death. The house and land remained in the family until 1875. (Archives of Ontario S 873)

altered and rebuilt beyond recognition. (On the grounds of the church, Lakeshore Road, Burlington)

World Championship Wheat

William Breckon received hearty congratulations from political figures as well as members of Canada's agricultural community when his Genesee grain won the World Wheat Championship at the Royal Agricultural Winter Fair in 1954. This was the first such win for an Ontario farmer. (On the grounds of W.E. Breckon School, 345 Tuck Drive, Burlington)

• CAMPBELLVILLE

Crawford Lake Indian Village Site

Sediment collected from Crawford Lake, a site of considerable scientific importance, has enabled archaeologists to make accurate datings of prehistoric sites and confirm the contributions made by native agricultural peoples to the region's changing environment. (At the entrance to the reconstructed Indian village, Crawford Lake Conservation Area, Regional Road 1 (Guelph Line), southeast of Campbellville)

• GEORGETOWN

John R. Barber and the Credit River Dynamo

The son of a prominent manufacturer and mill owner in the Credit valley, John Roaf Barber was reputedly the first in Canada to use hydro-electric power for industrial purposes when, in 1888, he installed a dynamo in the Credit River to augment the power of his paper mill. (At the former paper mill, 99 River Drive, Georgetown)

• MILTON

The P.L. Robertson Manufacturing Company

The first firm in the world to produce socket-head screws, the P.L. Robertson Company was estab-

lished in 1907. Socket-head screws found a ready
market among boat builders, electricians, furniture
companies, and the manufacturers of the Model T
Ford. (On the grounds of the Robertson Whitehouse
Company (successor to the P.L. Robertson Company),
97 Bronte Street, Milton)

• OAKVILLE
Colonel William Chisholm 1788-1842
After serving with the militia during the War of
1812, Chisholm settled in Nelson Township. On land
purchased from the Crown he established mills and
laid out a town plot which in time became the town
of Oakville. (In Lakeside Park, Navy and Front
Streets, Oakville)

Frederick Arthur Verner 1836-1928
Born in the village of Sheridan, Verner studied
painting in England, and in mid-life took up residence
there. Like Paul Kane, his elder contemporary
and idol, Verner travelled frequently in the
Canadian North West sketching the plains Indians
and the great buffalo herds. (At the entrance to
Sheridan College, off Trafalgar Road, Oakville)

The Winner of the First Queen's Plate
The Queen's Plate originally consisted of three one-
mile heats and was restricted to horses bred in
Canada West that had not won a race. At the first
running in 1860 Don Juan, a five-year-old bay,
earned the 50-guinea winner's purse for his owner,
James White of Bronte. (At the farm where Don
Juan was bred, opposite 1242 Bronte Road, on the
east side of Highway 25, just north of the Queen
Elizabeth Way, southwest of Oakville)

• ROCKWOOD
Toronto's Radial Railways
Electric railway lines radiating from Toronto began

operating in 1889. Sutton, West Hill, Port Credit, Woodbridge, and Guelph were connected to points on the outer edges of Toronto, but the lack of a central terminus weakened the transportation scheme and by 1930 most of the radials were out of service. (Near a relaid section of the Guelph electric railway line, at the Halton County Radial Railway Museum, Regional Road 1 (Guelph Line), about 13.5 km north of Exit 312 off Highway 401 – just south of Rockwood)

HAMILTON-WENTWORTH REGIONAL MUNICIPALITY

- ANCASTER
"The Bloody Assize" 1814
A special court was held at Ancaster toward the end of the 1812-14 war to deal with increasing instances of disloyalty among disaffected settlers. Of the fifteen men convicted of high treason, eight were executed. The trials became known as the Bloody Assize. (On the grounds of the Wentworth County Board of Education Memorial Building, 357 Wilson Street East, Ancaster)

The Founding of Ancaster
The community of Ancaster began to develop around the Rousseaux mills in the 1790s, and remained an important regional centre for small-scale, water-powered industries throughout the next century. (On the grounds of the township hall, 310 Wilson Street East, Ancaster)

- DUNDAS
Dundas Mills
The name of Dundas Mills was given to the saw- and grist-mills built on Spencer Creek in the 1790s and early 1800s. Other industrial and commercial structures were subsequently erected, and the resulting community became part of the town of Dundas in 1847. (On the grounds of the House of Providence, Governor's Road and Ogilvie Street (near the site of the former mills), Dundas)

The Founding of Dundas
The strategic location of Dundas at the head of navigation on Lake Ontario attracted many settlers and small businessmen to the area. Completion of the Desjardins Canal in 1837 stimulated further growth and by mid-century Dundas was a thriving

town. (In Dundas Riding Park, Cross and Alma Streets, Dundas)

The Desjardins Canal

The Desjardins Canal opened in 1837. By linking the community of Dundas to the shipping trade on Lake Ontario it contributed to the economic development of the region. With the completion of the Great Western Railway in 1853, however, the canal began to fall into disuse. (In Desjardins Centennial Park, East Street, Dundas)

Dundas Town Hall

Completed in 1849, this town hall is one of very few municipal buildings in the province surviving

---

A pleasure trip to Burlington Bay with music provided by the Ancaster Band officially opened the Desjardins Canal on August 16, 1837. (Archives of Ontario S 11915)

from the pre-1850 period. It was designed by a local contractor in the massive, unornamented Roman Classic style. Extensive interior renovations have been undertaken in the present century, but the handsome exterior remains largely unaltered. (On the grounds of the town hall, 60 Main Street, Dundas)

• GREENSVILLE
Upper Canada's First Paper Mill 1826
Two economic factors encouraged James Crooks to construct a paper mill on Spencer Creek: the growing domestic market and the high tariff imposed on imported paper. The mill operated under various owners until it was destroyed by fire in 1875. (Beside the creek, slightly upstream from the site of the former mill, Crooks Hollow Conservation Area, Crooks Hollow Road, just west of Greensville)

• HAMILTON
"The Burlington Races" 1813
On September 28, 1813 a heavily-armed American fleet attacked the British squadron off York (Toronto). After a running battle the British managed, with adroit seamanship, to bring their ships over the sand-bar to the safety of Burlington Bay. (In Harvey Park, York Boulevard near Dundurn Street, Hamilton)

Sir John Harvey 1778-1852
On the evening of June 5, 1813 Harvey led a contingent of 700 men in a surprise attack on an invading force of 3,000 American troops camped at Stoney Creek. The successful rout is generally considered to be the turning point in the 1812-14 war. (In Harvey Park (the site from which Harvey set out), York Boulevard near Dundurn Street, Hamilton)

George Hamilton 1787-1836

A shrewd businessman and prosperous landowner, Hamilton laid out a village plot at the Head of the Lake in 1815 which in time became the city that bears his name. When the settlement was designated the administrative centre of the Gore District, Hamilton donated land for the requisite court house. (In front of the court house, 50 Main Street East, Hamilton)

William Blair Bruce 1859-1906

A painter of remarkable versatility, Bruce was born and educated in Hamilton. From 1881 until his death he lived in Europe, exhibiting his work to critical acclaim in major salons throughout the Continent. (In Bruce Park, Brucedale and East Sixth Streets, Hamilton)

Horatio George Summers 1865-1941

For twelve successful seasons George Summers operated a pioneer summer theatre in Hamilton and managed its associated winter touring company. Both specialized in ever-popular melodramas and works of homespun humour. (Mountain Park Avenue and Upper Wentworth Street (the site of the former theatre complex), Mountain Brow Park, Hamilton)

Lieutenant Charles Davidson Dunbar, D.C.M. 1870-1939

An internationally renowned military piper, Dunbar saw action in the Boer War and the First World War, and was highly honoured for both his gallantry and his musicianship. (At the entrance to the armoury (where his regiment, the 91st Highlanders, was housed), James Street North, Hamilton)

William Sherring 1877-1964

One of Canada's finest marathon runners,

Hamilton-born Billy Sherring won an Olympic gold medal in Athens in 1906 by defeating fifty-five other runners on a gruelling 26-mile course. The Around-the-Bay Marathon, one of the oldest long-distance races in North America, has been renamed in his honour. (In the main foyer of the city hall, 71 Main Street West, Hamilton)

Bobby Kerr 1882-1963
A life-long resident of Hamilton, Bobby Kerr first gained prominence as a sprinter in the local Coronation Games in 1902. For more than a decade he dominated short-distance races in Canada, and in 1908 won a gold medal at the Olympics held in London. (In Bobby Kerr Park, Reno Avenue, Hamilton)

"Claremont Lodge" and "Auchmar" 1855
This attractive house and gate lodge were built for the Honourable Isaac Buchanan, a prosperous merchant and politician. The buildings are characteristic examples of the Cottage Gothic style of architecture. (On the grounds of the former gate lodge, 71 Claremont Drive, Hamilton)

Dundurn Castle 1832
Built by Allan Napier MacNab, a prominent military and political figure in Upper Canada, Dundurn Castle was named after the MacNab family's ancestral seat in Scotland. Restored and furnished to depict the lifestyle of its original inhabitants, Dundurn is now a public museum open to visitors year round. (On the grounds of the castle, Dundurn Park, Dundurn Street and York Boulevard, Hamilton)

"Whitehern"
Purchased by Dr. Calvin McQuesten in 1852, this handsome Victorian mansion remained the home of the McQuestens for more than a century. Restored

and furnished to reflect the lifestyle of this prosperous Hamilton family, Whitehern is operated as a historic house museum and is open to the public year round. (On the grounds of the house, 41 Jackson Street West, Hamilton)

Central Presbyterian Church
Erected in 1907-08 to replace an earlier building destroyed by fire, Central Presbyterian is reputedly the only church designed by architect John M. Lyle, one of the leading exponents in Canada of the Beaux-Arts style of design. (On the grounds of the church, 165 Charlton Avenue West, Hamilton)

Christ's Church Cathedral
An important ecclesiastical centre for the Niagara peninsula, Christ's Church was begun in 1835 and erected in stages as the congregation grew in size and prominence. Despite various alterations and renovations over the years, the building has retained its handsome nineteenth-century character. (On the grounds of the cathedral, 252 James Street North, Hamilton)

St. Mary's Pro-Cathedral
Built in 1859-60, St. Mary's is distinguished by a richly decorated interior that, despite alterations, retains much of its pre-Confederation character. (On the grounds of the pro-cathedral, Park and Sheaffe Streets, Hamilton)

St. Paul's Church
Completed in 1857, this Presbyterian church was designed by the prominent Ontario architect William Thomas. The interior carving, the tinted windows, and the massive stone spire distinguish St. Paul's as a fine example of Canadian Victorian church architecture. (On the grounds of the church, 70 James Street South, Hamilton)

Hamilton Central Public School

Opened in 1853 with a capacity to accommodate 1,000 students, this was the largest graded school in Upper Canada and one of the first to incorporate the educational reforms of Dr. Egerton Ryerson, the province's chief superintendent of schools. (In front of the school, 75 Hunter Street West, Hamilton)

McMaster University 1887

Established with funds bequeathed by the Honourable William McMaster, this university was incorporated in 1887, and opened in Toronto three years later. Inadequate facilities and the gift of land in Hamilton prompted the institution's relocation in 1930. (On the grounds of Gilmore Hall, McMaster University, 1280 Main Street West, Hamilton)

The Co-operative Union of Canada 1909

As a result of a meeting held in Hamilton in 1909, a national co-operative association was founded to co-ordinate the growing number of local co-operatives and unions being formed throughout the country. (Near the site of the organizing meeting, Gore Park, King and James Streets, Hamilton)

The Burlington Glass Works 1874

The Burlington Glass Works was one of the most significant producers of glassware in Canada. Various production and decorating techniques were used in the creation of lamps, containers and tableware – items highly prized by today's collectors and museums. (At the site of the former works, Burlington and MacNab Streets, Hamilton)

The Niagara Escarpment

A land formation of intriguing geological complexity, the escarpment stretches from central New York State to Manitoulin Island. It has influenced significantly the pattern of settlement and the development of communications systems in Ontario. (In the Sam Lawrence parking lot, Concession Street and Highcliffe Avenue, Hamilton)

• MOUNT HOPE
When You And I Were Young, Maggie
The words of this popular ballad were written by George Washington Johnson shortly before his marriage to Maggie Clark in 1864. The poem was set to music two years later. (On the grounds of Maggie Clark's childhood home, Nebo Road between Airport Road and Whitechurch Road, east of Highway 6, near Mount Hope)

Eileen Vollick 1908-1968
Following flight training in Hamilton, Eileen Vollick became the first woman in Canada to hold a private pilot's licence. This 1928 achievement effectively opened Canadian aviation to women. (Near the entrance to Hamilton Civic Airport, off Airport Road, Mount Hope)

• STONEY CREEK
The Battle of Stoney Creek 1813
In the early hours of June 6, 1813 some 700 British regulars launched a surprise attack on a large force of American troops at Stoney Creek. The successful rout was one of the decisive battles of the 1812-14 war. (In Battlefield Park, King Street and Highway 20, Stoney Creek)

John Willson 1776-1860
A prominent and influential politician and office holder, Willson settled in Saltfleet Township about 1797. He promoted many causes during his three decades of political life – among them religious and civil liberties, constitutional reform, and public support for education. (At his former home, now Liuna Gardens, 526 Winona Road North, Stoney Creek)

The First Women's Institute 1897

As a result of Erland Lee's organizing efforts, some 100 women from the surrounding district gathered on February 19, 1897 and, at the urging of Adelaide Hoodless, drafted a constitution for a society devoted to improving homemaking and child-care skills. The Women's Institutes movement subsequently gained world-wide participation. (At the former Lee home, now the Erland Lee Home Museum, 552 Ridge Road, about 5 km east of Highway 20 – about 2 km from Stoney Creek via New Mountain Road)

Adelaide Hoodless addressed a Farmers' Institute meeting in January 1897 and so impressed the women in the audience that within a matter of months the Women's Institute movement was born. (Archives of Ontario S 4332)

• WATERDOWN
Lionel Beaumaurice (Leo) Clarke, V.C. 1892-1916
For his courageous action in defending a trench on
the Somme battlefield on September 9, 1916 Leo
Clarke was awarded the Victoria Cross. Six weeks
later he was killed in action. (On the grounds of
the Royal Canadian Legion (Branch 551) building,
Hamilton Street, Waterdown)

HASTINGS COUNTY

• ACTINOLITE
The Founding of Actinolite
In the mid-1850s Billa Flint's mills on the Skoota-
matta River formed the nucleus of a small community first called Troy, and then Bridgewater.
About 1895 the village adopted the name Actinolite
after an asbestos-like material then being mined in
the area. (On the grounds of the United Church,
Store Street, just east of Highway 37, Actinolite)

• BANCROFT
The Monck Road
This colonization road was constructed between
1866 and 1873 for the dual purpose of opening up
a wilderness area to settlement and providing an
alternate, less vulnerable military route between the
upper Great Lakes and the Ottawa valley. It ran
from the vicinity of Lake Couchiching east to
present-day Bancroft. (In front of the Bancroft
Historical Museum, Station Street, Bancroft)

John Wesley Dafoe 1866-1944
A crusading journalist of international influence,
Dafoe was born near the hamlet of Purdy. As editor
of the *Winnipeg Free Press* from 1901 to 1944 he
championed many causes, among them the League
of Nations, low tariffs, and world peace. (In Lookout
Park, Highway 62 at Whiteduck Lake, just east of
Purdy – about 30 km northeast of Bancroft near
the Hastings/Renfrew county line)

• BELLEVILLE
Belleville
The construction of the Grand Trunk Railway
between Toronto and Montreal, a booming lumber
trade, and fertile agricultural land stimulated the
steady growth of Belleville throughout the nine-

teenth century. (In Victoria Park, just off South Front Street, along the waterfront, Belleville)

Belleville City Hall
A fine example of High Victorian architecture, the hall was erected in the 1870s to house the public market and administrative offices of the burgeoning community. Little altered over the years and remarkably well preserved, the building remains Belleville's most prominent landmark. (At the city hall, 169 Front Street, Belleville)

The Formation of the Methodist Church (Canada, Newfoundland, Bermuda) 1884
The official establishment of the Methodist Church resulted from a series of meetings held in Belleville in 1884, and was the culmination of years of debates and mergers between Methodist groups of British and American origin. (At Bridge Street United Church (the site of some of the meetings), Belleville)

Sir Mackenzie Bowell, K.C.M.G. 1823-1917
During his distinguished public career, Bowell combined journalistic interests, business activites and politics. A long-time resident of Belleville, he represented North Hastings for twenty-five years and served as prime minister of Canada from 1894 to 1896. (In front of his former home, 194 William Street, Belleville)

Albert College
In 1866 the Belleville Seminary, which had opened in 1857, was rechartered as Albert College, an affiliate of the University of Toronto. Five years later it became an independent, degree-granting institution. (At College Hill United Church, 16 North Park Street (the original site of the college), Belleville)

Albert Carman 1833-1917

Throughout his many-faceted career as a teacher and principal at the Belleville Seminary, and as a minister and bishop of the Methodist Episcopal Church, Carman was a forceful and eloquent proponent of Methodist education. His influence in both religious and educational circles makes him a major figure in the history of Methodism in Canada. (In front of Tabernacle United Church, 305 Church Street, Belleville)

The Ontario School for the Deaf

The first provincial school for deaf children, this residential institution combined elementary school

In 1896, following his stint as prime minister, Mackenzie Bowell (centre) repurchased the Belleville Intelligencer and continued as its publisher until his death at the age of ninety-four. (Archives of Ontario. Hastings County Historical Society Collection ACC 13281-90)

subjects with vocational training when it opened in 1870. Over the years ever-increasing enrolment has promoted the steady expansion of the school's facilities and curricula. (On the grounds of the school, now The Sir James Whitney School, 350 Dundas Street West, Belleville)

• DESERONTO
Christ Church 1843
Constructed by its Mohawk congregation to replace an earlier log chapel, Christ Church houses part of the communion plate that had been given to the Chapel Royal at Fort Hunter, New York by Queen Anne in 1712. The bell presented to the church in 1798 by George III has since been recast. (At the church, just off Highway 2 on the Tyendinaga Reserve, about 3 km west of Deseronto)

Oronhyatekha 1841-1907
A Mohawk of great renown and versatility, Oronhyatekha, who also called himself Peter Martin, combined a medical practice with activities as an orator, a marksman, and an organizer of humanist concerns, among them the Independent Order of Foresters. (On the grounds of Christ Church (where his grave is located), just off Highway 2 on the Tyendinaga Reserve, about 3 km west of Deseronto)

The Founding of Deseronto
Mill Point, as the community was known by 1850, took the name Deseronto in 1881 in honour of the Mohawk chief Deserontyon who had led the first settlers to the area following the American Revolution. (In Centennial Park, between Main Street and the waterfront, Deseronto)

Captain George Fraser Kerr, V.C., M.C., M.M. 1895-1929
A native of Deseronto, Kerr fought with the

Canadian Expeditionary Force in France throughout the 1914-18 war. For the single-handed capture of four machine-guns and thirty-one prisoners at Bourlon Wood in 1918 he was awarded the Victoria Cross. (In Centennial Park, between Main Street and the waterfront, Deseronto)

- ELDORADO
Ontario's First Gold Mine
The first gold mine in the province opened in 1867 as a result of a part-time prospector's chance discovery of gold on John Richardson's farm in the previous year. A substantial but short-lived gold rush ensued. (Near the site of the former mine, Highway 62, at the northern edge of Eldorado)

- MADOC
The Founding of Madoc
Mills and ironworks gave initial stimulus to the community of Madoc which, following the discovery of gold-bearing quartz in 1866, prospered for a time as an industrial centre. (At the Thomas Thompson Memorial Park, also called Cenotaph Park, St. Lawrence Street East, Madoc)

- MARMORA
The Marmora Ironworks 1823
Irishman Charles Hayes opened one of the earliest smelter/foundries in the province in 1823 and began producing pig iron from ore mined in the vicinity. Economic difficulties and transport problems dogged the venture and the works fell into ruin, although mining was resumed in the late 1860s and early '70s. (In Legion Park, just off Cameron Street at Highway 7, Marmora)

- MAYNOOTH
The Peterson Road
Constructed between 1858 and 1863, this coloniza-

tion road ran northeast from Muskoka to join the Opeongo Road in Renfrew County. Although poor soil dashed hopes for agricultural settlement along the route, the Maynooth-to-Combermere section proved a boon to lumbering in the area. (In front of the township hall, Highway 62, Maynooth – at the junction of Highways 127 and 62)

• ORMSBY
The Hastings Road
Running north from Madoc to Bancroft and bordered by free-grant lots, the Hastings Road, begun in 1854, successfully attracted settlers to the area. Poor soil and an unsympathetic climate prevented prosperous farming, however, and with the subsequent decline in lumbering most settlers abandoned their land. (Hastings Road and Highway 620, Ormsby – between Highway 62 and the Hastings/Peterborough county line)

• STIRLING
Asa Turner
An early Baptist missionary, Turner conducted services in pioneer homes, organized several congregations, and contributed substantially to the establishment of the Baptist Church in eastern Ontario during the early years of the nineteenth century. (On the grounds of Sidney Baptist Church, Baptist Church Road and Concession 8, off Highway 14, near Stirling)

Stone Church Hastings
Built in the 1850s by local Wesleyan Methodists, the church is one of three remaining cobblestone churches in Ontario. The interior underwent severe remodelling in the 1890s to conform to late-Victorian tastes, but the exterior remains largely unchanged. (On the grounds of the church, County Road 31, 3 km west of Highway 14, south of Stirling)

- TRENTON
Champlain's War Party 1615
In September 1615 Samuel de Champlain led a small party of Frenchmen, reinforced by a substantial force of Hurons and Algonkians, down the Trent River en route to attack an Onondaga village near present-day Syracuse. The ill-fated venture served mainly to increase the hostility of the Five Nations towards the French. (In Bayshore Park, Albert and Wharf Streets, opposite the Legion Hall, Trenton)

- TWEED
Merrill Denison 1893-1975
Designer, director, actor and playwright, Denison is perhaps best known for his series of historical radio plays, *The Romance of Canada*. The plays, which highlighted events in the lives of famous Canadians, were produced for the CBC in 1931-32 by Tyrone Guthrie, and marked the beginning of professional radio drama in Canada. (At the Tweed Playhouse (where many of his plays were performed), Tweed)

- BAYFIELD
The Founding of Bayfield
The second community established in the vast lands of the Huron Tract, Bayfield began life in the mid-1830s as a small milling centre. Construction of harbour facilities in the 1870s ensured the village's continued growth. (In Clan Gregor Square, Bayfield)

- BLYTH
The Founding of Blyth
The well-sited agricultural village of Blyth attracted a steady stream of settlers throughout the 1850s. Many small industries took advantage of the convenient water power in the area, and by 1870 the community had become an important regional market town. (In front of the memorial hall, 147 Queen Street North, Blyth)

- BRUSSELS
The Founding of Brussels
Originally known as Ainleyville after its founder William Ainley – and with a post office called Dingle – this thriving mill town adopted the somewhat more sophisticated name of Brussels in 1872 when it was incorporated as a village. (In front of the public library, Turnberry and Mill Roads, Brussels)

- CLINTON
The Founding of Clinton
A tavern at the junction of the London and Huron Roads marked the beginning of the village of Clinton, originally called The Corners. The absence of water power restricted early development, but the completion in 1858 of a rail line from Fort Erie to Goderich stimulated the community's industrial

growth. (On the grounds of Wesley Willis United Church, Mary and Victoria Streets, Clinton)

Horatio Emmons Hale 1817-1896
As a member of the Wilkes Expedition to the Pacific in 1838-42 Hale compiled a detailed report on linguistics and customs that is still regarded as fundamental to the study of Polynesian ethnology. Hale practised law in Clinton for forty years, during which time he undertook extensive studies of the language and customs of the Six Nations Iroquois. (On the grounds of St. Paul's Anglican Church, 49 Ontario Street, Clinton)

Dr. Robert Hamilton Coats 1874-1960
A native of the Clinton area, Coats worked as a journalist prior to his appointment in 1915 as Canada's first dominion statistician and controller of the census. He was responsible for drafting the legislation that three years later established the Dominion Bureau of Statistics. (On the grounds of Central Huron Secondary School, 165 Princess Street East, Clinton)

The Slomans and the CNR School on Wheels
Established in 1926, the school-on-wheels program offered academic instruction and social services to children and adults in the outlying regions of northern Ontario. One of the first teachers was Fred Sloman of Clinton who, with his wife Cela, travelled the Capreol-to-Foleyet line for thirty-nine years. (At the school car (now restored) which the Slomans used, Sloman Memorial Park, Victoria Terrace, Clinton)

• EGMONDVILLE
Colonel Anthony Van Egmond 1778-1838
A native of Holland and a veteran of the Napoleonic Wars, Van Egmond was one of the most prominent

early settlers in the Huron Tract. A strong supporter of William Lyon Mackenzie, he led the ill-fated skirmish at Montgomery's Tavern during the Rebellion of 1837. He was captured, and died in prison while awaiting trial. (At the entrance to the Egmondville Cemetery (where his grave is located), West Bayfield and Church Streets, Egmondville)

The Van Egmond House
Constructed about 1846 by Constant Van Egmond, the eldest son of Colonel Van Egmond, this handsome house combines well-proportioned characteristics of the Georgian and Classical Revival styles of architecture. The house has been restored with assistance from the Ontario Heritage Foundation, and is operated as a public museum by the Van Egmond Foundation. (On the grounds of the house, Centre and Bayfield Streets, Egmondville)

• EXETER
The Founding of Exeter
Mills constructed on the banks of the Aux Sables River in the 1830s provided the nucleus of the community of Exeter which, by 1860, had become the main market town in the district. (In Riverview Park, Main Street just south of the Ausable River bridge, Exeter)

The Right Honourable James G. Gardiner 1883-1962
Born in Hibbert Township, Gardiner was attracted to the Canadian West where he taught school for several years before entering politics in 1914. He served as premier of Saskatchewan for two terms, 1926-29 and 1934-35. (On the grounds of Thames Road United Church, Highway 83, east of Exeter)

Legend has it that William Dunlop, Warden of the Forests for the Canada Company, acquired the nickname "Tiger" while in India – by clubbing a tiger to death after throwing snuff in its eyes. (Archives of Ontario S 17142)

Yours truly

Dunlop

AUTHOR OF "SKETCHES OF UPPER CANADA"

- GODERICH
"Tiger" Dunlop 1792-1848
Surgeon, soldier, editor, and author, Dr. William Dunlop was one of Upper Canada's most colourful personalities. As an associate of John Galt, superintendent of the Canada Company, he was instrumental in opening up the Huron Tract for settlement. (At Dunlop's Tomb historic site, Highway 21, just north of Goderich)

Thomas Mercer Jones 1795-1868
Business experience gained in the mercantile trade in England stood Jones in good stead as commissioner of the powerful Canada Company (1829-52).

The Coat of Arms of the Canada Company. In 1826 the company purchased 2.5 million acres of land from the government, approximately half of which lay in the area known as the Huron Tract. (Archives of Ontario S 16259)

He was responsible for administering settlement of the million-acre Huron Tract, and from his headquarters in Goderich wielded unrivalled authority in the area. (In Harbour Park, West Street, Goderich)

The Founding of Goderich
As Warden of the Forests for the Canada Company, William "Tiger" Dunlop recognized the potential for harbour facilities at the mouth of the Maitland River. In 1827 he laid out a town site to serve as a port and service centre for the western section of the Huron Tract, and named the community Goderich. (In Harbour Park, West Street, Goderich)

The Great Storm of 1913
One of the worst storms in the history of the Great Lakes raged for three days in November 1913 during which nineteen vessels were destroyed and 244 lives lost. Lake Huron bore the brunt of the storm's fury, and extensive salvage operations were conducted along the length of the county's shoreline. (At Cobourg and Lighthouse Streets, Goderich)

The British Commonwealth Air Training Plan
Inaugurated in 1939 at the outset of the Second World War to provide air training safely removed from active war zones, the plan was administered by Canada with financial assistance from other Commonwealth countries. The Goderich school at Sky Harbour was one of thirty-eight training units established in Ontario during the war years. (At Sky Harbour Airport, Highway 21, Goderich)

• ST. JOSEPH
Narcisse M. Cantin 1870-1940
Entrepreneur, inventor, cattle trader, and the founder of St. Joseph, Narcisse Cantin spent much energy

and money in promoting the idea of a canal to link Lakes Huron and Erie. The canal was never built but extensive publicity about the scheme gave significant impetus to the broader idea of a Great Lakes seaway system. (At the junction of Highways 21 and 84, St. Joseph)

• SEAFORTH

The Founding of Seaforth

Anticipating construction of a rail line through the region, the Sparling brothers acquired most of the present site of Seaforth in the early 1850s and laid out a town plot. Advantageously situated on both the railway and the Huron Road, Seaforth soon became an important shipping point for local grain and produce. (At the west entrance to Victoria Park, Victoria and Gouinlock Streets, Seaforth)

The Honourable William Aberhart 1878-1943

Founder of the Social Credit party and premier of Alberta from 1935 to 1943, Aberhart grew up in Huron County and attended high school in Seaforth. He combined a teaching career with activities as a lay preacher and broadcaster until he entered politics. (At Seaforth and District High School, 58 Chalk Street North, Seaforth)

• WINGHAM

The Founding of Wingham

Ideally located at the convergence of two branches of the Maitland River, Wingham became a prominent supply and distribution centre for the agricultural and lumbering hinterland. Railway expansion in the 1870s stimulated further growth and the village tripled its population in a five-year period. (At the Wingham Museum, 273 Josephine Street, Wingham)

• ZURICH
Sir John Stephen Willison 1856-1927
An influential political journalist and proponent of imperial federation, Willison, who was born near Zurich, began his career with the *London Advertiser*. He worked on several major newspapers, writing about Canadian affairs with detachment and clarity. His published works include a biography of Sir Wilfrid Laurier. (On the grounds of the community centre, 30 Main Street, Zurich)

KENORA DISTRICT

- HUDSON
Canada's Pioneer Airlines
Western Canada Airways, based at Hudson in 1926, was one of the earliest airlines established in the country. Along with other pioneer companies it stimulated the development of the northern region and laid the groundwork for commercial aviation in Canada. (Near the fire hall, Main Steet, Hudson – west of Sioux Lookout on Highway 664)

- KENORA
Rat Portage Post
About 1836 the Hudson's Bay Company built a small fur trading post on Old Fort Island, situated below the falls on the eastern outlet of Lake of the Woods. Twenty-five years later the post was moved to the mainland where it formed the nucleus of the community of Rat Portage, later renamed Kenora. (In McLeod Park, Highway 17 West, Kenora)

The Wolseley Expedition 1870
Colonel Garnet Wolseley led an expedition of 1,200 men west in 1870 to quell the Métis rebellion at Fort Garry. Travelling via the Great Lakes and roughly following the route of the voyageurs, the expedition reached Rat Portage in mid-August. (At the Travel Centre on Highway 17, just west of Kenora)

The Reverend Albert Lacombe, O.M.I. 1827-1916
An Oblate missionary, Father Lacombe established several missions in western Canada among the Cree, Blackfoot, and Métis peoples. From his mission headquarters at Rat Portage he also ministered to CPR construction crews as far west as Winnipeg from 1880 to 1882. (On the grounds of the Church of Notre Dame du Portage, First Street North, Kenora)

The Ontario Boundary Dispute

Following acquisition in 1869 by the Dominion of Canada of the territories of the Hudson's Bay Company, the western and northern boundaries of the province of Ontario became a matter of ongoing dispute. The matter was finally settled in 1884. (On the grounds of the Lake of the Woods Museum, Water Street, Kenora)

The Kenora Thistles

In a best-of-three challenge, the Kenora Thistles hockey team ably defeated the Montreal Wanderers

Rivalry between the Hudson's Bay Company and the North West Company was so fierce during the 1790s that apparently a secret opening was cut in the palisade at Osnaburgh House (shown here at a later date) to permit fur-laden traders to enter the post under cover of darkness. (Archives of Ontario S 7519)

to win the Stanley Cup in 1907. Competition rules being less formal at that time, the Wanderers re-challenged the Thistles two months later and won back the cup. (In Memorial Park, Main Street, Kenora)

- ## OSNABURGH HOUSE
  ### *Osnaburgh House 1786*
  Constructed on Lake St. Joseph to counter the activities of the North West Company, this Hudson's Bay Company post proved highly profitable and was maintained even after the merger of the two rival companies in 1821. In the 1930s when the site was flooded following the construction of a hydro dam at Rat Rapids, the post was relocated to the northeast. (In the settlement of Osnaburgh House – on Highway 599 about 38 km south of Pickle Lake)

- ## RED LAKE
  ### *Red Lake House*
  In 1790 the Hudson's Bay Company set up a trading post on Red Lake in order to compete more effectively with the Nor'Westers who had been trading in the area for several years. Closed, reopened, and relocated numerous times, the post was finally located in the town of Red Lake in 1933. (In front of the municipal offices, 117 Howey Street, Red Lake)

The Founding of the Red Lake Mining District
The discovery of gold at Red Lake in the 1920s stimulated much activity in the region and within a few years intrepid bush pilots were flying men and supplies to otherwise inaccessible mining sites. By 1961 gold valued at more than $200 million had been extracted from the district. (At the junction of Highways 105 and 125, southeast of Red Lake)

• SIOUX LOOKOUT
Umfreville's Exploration 1784
Commissioned by the North West Company to find an alternative to the traditional canoe route to the West (which passed through American-held territory), Edward Umfreville successfully made his way up the Nipigon River and west through a web of rivers to present-day Manitoba. (In McKenzie Park, Highway 72, about 5 km south of Sioux Lookout)

- BLENHEIM
The Founding of Blenheim
The opening in 1847 of Rondeau harbour and the completion of a road from the port to Chatham stimulated lumbering in the area, which in turn spurred the growth of the small crossroads community of Blenheim. (At the municipal building, 35 Talbot Street West, Blenheim)

Harry G.B. Miner, V.C. 1891-1918
During a Canadian attack near Amiens on August 8, 1918 Corporal Miner captured a machine-gun post single handed. For his conspicuous bravery on this and other occasions, the Cedar Springs native was awarded, posthumously, the Croix de Guerre and the Victoria Cross. (On the grounds of the United Church, Cedar Springs – at the junction of Highway 3 and County Road 10, southwest of Blenheim)

- BOTHWELL
The Founding of Bothwell
George Brown, one of the Fathers of Confederation, owned some 4,000 acres of land in Kent County. After the Great Western Railway constructed a line and a station on his property in 1855, he had a town plot surveyed. The resulting community, named Bothwell, developed quickly. Its economic prosperity was further enhanced by the discovery of oil some years later. (On the grounds of the town hall, 320 Main Street, Bothwell)

- CHATHAM
The Chatham Blockhouse 1794
Constructed by order of Lieutenant-Colonel Simcoe in 1794, the Chatham blockhouse was garrisoned for a few years and then abandoned. In 1798 the building was moved to Sandwich (Windsor) to serve as the

court house and jail for the Western District. (At the original site of the blockhouse, near the band-stand in Tecumseh Park, William Street South and Stanley Avenue, Chatham)

John Brown's Convention 1858
In May 1858 the American abolitionist John Brown held a three-day series of meetings in Chatham (a terminus on the underground railroad) to organize support for his plan to liberate the southern slaves. First Baptist Church was the site of one of these meetings. (On the grounds of the church, 135 King Street East, Chatham)

Kent County Court House
Constructed in 1848-50 of white limestone, the court house was designed by William Thomas in the Neoclassical style – a style common to many nineteenth-century public buildings in Ontario. The building still houses the county courts, although other administrative functions have been trans-ferred elsewhere. (In front of the court house, 21 Seventh Street, Chatham)

• DRESDEN
The Josiah Henson House
Born on the farm of a slave-owner in Maryland, Josiah Henson (1789-1883) escaped to Upper Canada at the age of forty-one. In 1841, with a group of abolitionists, he established a vocational school for fugitive slaves near present-day Dresden. Even after the abolition of slavery Henson remained in Canada. His house is now a museum. (On the grounds of the house, west of Highway 21, Dresden)

The Founding of Dresden
A sawmill and grist-mill in operation by 1850 provided the basis for the small community of Dresden. Extensive timber resources and the poten-

tial for navigation on the Sydenham River stimulated development, and by 1871 the village was a major commercial centre in that part of the county. (At the town hall, 485 St. George Street, Dresden)

• PAIN COURT
Pain Court
One of the earliest French-speaking settlements in southern Ontario, Pain Court was founded by squatters from the Detroit area who began to settle in the region in the 1780s. It derived its name from the small loaves of bread which the impoverished parishioners offered to Roman Catholic missionaries. (At the Church of the Immaculate Conception, Pain Court – west of Chatham at the intersection of County Roads 34 and 35)

• PALMYRA
The Honourable David Mills 1831-1903
During his years in federal politics Mills held two cabinet posts: minister of the interior and minister of justice. An expert in constitutional and international law, he lectured and wrote extensively on these subjects. (Near the Mills family homestead, Highway 3, just east of Palmyra)

• RIDGETOWN
The Founding of Ridgetown
Economic growth was slow in this small agricultural community until the Canada Southern Railway made Ridgetown a stop on its Fort Erie-to-Amherstburg line in 1872. Then the village became an important depot for local grain and lumber shipments. (On the grounds of the public library, Main Street, Ridgetown)

• RONDEAU PROVINCIAL PARK
The Wilkins Expedition 1763
En route to relieve the British post at Detroit which

was under siege by a force of Indians led by Pontiac, a fleet of small boats commanded by Major John Wilkins encountered a violent storm off Rondeau Point in November 1763. Most of the supply ships were lost and the expedition had to abandon its objective and return to the garrison at Niagara. (At the Rondeau Interpretive Centre, at the foot of Highway 51)

• SOUTH BUXTON
The Buxton Settlement 1849
The founder of the Buxton Settlement was the Reverend William King, an Irish-born Presbyterian minister who, in 1848, came to Upper Canada from Louisiana with fifteen slaves. They formed the nucleus of the settlement which, fifteen years later, contained about 1,000 freed and fugitive slaves living on some 6,700 acres in Raleigh Township. (On the grounds of St. Andrew's United Church (a parish established by King in the heart of the settlement), South Buxton – at the intersection of County Roads 6 and 8)

• THAMESVILLE
New Fairfield 1815
In 1792 Fairfield, a Moravian missionary settlement of Delaware Indians, was established on the north bank of the Thames River. Destroyed in 1813 by invading American forces, the mission was re-built on the south side of the river after the war. (On the grounds of the church on the Moravian Indian Reserve, County Road 18, near Thamesville)

• TILBURY
St. Peter's Roman Catholic Church
Built to serve the second-oldest Roman Catholic parish in southwestern Ontario, St. Peter's was erected in 1896 to replace an earlier building destroyed by fire. Eighteen murals by the noted

Canadian artist, Marie Georges Delfosse, grace the interior. (On the grounds of the church, River Road, Tilbury East Township – northeast of the town of Tilbury)

- ## WALLACEBURG
The Baldoon Settlement 1804-1818
In 1804 fifteen families from Scotland optimistically settled near the St. Clair River in a community sponsored by Lord Selkirk. Flooding, malaria, and invading American forces during the War of 1812 took their toll, however, and by 1818 the few settlers who remained had moved to higher ground. (On the grounds of 7057 Dufferin Avenue (Highway 40), west of Wallaceburg at the approach to the Walpole Island bridge)

The Founding of Wallaceburg
Several early settlers at "The Forks" were Highlanders from the ill-fated Baldoon Settlement. When a post office was opened in 1837 the community, situated at the forking of the Sydenham River, was renamed in honour of the Scottish hero Sir William Wallace. (In Library Park, James and Nelson Streets, Wallaceburg)

James Paris Lee 1831-1904
A major contribution to firearms design was made in 1878 when the inventor James Lee developed the box magazine, a significant improvement on the standard tube magazine which held cartridges under the gun barrel. Tradition has it that the invention took place in Wallaceburg while Lee was visiting his brother. (In Civic Square Park, Highway 40, Wallaceburg)

LAMBTON COUNTY

- ARKONA
The Founding of Arkona
Situated at a well-travelled crossroads in the midst
of a fertile agricultural region, Arkona was reportedly one of the largest villages in Lambton County
during the 1870s. Pining perhaps for a glimpse of
the sea, the early settlers, some of whom were of
German extraction, named this inland village after
a lighthouse point in Germany. (At the fire hall,
Victoria and North Streets, Arkona)

- BRIGHTS GROVE
Canada's First Commune
The first communal settlement in Canada was
established in 1829 by Henry Jones, an ardent
follower of the renowned social reformer Robert
Owen. The short-lived commune was situated on
a 1,000-acre tract of land in the vicinity of present-
day Brights Grove. (On the grounds of the public
school, Hamilton Road, Brights Grove – near Sarnia
on County Road 7)

- FOREST
The Founding of Forest
In 1859 the Grand Trunk Railway opened a station
at the junction of three townships on the Guelph-
to-Sarnia line. Situated in dense bush, the station
was called Forest; the name was retained even after
the trees had been felled and the community had
developed into a trans-shipment centre. (In front
of the town hall, 40 King Street West, Forest)

- IPPERWASH PROVINCIAL PARK
The Indian Flint Bed
Outcroppings of chert along the shoreline of Lake
Huron provided aboriginal inhabitants with flint for
fashioning arrow points and spearheads. Scientific

analysis suggests that these flint beds were used from 700 BC until the advent of European trade goods in the seventeenth century. (In front of the water station in Ipperwash Provincial Park – 3 km north of Highway 21 on County Road 6)

- MOORETOWN
  ### Old Trinity 1842-1881
  The bright tin steeple of Lambton County's first Anglican church served for many years as a guide to mariners plying the St. Clair River. The foundation of Old Trinity proved less reliable, however – being made of logs in lieu of stones – and the church was demolished in 1881. (At the site of the former church, in the old Sutherland Cemetery, Mooretown – about 15 km south of Sarnia on County Road 33)

- PETROLIA
  ### The Founding of Petrolia
  The first oil well at Petrolia was brought into production in 1860 and by the middle of the decade the village had become the major oil-producing centre in Canada. Phenomenal gushers like those at Oil Springs were never struck here, but the wells at Petrolia yielded a steady output of oil for many years. (At the town hall, 411 Greenfield Street, Petrolia)

- POINT EDWARD
  ### The Voyage of the Griffon 1679
  Built by Sieur de La Salle to service the fur trade, the *Griffon* was the first European ship to sail Lakes Erie, Huron, and Michigan. On its maiden voyage

---

During the original oil boom at Petrolia between 1865 and 1872 the town depended almost entirely on the production of oil for its survival. (Archives of Ontario S 4748)

from Niagara to Green Bay in 1679 the vessel reportedly encountered much difficulty in the swift current of the St. Clair River. (Michigan Avenue at the Bluewater Bridge (in the vicinity where the ship was hauled through the current by its crew), Point Edward)

The Founding of Point Edward
Originally reserved for use as a military base, Point Edward was made the western terminus on the Grand Trunk line from Rivière du Loup in 1859. Strategically located at the point where the St. Clair River flows out of Lake Huron, the village became an important point of transfer for both people and goods travelling east and west. (At the municipal office, 36 St. Clair Street, Point Edward)

• RUTHERFORD
Donald Allerton Johnston 1874-1957
Born and raised on a farm near the village of Rutherford, Johnston emigrated to Detroit, Michigan where he became a prominent business leader. In 1915 he played an instrumental role in founding the Kiwanis Club. This community-service organization rapidly established branches throughout the United States and Canada. (On County Road 1, just off Highway 21, Rutherford)

• SARNIA
Froome and Field Talfourd
The Talfourd brothers immigrated from England in 1832 and took up neighbouring lots in Moore Township. After Field moved to the United States, Froome laid out the town plot of Froomefield on their combined property and took an active part in local administrative affairs. (At Froomefield Pioneer Cemetery, County Road 33 and Church Street, Sarnia)

The International Boundary

As early as 1783, the end of the American Revolution, the St. Clair River was designated an international boundary line. Under the terms of the 1814 Treaty of Ghent a detailed survey was undertaken north to Lake of the Woods and the boundary line was delineated. (On the grounds of the Shell Canada Marketing Terminal, County Road 33, Froomefield, Sarnia)

The Founding of Sarnia

Stimulated by regional lumbering, oil drilling, and rail traffic, the community of Sarnia had developed, by 1880, into a major trans-shipment point for grain, coal, oil, and lumber. (In Alexander Mackenzie Park, Front Street, Sarnia)

Ontario's Oil Refining Industry

With the discovery in the 1850s of significant oil deposits in Enniskillen Township, wells were drilled and refineries established at Oil Springs and Petrolia as well as Sarnia. (At the main office of the Imperial Oil Refinery, Christina and Clifford Streets, Sarnia)

The Mackenzie House and Family

The seven Mackenzie brothers played prominent roles in the business and political life of Lambton County in the nineteenth century. John Mackenzie purchased land in Sarnia in 1856, and until 1902 members of his family lived in a house that possibly had been built by his brother Alexander. The latter, a building contractor by trade, served as Canada's second prime minister from 1873 to 1878. (At the house, 316 Christina Street North, Sarnia)

The St. Clair Tunnel

Built during 1889-91 by the Grand Trunk Railway to link Sarnia with Port Huron, Michigan, the St. Clair Tunnel was the first international submarine railway tunnel in North America. An engineering feat that attracted much popular attention, the tunnel was constructed at a cost of $2.5 million. (Adjacent to the tunnel, St. Andrew Street, Sarnia)

- THEDFORD
The Founding of Thedford
An early stop on the Grand Trunk line, which was constructed through the Huron Tract during the late 1850s, Thedford – known for a time as Widder Station – became an important nineteenth-century shipping point for square timber, grain, and cattle. (In Thedford Park, Main and King Streets, Thedford)

LANARK COUNTY

- ALMONTE
Auld Kirk 1836
Constructed by the local congregation of The Established Church of Scotland, *Auld Kirk* was attended by Presbyterian settlers from several neighbouring townships. The sturdy stone church still stands, a fitting memorial to its hardy founders. (On the grounds of the church, County Road 16, about 1 km west of Highway 15, Almonte)

The Founding of Almonte
The establishment during the 1850s of several woollen mills and the construction of a railway line to Brockville stimulated the economic growth of Almonte. By 1870 the village was one of the leading centres in Ontario for the manufacture of woollen cloth. (At the town hall, 14 Bridge Street, Almonte)

The Rosamonds in Almonte
James Rosamond and his sons Bennett and William were instrumental in the development of a thriving woollen industry in the Mississippi River valley during the nineteenth century. By 1890 Almonte was reputedly the seat of the woollen trade in Canada. (At a former Rosamond mill building, 7 Mill Street, Almonte)

The Mill of Kintail and Robert Tait McKenzie
Surgeon, physical educator, and noted sculptor, McKenzie was responsible for the design of many war memorials in Canada, the United States and Great Britain. In 1930 he renovated the old Baird mill for use as a studio, renaming it after his ancestral home. The Mill of Kintail is now a museum. (At the mill on the Indian River, on the 8th Line of Ramsay Township, about 6.5 km northwest of Almonte)

Dr. James Naismith 1861-1939

Born and raised in Ramsay Township, Naismith creatively combined two professions: physical educator and medical doctor. In 1891, responding to the need for an indoor team sport to occupy students during the winter months, Naismith devised the game of basketball – initially using a soccer ball and two half-bushel peach baskets. (At his childhood home, Highway 15, just north of Clayton Road, about 4.5 km northwest of Almonte)

• CARLETON PLACE

The Ballygiblin Riots 1824

Religious and racial animosity provided the background for a series of riots at Carleton Place during April and May 1824. Peace was restored by Colonel James Fitzgibbon who censured the militia for aggravating the settlers' unrest. (On the grounds of the town hall, 175 Bridge Street, Carleton Place)

The Founding of Carleton Place

Originally called Morphy's Falls, this settlement on the Mississippi River took the name of Carleton Place in 1830 when a post office was opened. The construction of railway lines from Brockville and Ottawa later in the century greatly stimulated the community's growth. (In Centennial Park, Flora Street, Carleton Place)

Captain A. Roy Brown, D.S.C. 1893-1944

A native of Carleton Place, Captain Brown flew with the Royal Naval Air Service in the First World War. He is credited with shooting down Germany's leading fighter pilot, Captain von Richthofen commonly known as the "Red Baron". (In Memorial Park, Franklin and Beckwith Streets, Carleton Place)

• FRANKTOWN

The Reverend George Buchanan 1761-1835

The first resident clergyman in Beckwith Township,

Buchanan served the area's inhabitants as minister, teacher and physician for eleven years. When his Presbyterian congregation erected a stone church in 1833, some parishioners insisted that services be conducted strictly according to the Church of Scotland and Buchanan, a Secessionist, was barred from preaching there. (On the grounds of St. Paul's United Church (a successor to the 1833 church), Highway 15, Franktown)

The Rectory of Beckwith

St. James' Church, Beckwith (later Franktown) was completed about 1828 and is one of the oldest remaining Anglican churches in eastern Ontario. The rectory of Beckwith was created in 1836 and at one time served a parish that extended from Smiths Falls to Pakenham. (On the grounds of St. James', Church Street, Franktown)

• LANARK

The Lanark Settlement 1820

More than 3,000 settlers, many of them unemployed weavers from Scotland and discharged soldiers, were established on recently surveyed townships in the Bathurst District during 1820 and 1821. A depot was established at present-day Lanark to serve as the centre of the settlement. (On the grounds of the town hall, 75 George Street, Lanark)

The Dalhousie Library

In 1828 the St. Andrew's Philanthropic Society of Dalhousie Township founded the first public library in the Bathurst District and persuaded Lord Dalhousie, governor-general of Canada, to make a substantial donation of money and books. (On the grounds of the community hall (where the local library is now housed), just off County Road 8, Watsons Corners – west of Lanark)

• PERTH

The Perth Military Settlement 1816

Scottish immigrants and soldiers discharged from the Glengarry Light Infantry and other regiments formed the majority of early settlers in the Perth Settlement. Within six months of its formation, the settlement contained some 1,500 people. (In Stewart Park, behind the town hall, 80 Gore Street East, Perth)

Malcolm Cameron 1808-1876

A successful businessman and politician, Cameron co-founded the *Bathurst Courier* in Perth in 1834, and two years later entered politics. He represented several ridings, including Lanark, during his long career, and was an early leader in the Clear Grit movement. (In Stewart Park, behind the town hall, 80 Gore Street East, Perth)

Alexander Morris 1826-1889

Born in Perth, Morris spent most of his professional life in the political arena. A strong advocate of Confederation, he represented South Lanark in the federal legislature, served as lieutenant-governor of Manitoba and the North-West Territories, and in his later years was a member of the Ontario legislature. (In Stewart Park, behind the town hall, 80 Gore Street East, Perth)

The Last Fatal Duel 1833

The participants in the last fatal duel fought in Upper Canada were two law students, John Wilson and Robert Lyon. Disparaging remarks by Lyon about Miss Elizabeth Hughes prompted the duel, in which Lyon was mortally wounded. (In front of the Inderwick House (the house to which the wounded Lyon was taken; now the property of the Ontario Heritage Foundation), 66 Craig Street, Perth)

District Court House and Gaol 1843
Designed in the Neoclassical style by Malcolm McPherson of Perth, the second Bathurst District court house was built on the same site that the first had occupied. Since 1861 the building has served as the court house for the County of Lanark. (On the grounds of the court house, 43 Drummond Street East, Perth)

Herbert Taylor Reade, V.C. 1828-1897
A native of Perth, Reade served as assistant surgeon with the 61st (South Gloucestershire) Regiment during the Indian Mutiny of 1857. For his gallantry on two occasions during that conflict he was awarded the Victoria Cross. (At the Royal Canadian Legion (Branch 244) building, 26 Beckwith Street East, Perth)

The Reverend William Bell 1780-1857
One of the most influential Presbyterian clergymen in Upper Canada, Bell ministered to settlers in the Lanark region for forty years, using Perth as his headquarters. His writings and journals provide a valuable record of life in the province at that time. (On the grounds of St. Andrew's Presbyterian Church, Drummond and North Streets, Perth)

The Haggarts
John Haggart, a stone mason, came to Upper Canada from Scotland in the 1820s and established a milling complex on the Tay River. His son John was the mayor of Perth before serving for forty years as the federal member for South Lanark. (On the grounds of the Haggart-Shortt House, 41 Mill Street, Perth)

The Summit House
Built in 1823 by James Boulton, one of the first lawyers to set up practice in Perth, the Summit

House reflects the fashionable Adamesque style which had developed in England in the eighteenth century. An unusual feature of the house is the use of brick, which had not yet become a popular building material. (Near the house, Harvey and Drummond Streets, Perth)

The McMartin House
A rare example of the American Federal style of architecture in Ontario, the McMartin House was constructed about 1830. Now owned by the Ontario Heritage Foundation, the house has been restored and its interior space adapted for use by community groups. (On the grounds of the house, Gore and Harvey Streets, Perth)

The McMartin House in Perth was owned between 1871 and 1883 by William O'Brien (shown here on his front steps), a local shoe manufacturer. (Archives of Ontario S 7457)

- SMITHS FALLS
  ### The Rideau Waterway
  Constructed between 1826 and 1832 for military purposes – but used mainly for commerce – the Rideau waterway together with the lower Ottawa River formed the first canalized route from Montreal to the Great Lakes. (In Victoria Park, Lombard Street and Highway 29, Smiths Falls)

LEEDS AND GRENVILLE UNITED COUNTIES

• BROCKVILLE

Forsyth's Raid 1813
Brockville offered virtually no resistance to Major Benjamin Forsyth's surprise attack in February 1813 and his American raiders made off with a quantity of arms and supplies. Retaliation came two weeks later, however, with a successful British attack on Ogdensburg, New York. (On Blockhouse Island, Market Street South, south of Water Street, Brockville)

Blockhouse Island
Known briefly as Hospital Island during the 1832 cholera epidemic when victims of the disease were housed there, the island was used for defence purposes later in the decade when a blockhouse was constructed to discourage raids by rebel sympathizers from across the St. Lawrence. (On the island, Market Street South, south of Water Street, Brockville)

The Brockville Tunnel 1860
The railway tunnel running under the city of Brockville was constructed between 1854 and 1860 to give the Brockville and Ottawa Railway access to the river front. The oldest railway tunnel in Canada, it was used by steam locomotives until 1954. (In the park at the tunnel doors, Water Street, Brockville)

Johnstown District Court House and Gaol
Completed by 1843 to replace an earlier district headquarters in poor repair, this building is one of the finer court houses remaining in Ontario from the pre-1845 period. Alterations over the years have not obscured its original Neoclassical design. (In Court House Square, Church Street, Brockville)

William Buell, Sr. 1751-1832

At the close of the American Revolution Buell, who had served as an officer in the King's Rangers, settled with his family on a Crown grant in present-day Brockville. He contributed significantly to the development of the town by subdividing his holdings and donating land for churches and a court house. (On the grounds of the Buell-Fitzsimmons Home, Water Street West at Home Street, Brockville)

Ogle Robert Gowan 1803-1876

A year after coming to Upper Canada and settling in the Brockville area, Gowan founded the Grand Orange Lodge of British North America in 1830. A shrewd strategist and politician, the enigmatic Irishman used his newspaper, the *Brockville Statesman*, to promote his political views. (Courthouse Avenue, Brockville)

James Morris 1798-1865

A prominent politician and long-time resident of Brockville, Morris became the first Canadian post-master-general in 1851 when responsibility for that service passed from the British government. He introduced the first Canadian stamps – designed and engraved by Sandford Fleming – and standardized postal rates. (At the county court house, Church Street, Brockville.

George Chaffey 1848-1932

An early promoter of large-scale irrigation, George Chaffey was born in Brockville. Both entrepreneur and engineer, Chaffey worked in various places in the United States and Canada before undertaking, with his brother William, major irrigation projects in Australia during the late 1880s and early 1890s. (In Victoria Park, Pearl and Park Streets, Brockville)

- BURRITTS RAPIDS

The Founding of Burritt's Rapids

Milling was the main activity in this pioneer community named in honour of its founding family. Construction of the Rideau Canal stimulated the centre's growth for a time, but lack of railway connections ultimately led to economic decline. (On the grounds of the community hall, Main Street near the bridge, Burritts Rapids)

Christ Church

Constructed in the early 1830s on land donated by Daniel Burritt, Christ Church served an Anglican congregation which had been active in the area since about 1822. The simple, Gothic Revival design of this small frame church is typical of many early rural churches in the province. (On the grounds of the church, County Road 3, Burritts Rapids)

- CARDINAL

The Founding of Cardinal

The grist-mill built at Point Cardinal by Hugh Munro in 1796 attracted other small industries to capitalize on the water power offered by the Galops Rapids. By 1864 Cardinal boasted many prominent business concerns, notably the McLatchie foundry and the Canada Starch Works. (At the junction of Highway 2 and Bridge Street, Cardinal)

St. Paul's Church

Completed by 1833, St. Paul's was constructed at the urging of the Reverend Johann Weagandt, a Lutheran-turned-Anglican whose change of faith caused much controversy in the Williamsburg area. All that remains of the small stone church is the tower. (At the site of the former church, St. Paul's cemetery, Highway 2, just east of Cardinal)

- CHAFFEYS LOCKS
Chaffey's Mills
After Benjamin and Samuel Chaffey established an extensive milling complex along the Rideau River in the 1820s, a small settlement known as Chaffey's Mills flourished briefly, until construction of the Rideau Canal necessitated the flooding of the mill site. Shipping, and later tourism, helped to maintain the small community. (At Chaffeys Locks, County Road 9, southwest from Highway 15)

- DELTA
Dr. Lorne Pierce 1890-1961
A prolific writer and ardent promoter of Canadian literature, Dr. Pierce, who was born in Delta, was the editor of The Ryerson Press from 1920 to 1960. He set up several university scholarships and established an excellent Canadian literature collection at Queen's University. (On the grounds of the United Church in Delta – Highway 42 west of Athens)

- FRANKVILLE
Louise C. McKinney 1868-1931
Born and raised in Leeds County, McKinney moved to Alberta in 1903. She was a strong advocate of temperance and female suffrage, and with her election to the provincial legislature in 1917 became the first woman in the British Empire to gain a parliamentary seat. (On the grounds of the Kitley Historical Museum, Highway 29, Frankville)

- GANANOQUE
The Raid on Gananoque 1812
An important forwarding point for shipping between Montreal and Kingston, Gananoque was subjected to a devastating raid during the War of 1812 by a contingent of American forces led by Captain Benjamin Forsyth. Subsequently a block-

house was constructed to strengthen Gananoque's defences. (On the grounds of the Gananoque Power Company, 5 King Street East, Gananoque)

Colonel Joel Stone 1749-1833

A loyalist during the American Revolution, Stone came to Canada in 1786 and established a milling complex on the Gananoque River. The small settlement that developed around these mills formed the nucleus of present-day Gananoque. (In front of the town hall, 30 King Street East, Gananoque)

The Gananoque Town Hall

Built in the early 1830s, the town hall in Gananoque was originally the home of John McDonald, a local landowner and merchant. The handsome Neoclassical structure remained in the possession of the family until 1911 when it was deeded to the community. (In front of the town hall, 30 King Street East, Gananoque)

"Pirate" Johnston 1782-1870

A Canadian renegade, William Johnston settled in New York State during the War of 1812. He set up a base in the Thousand Islands as a trader and smuggler and from there, during the disturbances of 1837-38, led many armed raids on communities along the Canadian shore. (In the waterfront park, Water Street, just east of Main Street, Gananoque)

Thousand Islands International Bridge

Opened in 1938 by Prime Minster Mackenzie King and President Roosevelt, this international bridge system comprises five separate bridges with connecting viaducts and highways, which together cover a distance of about thirteen kilometres. (At the tourist information booth on Hill Island – off

Highway 401 at turnoff 661, about 15 km east of
Gananoque)

• JOHNSTOWN
Johnstown 1789
Many prominent loyalists settled in Johnstown, and
between 1793 and 1808 it was the administrative
centre for the Eastern District. The town's shallow
harbour, however, prevented extensive development. (On the south side of Highway 2, near
Highway 16, Johnstown)

• JONES FALLS
Lieutenant-Colonel John By, R.E.
Between 1802 and 1811 John By (c.1779-1836) was
posted at Quebec City with the Royal Engineers.
The experience he gained working on the construc-
tion of martello towers and several small canals on
the St. Lawrence proved indispensable later when
he was appointed to superintend construction of the
Rideau Canal. (Near the locks at Jones Falls – on
County Road 11 west from Highway 15)

• KEMPTVILLE
The Honourable G. Howard Ferguson 1870-1946
Born in Kemptville, Ferguson practised law prior
to entering provincial politics in 1905. Following his
term as Ontario's ninth prime minister (1923-1930)
he served as Canadian high commissioner to the
United Kingdom. (Van Buren Street, just south of
Prescott Street, Kemptville)

• LANSDOWNE
Elizabeth Rabb Beatty 1856-1939
Elizabeth Beatty spent most of her early years in
Lansdowne and taught school in Leeds County
before studying medicine at Queen's University.
Supported by the Presbyterian Church, Dr. Beatty
practised in Indore, Central India from 1884 to 1891

where, with Dr. Marion Oliver, she established a hospital for women. (In front of her former home, Prince and Beatty Streets, Lansdowne)

• LYNDHURST
The Founding of Lyndhurst
An iron smelter operating on the Gananoque River by 1801 gave rise to a small industrial community called, unimaginatively, Furnace Falls. The ironworks were destroyed by fire ten years later, but several mills were established and by 1846 the settlement had been renamed Lyndhurst. (At the stone bridge, Charles Street, Lyndhurst)

• MAITLAND
The Founding of Maitland
The site of a shipyard during the latter half of the eighteenth century, Maitland was a convenient point of access to the Rideau area and flourished during the construction of the canal between 1826 and 1832. The attractive village still contains many early buildings. (Highway 2, east of Church Street, Maitland)

St. James' Church 1826
One of the oldest parish churches in the Anglican Diocese of Ontario, St. James' was begun in 1826 and consecrated four years later. Although somewhat altered by renovations, the church remains a pleasing example of early Gothic Revivial architecture. (On the grounds of the church, Church Street, Maitland)

Lieutenant-Colonel Thain Wendell MacDowell, V.C., D.S.O. 1890-1960
The courage and quick thinking displayed by Mac-Dowell during the battle of Vimy Ridge in April 1917 gained his battalion its objective, and earned the young soldier from Maitland the Victoria Cross.

As a civilian after the war MacDowell worked in the civil service and later entered the mining industry. (At the intersection of Maitland Road and Highway 2, Maitland)

Dr. Solomon Jones 1756-1822
Jones served as a surgeon's mate with various loyalist units during the American Revolution and at the conclusion of the war received a large land grant in Augusta Township. "Homewood", the Georgian-style residence he built in 1800 overlooking the St. Lawrence River, is now owned by the Ontario Heritage Foundation and is operated as a museum by the Grenville County Historical Society. (On the grounds of Homewood, Highway 2, about 3 km east of Maitland)

• MERRICKVILLE
The Founding of Merrickville
William Merrick, a loyalist from Massachusetts, acquired a sawmill at Great Falls in 1793 and soon built additional mills. A community began to develop called, logically enough, Merrick's Mills. Construction of the Rideau Canal attracted other small industries and an organized village was soon in evidence. (On the grounds of the municipal building, Main Street at Elgin, Merrickville)

The Merrickville Blockhouse 1832
Completed in 1832 to accommodate some fifty men, this blockhouse formed part of a large-scale defence system along the Rideau Canal. It was never the scene of military action, however, and through the years the structure has served as lockmaster's quarters, a church, and a canal-maintenance building. (At the blockhouse, Main and Mill Streets, Merrickville)

• NEWBORO
The Royal Sappers and Miners
In 1827 two companies of the British Army's construction corps, the Royal Sappers and Miners, were raised specifically to work on the Rideau Canal. They built locks and military structures primarily in the Bytown (Ottawa) area and at the Isthmus (Newboro). (At St. Mary's Cemetery, Highway 42, Newboro)

The Founding of Newboro
A major construction camp during the building of the Rideau Canal, Newboro became a trade centre for the region's lumbering industry and agriculture.

The excavation of a three-kilometre cut across the Isthmus (later Newboro) to join Rideau Lake and Mud Lake was a major undertaking requiring the expertise of the Royal Engineers and a workforce estimated at close to 1,000. (Archives of Ontario. Thomas Burrowes Sketch #36. 1841)

Its growth was further stimulated during the latter part of the nineteenth century when iron ore from local mines was shipped via the canal to smelters in Pittsburgh and Cleveland. (At the war memorial, Drummond Street (Highway 42), Newboro)

• PHILLIPSVILLE
James Philips
An early store and tavern owner in present-day Phillipsville, James Philips (c.1800-1838) became active in politics and rose to local prominence as a Reformer in the 1830s. He was killed at the Battle of the Windmill in 1838. (In Phillipsville – Highway 42, southeast of Highway 15)

• PRESCOTT
The Forwarding Trade at Prescott
Prior to the construction of canals to bypass the hazardous Galops Rapids, goods and passengers travelling between the Great Lakes and Montreal were trans-shipped or "forwarded" at Prescott. During the first half of the nineteenth century many firms constructed shipyards, wharfs and warehouses along the waterfront. (At the Forwarders' Museum, Centre and Water Streets, Prescott)

The Prescott Barracks and Hospital
One of the few surviving buildings used for military purposes during the War of 1812, this stone house was built about 1810 by Colonel Edward Jessup. As a combined hospital and barracks store it formed part of the strategic Prescott garrison. (At the former barracks, known locally as the Fetterly House, 356 East Street, Prescott)

The Capture of Ogdensburg 1813
On February 22, 1813 a British and Canadian force under the command of Lieutenant-Colonel "Red George" Macdonell set out from Prescott and

crossed the frozen St. Lawrence to attack the American military post at Ogdensburg. After a spirited battle, the garrison was overcome and Ogdensburg fell. (In the Public Utilities Park, at the foot of Sophia Street, Prescott)

Major James Morrow Walsh 1840-1905

A native of Prescott, Walsh gained fame in western Canada as an officer in the North-West Mounted Police. His negotiations with Chief Sitting Bull led to the amicable return to the United States of the 5,000 Sioux who had sought refuge in Canada during 1876-1877. (In Centennial Park, King Street West, Prescott)

The Bytown and Prescott Railway Company 1850

The railway that opened between Prescott and Bytown (Ottawa) on Christmas Day 1854 gave the latter community an important link with shipping on the St. Lawrence as well as with the Grand Trunk Railway, and was undoubtedly a factor in the choice of Ottawa as the country's capital. (Opposite Fort Wellington, Highway 2, Prescott)

Colonel Edward Jessup 1735-1816

At the outbreak of the American Revolution Edward Jessup, with his brother Ebenezer, raised and commanded the loyalist corps known as Jessup's Rangers. He received a large land grant at the close of the war, part of which later became the town site of Prescott. (On the grounds of Fort Wellington, Highway 2, Prescott)

Justus Sherwood 1747-1798

A native of Connecticut, Sherwood joined the loyalist forces during the American Revolution. He came to Augusta Township in 1784 and, by assisting former members of Jessup's Rangers in taking up land in the region, played a prominent role in the settlement of Grenville County. (At the junction of Highway 2 and Merwin Lane, just west of Prescott)

The Blue Church

This small wooden chapel, painted blue, was built in 1845 to replace an earlier structure badly damaged by fire. Used mainly as a funeral chapel, it stands today as a memorial to the many early settlers whose graves can be found in the adjacent churchyard. (At the church, on the north side of Highway 2, about 3 km west of Prescott)

• ROEBUCK

Roebuck Indian Village Site

Some 500 years ago an eight-acre site near present-day Roebuck contained the palisaded village of an Iroquoian agricultural community. Archaeological excavations have uncovered stone tools such as scrapers and adzes, bone needles and knives, pottery vessels and earthenware pipes, but very few weapons. (At the archaeological site, County Road 21, just east of Roebuck)

• SPENCERVILLE

The Founding of Spencerville

Peleg and David Spencer's mills on the banks of the South Nation River formed the nucleus of a small pioneer community that by the middle of the nineteenth century contained a variety of small industries and was the site of an annual agricultural fair. (In front of the township hall, Centre Street, Spencerville)

• TOLEDO

Abel Stevens

Within two years of moving to Upper Canada from Vermont and settling in Leeds County in 1796,

Stevens (c.1750-c.1826) had encouraged some 100 loyalist families to locate in Kitley and Bastard Townships. He built mills at several sites along the Gananoque River and was involved in the establishment of an ironworks at present-day Lyndhurst. (At the cemetery at Bellamy's Lake (within the lands he helped to settle), west of Toledo – County Road 8, west of Highway 29)

• WESTPORT
The Perth Road
Surveyed in 1852 to encourage settlement in isolated townships between Perth and Kingston, the Perth Road was passable as a winter road by 1855. Today, County Road 10 essentially follows the original route. (County Road 10, about 1.5 km south of Westport)

The Brockville, Westport and Sault Ste. Marie Railway
In 1888, four years after receiving its charter, this railway was operating between Brockville and Westport. Lack of funds prevented extension of the line to Sault Ste. Marie as originally intended, but local trains continued to run – under various owners – until 1952. (Near the former railway station, Highway 42, Westport)

The Founding of Westport
Sawmills built during construction of the Rideau Canal formed the nucleus of the hamlet of West Port. Completion of a railway line from Brockville in 1888 helped to foster further development of this rural community. (At the town hall, Bedford Street, Westport)

LENNOX AND ADDINGTON COUNTY

• ADOLPHUSTOWN

The Loyalist Landing Place 1784
In 1783 some 250 loyalist refugees led by Peter Van Alstine sailed from New York City bound for a new life in a new country. After wintering at Sorel they proceeded up the St. Lawrence River to their destination in Adolphustown Township on the Bay of Quinte. (In the park on Highway 33, Adolphustown)

The Loyalist Memorial Church
The Anglican Church of St. Alban-the-Martyr was constructed between 1884 and 1888, funded by public subscriptions, to commemorate loyalists of all denominations who had come to the Bay of Quinte in 1784. (At the church, Highway 33, just west of County Road 8, Adolphustown)

Lieutenant-Colonel James Rogers 1726-1790
A veteran of the Seven Years War and the American Revolution, Rogers led a party of some 300 disbanded King's Rangers and their families to the Bay of Quinte in 1784 where they were granted land in Fredericksburgh Township. (On the grounds of St. Paul's Anglican Church, Highway 33, Sandhurst – just east of Adolphustown)

The Reverend Robert James McDowall 1768-1841
Ordained by the Dutch Reformed Church at Albany, McDowall was sent to Canada to minister to settlers in the Bay of Quinte region in 1798. For more than forty years he travelled throughout central Upper Canada preaching, performing marriages, and spreading the doctrine of Presbyterianism. (Near the McDowall Memorial Cemetery (where his grave is located), Highway 33, Sandhurst – just east of Adolphustown)

The Quakers of Adolphustown

The Quakers who settled in Adolphustown Township in 1784 came mainly from New York State, and formed one of the earliest Quaker communities in the province. Although they were not "loyalists", since they had refused to bear arms for either side in the American Revolution, they were readily accepted into the predominantly loyalist community at Adolphustown. (At the Quaker cemetery on Hay Bay Road, about 4 km north of Adolphustown)

Hay Bay Church 1792

In 1792 the congregation at Hay Bay built the first Methodist chapel in Upper Canada. The small frame

---

According to local legend the 1798 Quaker meeting house at Adolphustown was used as a barracks during the War of 1812. This building, of similar construction, replaced it in 1868. Today only a small burying ground marks the site. (Archives of Ontario S 954)

meeting house was used for worship until about 1860 when it became, for a time, a storehouse for crops. Re-acquired by the Methodists in 1910, it has since been restored and is now maintained by the United Church of Canada. (On the grounds of the church, Hay Bay Road, about 4 km north of Adolphustown)

• AMHERST ISLAND
Daniel Fowler 1810-1894
A long-time resident of Amherst Island, Fowler received much public acclaim for his watercolours. He painted local landscapes, flowers, and still-life compositions in a highly realistic style enhanced by a strong sense of colour. (On the grounds of his former home, Concession Road 1, near Emerald, Amherst Island)

• AMHERSTVIEW
The Fairfield House
Built by William Fairfield, Sr., a loyalist from Vermont, this handsome clapboard house was completed, according to tradition, in 1793. Six generations of Fairfields occupied the house over the next 150 years. Maintained by the St. Lawrence Parks Commission since 1959, the house has been restored and is now a public museum. (In Fairfield Historical Park, Amherstview – Highway 33, just east of County Road 6)

Madeleine de Roybon d'Allonne
The daughter of a French nobleman, Madeleine de Roybon (c.1646-1718) came to Fort Frontenac (Kingston) about 1679. On land granted to her by La Salle she built a house and barns, grew crops and grazed cattle, and established a small trading post. She was the first known female landholder in present-day Ontario. (On her former land holding, Highway 33, east of the floating bridge at Parrott Bay – just west of Amherstview)

Lieutenant-Colonel Edwin Albert Baker
1893-1968

As a result of being blinded while serving with the Canadian Army in Belgium in 1914, Baker devoted his life to the rehabilitation and training of blind people. He played an instrumental role in the formation of the CNIB in 1918 and served as its managing director for more than forty years. (At Beulah United Church (near his birthplace), Highway 33, west of the floating bridge, just west of Amherstview)

• BATH

The Hawley House

Built in the 1780s by Captain Jeptha Hawley, a loyalist from Vermont, the Hawley House is probably the oldest remaining house in the Bay of Quinte area and one of the oldest in the province. The stone portion of the building was added the following decade to provide living quarters for the Reverend John Langhorn, the first resident Anglican clergyman in the district. (On the grounds of the house, 531 Main Street, Bath)

The Bath Academy 1811

Founded in 1811 by means of local subscriptions, the Bath Academy operated briefly as a public school before being requisitioned as a military barracks during the War of 1812. It later re-opened and by offering an extensive curriculum gained an excellent reputation for scholarship. (On the grounds of the municipal office, 352 Academy Street, Bath)

The Reverend John Langhorn 1744-1817

Born in Wales, Langhorn was appointed missionary to the Bay of Quinte in 1787 and became that region's first resident Anglican clergyman. A man of strong, if eccentric, character, Langhorn energetically served the area for twenty-six years from his headquarters in Ernestown (Bath). (On the grounds of St. John's Anglican Church (one of the parishes he served), 212 Church Street, Bath)

The Founding of Bath
One of the oldest communities in Ontario, Bath was first settled in 1784 by soldiers discharged from Jessup's Rangers. A sheltered harbour and road connections with Kingston stimulated economic development and by mid-century Bath was a prosperous point of trade. (In Centennial Park, Main and Fairfield Streets, Bath)

The Escape of the Royal George 1812
In the first significant naval action on the Great Lakes during the War of 1812 the British warship *Royal George* escaped its American pursuers by adroitly navigating the gap between Prince Edward County and Amherst Island. After an exchange of fire in Kingston harbour the following day, the American fleet was forced to withdraw. (Highway 33, opposite the gap, about 5 km west of Bath)

- ## CAMDEN EAST
Sir Gilbert Parker 1862-1932
A native of Camden East, Parker pursued a career in journalism in Australia before moving to England in 1889. There he gained a considerable reputation as a writer of historical novels, many of which were set in French Canada. Probably the best-known of his works is *The Seats of the Mighty*. (On the grounds of St. Luke's Anglican Church, County Road 4, Camden East)

- ## CONWAY
Hazelton Spencer 1757-1813
After fighting with the loyalist forces in the American Revolution, Spencer settled in Fredericksburgh Township in 1784. He represented the region in the

province's first parliament, and from 1794 until his death held the prestigious post of lieutenant of the County of Lennox. (Near his former farm, Highway 33, just west of Conway)

- KALADAR
The Addington Road
Extending northward to meet the Peterson Road, the Addington Road was part of a network of government roads built to encourage settlement in the southern region of the Precambrian Shield. It was built in two stages, in 1854-57 and in 1863-64. (Near the route of the former colonization road, Highway 41 at Highway 7, Kaladar)

- NAPANEE
The Napanee Mills
A sawmill and grist-mill built in the 1780s by Robert Clark were purchased in 1799 by Richard Cartwright, a prominent Kingston merchant. The mills served settlers as far west as the Trent River and formed the nucleus of the community of Napanee. (In Springside Park, Dundas Street (Highway 2), Napanee)

The Macpherson House
A fine example of late Georgian architecture, the Macpherson House was built some time prior to 1830 by Allan Macpherson, Napanee's first postmaster and a prominent personality in the community. The house is now a public museum operated by the Lennox and Addington Historical Society. (On the grounds of the house, 180 Elizabeth Street, Napanee)

- NEWBURGH
John Thomson 1837-1920
After serving an apprenticeship as a paper-maker in New Jersey, John Thomson worked for a number of American and Canadian firms while perfecting

his revolutionary process for producing paper from wood pulp. In 1872 he and his brother James established the Newburgh Paper Mills. (In front of the municipal office, Main Street, Newburgh – at the junction of County Roads 2 and 11)

Sir Allen Bristol Aylesworth 1854-1952
A native of Newburgh, Aylesworth was elected to the federal parliament in 1905 and held a number of appointments in the Laurier cabinet. He also served as a Canadian member of the Alaska Boundary Tribunal in 1903 and as a British representative at the North Atlantic Fisheries Arbitration in The Hague in 1910-11. (At the municipal office, Main Street, Newburgh)

MANITOULIN DISTRICT

• KILLARNEY
The Founding of Killarney
In 1820 the fur trader Etienne de la Morandière moved to the site of present-day Killarney – then known as Shebahonaning. He cleared land, planted crops, and even imported cattle. The remote settlement he founded continued to develop over the years despite the fact that until Highway 637 was opened in 1962 it was accessible only by water. (On the grounds of the municipal building, 31 Commissioner Street, Killarney)

• LITTLE CURRENT
Hudson's Bay Post 1856
Faced with declining trade on the mainland following the establishment of permanent Indian settlements on Manitoulin Island, the Hudson's Bay Company built a substantial post at Little Current in 1856. Because of opposition from the island's native inhabitants and resident missionaries, however, the company's licence was revoked before trade began. (Near the site of the former post, Manitowaning Road and Water Street, Little Current)

The Jesuit Mission to Manitoulin 1648-50
The first recorded European resident of Manitoulin Island was Father Joseph Poncet, S.J., who established a mission to serve the island's Algonkian-speaking people in 1648. The mission was abandoned in 1650, however, following the destruction of the Huron nation by the Iroquois. (At Ten Mile Point, Highway 6, about 16 km south of Little Current)

Dreamer's Rock
A shallow depression at the summit of a tall quartzite rock served as the site for a rite of passage

for Indian youths approaching the age of puberty. Reclining in solitude in the elongated hollow, a boy would fast, and through dreams receive visions of the future from his guardian spirit. (At the rock, Whitefish River Indian Reserve, Birch Island Lodge Road, east off Highway 6 about 12 km northeast of Little Current)

The Route of the Voyageurs

The historic canoe route from Montreal to Sault Ste. Marie via the Ottawa River, Lake Nipissing, the French River and the North Channel was, in all likelihood, used for centuries by the continent's native inhabitants. In recorded history, numerous explorers, missionaries and fur traders guided their

Dreamer's Rock, or the fasting rock, on Manitoulin Island was a legendary site for the ancient Indian rite of dream visitation. (Archives of Ontario S 1055)

canoes through the channel at Swift Current. (At Swift Current Channel, Highway 6, about 15 km northeast of Little Current)

• MANITOWANING
The Manitowaning Indian Treaties
The treaties of 1836 and 1862 between chiefs of the Ojibwa and Ottawa nations and the government greatly influenced the future of Manitoulin. The first designated the entire island as a reserve for all Indians wishing to settle there, while the second treaty opened Manitoulin, exclusive of its eastern peninsula, to general settlement. (On the grounds of the Assiginack Museum, Arthur and Nelson Streets, Manitowaning)

The Manitowaning Mission
The first permanent Anglican mission on Manitoulin Island was established in 1838 as an outpost of the Diocese of Toronto. Between 1845 and 1849 the small Indian congregation led by the Reverend F.A. O'Meara built St. Paul's Church – the oldest remaining church in the Manitoulin-Algoma area. (On the grounds of St. Paul's Anglican Church, Spragge Street, Manitowaning)

MIDDLESEX COUNTY

- AILSA CRAIG
Ailsa Craig
Named after a small Scottish island, Ailsa Craig
prospered as a point of trade on the Grand Trunk
Railway, and by 1870 was the site of the largest cattle
market west of London. (At the community centre,
Highway 7 and Jameson Street, Ailsa Craig)

- DELAWARE
Ebenezer Allan 1752-1813
Having fought with the loyalist forces in the
American Revolution, Allan came to Upper Canada
in 1794 where he obtained 2,000 acres of land on
the site of present-day Delaware. Disputes with
authorities over land deals, however, led to disaf-
fection, and during the War of 1812 he supported
the American invaders. (In the municipal park,
County Road 3 and Wellington Street, Delaware)

Gideon Tiffany 1774-1854
One of the earliest printers in Upper Canada,
Tiffany, with his brother Silvester, founded the
province's first independent newspaper at Niagara
in 1799. When it failed, he moved to Delaware
Township where he became a prominent landowner
and office holder. (In the municipal park, County
Road 3 and Wellington Street, Delaware)

- LONDON
The Founding of London
In 1793 Lieutenant-Governor Simcoe reserved the
site at the forks of the Thames for the capital of
Upper Canada. York became the seat of govern-
ment, however, and the townsite of London began
to develop only after 1826 when it was selected as
the judicial and administrative centre of the London
District. (In the northeast corner of Court House
Square, Dundas and Ridout Streets, London)

Eldon House

The oldest remaining house in London, Eldon House was built in 1834 by a retired naval officer, Captain John Harris. For many years it was the centre of social and cultural life in the community, and is now a public museum, having been given to the City of London by the Harris family in 1960. (At the house, 481 Ridout Street North, London)

The Reverend William Proudfoot 1788-1851

An energetic Presbyterian missionary and church leader, Proudfoot served a parish in Scotland before coming to Upper Canada in 1832 and settling in London the following year. He made numerous preaching tours and organized congregations in both Canada and the United States. (On the grounds of First St. Andrew's United Church (the successor to the London congregation Proudfoot organized), 350 Queens Avenue, London)

Josiah Blackburn 1823-1890

An astute businessman with a flair for political writing, Blackburn founded the *London Free Press and Daily Western Advertiser* in 1855. He continued to publish that paper until his death, as well as maintaining a controlling interest in several other newspapers. (At his former residence, now the London Squash Racquets Club, 76 Albert Street, London)

Richard Maurice Bucke, M.D. 1837-1902

While superintendent of the London Asylum for the Insane (1877-1902), Bucke gained a substantial reputation for his innovative treatment of mental disorders. The author of *Cosmic Consciousness* (1901), he also earned renown for his speculations on the philosophy of religion. (Beside the Chapel of Hope, on the grounds of the London Psychiatric Hospital, 850 Highbury Avenue, London)

Sir Adam Beck 1857-1925

A prominent politician in the London area, Beck was responsible for introducing a bill in the provincial legislature in 1906 which established the Hydro-Electric Power Commission of Ontario. He served as chairman of that body until his death. (At the site of his former home, Richmond Street near Oxford, London)

Paul Peel

A native of London, Paul Peel (1860-92) studied painting in Philadelphia and in England before moving to Paris. His romantic, warm-toned canvases hang in several major Canadian galleries and private collections. (At the Dundas Street entrance to the London Regional Art Gallery, 421 Ridout Street North, London)

St. Paul's Cathedral 1846

Solidly built of brick to replace a more vulnerable wooden structure, St. Paul's Anglican Church was designed by the renowned architect William Thomas. In 1857, with the creation of the Diocese of Huron, St. Paul's was designated a cathedral. (On the grounds of the cathedral, Richmond Street and Queens Avenue, London)

St. Peter's Cathedral Basilica

Designed by church architect Joseph Connolly in the thirteenth-century French-Gothic style, and built between 1880 and 1885, St. Peter's was designated a minor basilica by the Vatican in 1961. Recent alterations have not marred the majestic proportions of the cathedral's original design. (On the grounds of the cathedral, 196 Dufferin Avenue, London)

The Right Reverend Isaac Hellmuth 1817-1901

Born and educated in Poland, Hellmuth came to

Canada in 1844 where he was ordained in the Church of England. The second bishop of Huron, he was instrumental in founding the University of Western Ontario in 1878 and served as that institution's first chancellor. (At the rear of the administration building, Wellington Drive, University of Western Ontario campus, London)

Huron College 1863
Founded by Benjamin Cronyn, first bishop of Huron, this college provided theological training and instruction in the liberal arts. In 1881 Huron College was affiliated with the University of Western Ontario. (On the outside north wall of Huron College Chapel, Western Road, opposite the community centre, University of Western Ontario campus, London)

The British Garrison in London
Established to guard against border raids in the wake of the Rebellion of 1837, the British garrison contributed significantly to London's economic and social life. The troops were withdrawn in 1853, but with the threat posed by the American Civil War the garrison was re-occupied during the 1860s. (In Victoria Park (formerly the old military reserve), bounded by Dufferin Avenue, Central, Wellington and Clarence Streets, London)

The Victoria Boat Disaster 1881
One of the worst marine disasters in Canada occurred on May 24, 1881 when the excursion steamer *Victoria* sank in the Thames River. Overcrowded with excited holiday-makers, the flat-bottomed boat overturned and close to 200 of its 600 passengers were drowned. (Near the site of the disaster, Riverside Park, London)

Blackfriars Bridge

The oldest known wrought iron bridge in Ontario, Blackfriars was constructed in 1875 to replace a less reliable wooden structure. A fine example of truss construction, the bowstring arch bridge remains in regular use. (At the riverside walkway beside the bridge, Blackfriars Street, London)

The Lawson Site

Archaeological excavations have revealed that a prehistoric Neutral Indian village existed on this site about 1500. Named after the owners of the land when excavations began in the 1920s, the site is now owned by the University of Western Ontario. (At the entrance to the reconstructed Indian village, east of the Museum of Indian Archaeology, 1600 Attawandaron Road, London)

The Tolpuddle Martyrs

Six agricultural labourers in Tolpuddle, England were condemned to penal servitude in 1834 for organizing a union of fellow workers. The case, which caused much public indignation, marked a turning point in British labour laws. Most of the "martyrs" eventually settled in Upper Canada. (In Siloam Cemetery (where the grave of George Loveless, one of the martyrs, is located), County Road 31, north of London)

• LUCAN
The Wilberforce Settlement 1830

A group of fugitive slaves from Cincinnati, aided by Quakers in Ohio, purchased 800 acres in Biddulph Township from the Canada Company in 1830. Within three years, thirty-two families were living in the settlement, which was named after the British abolitionist William Wilberforce. (On the grounds of the post office, 179 Main Street (within the area of the former settlement), Lucan)

The Founding of Lucan

In anticipation of construction of the Grand Trunk Railway to Sarnia, the site of Lucan was subdivided into lots, the first of which were sold in 1855. Mills, stores and hotels were built and with the completion of the rail line, Lucan, as its founders had hoped, prospered. (On the grounds of the community centre, 263 Main Street, Lucan)

- NAIRN

Sir George W. Ross 1841-1914

Born near Nairn, George Ross was a teacher and school inspector before he entered politics in 1872. He served as minister of education in the Mowat government and, following the retirement of A.S. Hardy, became the fifth prime minister of Ontario (1899-1905). (On the grounds of East Williams Memorial Public School, Queen Street, Nairn – County Road 19 south of Highway 7)

- NEWBURY

The Founding of Newbury

A railway station on the line from Niagara Falls to Windsor provided the nucleus around which Newbury began to develop in the 1850s. It soon became an important shipping point for square timber, and by 1872 boasted a population of 800. (On the grounds of the public library, 48 Hagerty Road, Newbury)

- PARKHILL

The Founding of Parkhill

Despite construction of a railway station at the site of Parkhill in 1860, the community was slow to develop. A grist-mill and other small industries were established some years later, which gave Parkhill a firmer economic base and fostered its growth. (On the grounds of the municipal offices, 229 Main Street, Parkhill)

- ## STRATHROY
The Founding of Strathroy
The sawmill and grist-mill that John Buchanan built on the Sydenham River in 1836 formed the basis of a settlement named after Buchanan's birthplace in Ireland. Construction of a rail line through Strathroy twenty years later ensured the community's continued development. (On the grounds of the town hall, 52 Frank Street, Strathroy)

The Honourable Edward Blake 1833-1912
A distinguished lawyer and brilliant orator, Blake, who was born near Strathroy, served briefly as prime minister of Ontario in 1871-72. He later held several cabinet posts in the federal government and was leader of the Liberal party for eight years. (On the grounds of the town hall, 52 Frank Street, Strathroy)

General Sir Arthur William Currie 1875-1933
A native of Strathroy, William Currie was one of Canada's most distinguished military figures. He saw action throughout the First World War and in 1917 was appointed commander-in-chief of the Canadian Corps in Europe. (On the grounds of Strathroy District Collegiate Institute (which Currie attended), 96 Kittredge Avenue East, Strathroy)

St. Mary's Church
In the 1830s many veterans of British military and naval service commuted their pensions to purchase land in Adelaide Township. Largely members of the Church of England, they soon erected St. Mary's – now the oldest remaining church in Middlesex County. (On the grounds of the church, Concession Road 5 and 6, one road west of County Road 6, outside the community of Napier – southwest of Strathroy)

MUSKOKA DISTRICT

• BALA

The Precambrian Shield
The shield is one of the oldest rock formations in the earth's crust and covers about two-thirds of the surface area of Ontario. Although the shield was unsuitable for agricultural settlement, its lakes, forests and mineral resources proved to be the foundation of the province's economic development. (In the parking lot, Highway 169, Bala)

The Founding of Bala
Soon after settling at the site of present-day Bala in 1868 Thomas Burgess opened a sawmill and store to serve the area's scattered settlers. The Musquosh Road from Gravenhurst and, many years later, railway connections helped to establish the village as a popular summer resort. (In Bala Falls Park near the Moon River bridge, Highway 169, Bala)

• BAYSVILLE

Explorers of Muskoka and Haliburton
In the decades following the War of 1812 various expeditions explored the wilderness between the Ottawa River and Lakes Simcoe and Muskoka seeking a route across Upper Canada less open to attack than the vulnerable region along the St. Lawrence River and Lake Ontario. (Near the government wharf, opposite Lincoln Lodge Hotel, Highway 117, Baysville)

The Founding of Baysville
A sawmill built by William Brown in the 1870s was the focal point of the small community that developed on the sawyer's sub-divided landholdings. Good road and steamboat connections helped to turn Baysville into a popular haven for vacationers and sportsmen. (Near the government wharf, opposite Lincoln Lodge Hotel, Highway 117, Baysville)

• BRACEBRIDGE
The Founding of Bracebridge
Once the Muskoka colonization road had been completed to the first falls on the north branch of the Muskoka River by 1862, entrepreneurs began to take advantage of the area's water power and soon a small community was in evidence. With the advent of steamship service on Lake Muskoka a few years later, Bracebridge prospered as the main distribution centre for the region. (In Memorial Park, bordered by Manitoba, Kimberly and Parklane Streets, Bracebridge)

Woodchester Villa at Bracebridge (shown here shortly after its construction in 1882) was designed in part to incorporate some of the theories of the American architectural philosopher and phrenologist Orson Fowler. (Archives of Ontario ACC 15963-8)

Woodchester Villa

Known locally as the "Bird Cage", this octagonal house was built in 1882 by Henry James Bird, and contained many innovative features aside from its unusual shape. Restored and furnished by the Bracebridge Historical Society, Woodchester Villa is now a public museum. (On the grounds of the house, Muskoka Road, Bracebridge)

• GRAVENHURST
The Muskoka Road 1858

In an attempt to open the northern bushland to settlement, the government constructed numerous colonization roads, offering free land grants flanking the routes to settlers willing to clear a specific

Steamboating on the Muskoka waterways was a thriving enterprise, as evidenced by this photograph of the Sagamo taking on passengers at Port Carling in 1908. (Archives of Ontario S 3627A)

acreage. Begun at Washago in 1858, the Muskoka
Road was completed north to the site of present-
day Bracebridge within three years. (In Kahshe
River Park, Highway 11, about 8 km south of
Gravenhurst)

The Founding of Gravenhurst

The construction of a colonization road in the 1850s
and the launching of steamboating on the Muskoka
lakes during the following decade ensured the
economic prosperity of Gravenhurst. The town's
location at the northern terminus of the Toronto,
Simcoe and Muskoka Junction Railway further
consolidated its position as the "Gateway to Muskoka". (In front of the municipal building, 190
Harvie Street, Gravenhurst)

Steamboating in Muskoka 1866-1959

The introduction of steam navigation on the Muskoka lakes contributed significantly to the rapid
development of Muskoka as a lumbering and resort
area. Enormous log booms were towed to the
sawmills at Gravenhurst by tugboats, and excur-
sionists and travellers explored the lakes on passenger vessels whose names still haunt the region
– *Wenonah, Ahmic, Sagamo, Segwun.* (In Sagamo Park,
Highway 169, Gravenhurst)

The Toronto, Simcoe and Muskoka Junction
Railway Company

Begun at Barrie in 1870, this rail line did not reach
Gravenhurst until five years later, having been
hampered by rugged terrain and constant financial
troubles. The completed line, which connected with
steamboat service on the lakes, contributed substantially to the economic development of the region.
(At the CNR station, Brock and Second Streets,
Gravenhurst)

Dr. Henry Norman Bethune 1890-1939

Humanitarian, surgeon and revolutionary, Bethune was born at Gravenhurst and educated at Toronto. Concern with social and political issues took him to Spain in 1936 and then to China where, until his death, he worked unsparingly as a surgeon with the Revolutionary Army. (At his birthplace, now the Bethune Memorial House Museum, 235 John Street, Gravenhurst)

• HUNTSVILLE

The Founding of Huntsville

Begun as a small agricultural settlement in the late 1860s largely through the efforts of Captain George Hunt, Huntsville continued to develop throughout

Built by members of the congregation who also provided the logs, the Madill Church near Huntsville stands today as a sturdy memorial to the area's first settlers. (Archives of Ontario ACC 16856-22007A)

the century, stimulated to a great extent by the engineering of a navigable water route to Port Sydney and the construction of a rail line from Gravenhurst. (In front of the town hall, 37 Main Street East, Huntsville)

The Madill Church 1873
Contemporary with the pioneer settlement era of the Muskoka region, this small, squared-timber church is one of very few churches of its type remaining in Ontario. Land was donated by John Madill, an early settler in the area, and the church was built by a Wesleyan Methodist congregation. (At the church, Madill Church Road, just west of Highway 11 about 6 km south of Huntsville)

• MUSKOKA FALLS
The Peterson Road
Named after surveyor Joseph Peterson and built between 1858 and 1863, this colonization road ran from the Opeongo Road west to Muskoka Falls and was part of the government's network of settlement roads. Poor soil thwarted attempts at large-scale agricultural development along the route, but parts of the old road have been incorporated into the present highway system. (On the grounds of Muskoka Falls Community Church, Vankoughnet Road, just east of Highway 11, Muskoka Falls)

• PORT CARLING
Port Carling
Originally called Indian Village, Port Carling was renamed in 1869 in honour of John Carling, Ontario's first minister of public works. Construction of locks between Lake Muskoka and Lake Rosseau greatly aided the economic development of the small port. (In the park beside the locks, Lock Street, Port Carling)

NIAGARA REGIONAL MUNICIPALITY

- CHIPPAWA
Fort Chippawa 1791
Built to protect the southern end of the Niagara portage road, Fort Chippawa (also called Fort Welland) originally consisted of a log blockhouse surrounded by a stockade. Before the fort was abandoned sometime after the 1812-14 war, a barracks, storehouse, officers' quarters and earthworks had been added. (In the park on the north bank of the Welland River (near the site of the former fort), Chippawa)

The Founding of Chippawa
Situated on Chippawa Creek at the end of the portage road from Queenston, Chippawa retained its original name even though the creek was renamed the Welland River in 1793. Severely damaged during the War of 1812, the village revived following construction of the first Welland Canal. (In Cummington Square, near the former town hall, Chippawa)

The Raid on Fort Schlosser 1813
At daybreak on July 5, 1813 a British and Canadian force crossed the Niagara River from Chippawa to attack the American depot on the opposite shore. The success of this raid inspired a series of similar incursions along the frontier. (In King's Bridge Park, Chippawa)

The Church of the Holy Trinity
The first Anglican church on this site was burned by supporters of William Lyon Mackenzie following the Rebellion of 1837. The present church was built in the 1840s and over the next few decades numbered among its worshippers Laura Secord, Jenny Lind and the Prince of Wales. (On the grounds of the church, 7820 Portage Road South, Chippawa)

The Destruction of the Caroline 1837

Under cover of darkness on the night of December 29, 1837 a group of volunteers commanded by Captain Andrew Drew, R.N. captured the American schooner *Caroline* which had been supplying Mackenzie's rebel forces on Navy Island. The ship was set on fire and sank in the Niagara River. (Niagara River Parkway, about 2 km south of Chippawa, opposite Navy Island)

- CRYSTAL BEACH
The Capture of the Somers and Ohio

On the night of August 12, 1814 two armed American schooners were successfully captured by a small British fleet masquerading as supply craft. This

This engraving of the Caroline set ablaze in the Niagara River formed the title page of Volume II of J.C. Dent's The Story of the Upper Canadian Rebellion, published in 1885. (Archives of Ontario S 13291)

daring exploit was the last naval action fought on the Great Lakes in the 1812-14 war. (In the park on Derby Road and Queen's Place (near the site from which the British fleet embarked), Crystal Beach)

• FONTHILL
St. Johns
Benjamin Canby's 1792 sawmill on Twelve Mile Creek formed the nucleus of the community of St. Johns, for several years the leading mill-centre in the Niagara region. Construction of the Welland Canal and the consequent emergence of small industries along its length, however, had undermined St. Johns' prosperity by 1850. (On the grounds of the St. Johns Outdoor Study Centre, 2984 Holland Road, St. Johns – northwest of Fonthill)

• FORT ERIE
Mackenzie's Crossing 1837
After the defeat of his "Patriot" forces at Montgomery's Tavern, William Lyon Mackenzie fled to the United States, crossing the Niagara River near Fort Erie with the assistance of Samuel McAfee and his family. (Niagara River Parkway and Thompson Road (near the site of his crossing), about 6 km north of Fort Erie)

• GRIMSBY
Neutral Indian Burial Ground
Discovered in 1976, this burial ground revealed to archaeologists an invaluable record of the burial customs and material culture of the little-known Neutral peoples, a confederacy of Iroquoian tribes that had inhabited this region before 1655. After six months of excavation and study, all remains were reinterred. (In Centennial Park (just east of the burial ground), Grimsby)

The First Town Meeting 1790
The town meeting held on April 5, 1790 at present-

day Grimsby (then called Township #6) marked the beginning of local self-government in what is now Ontario. Such matters as the height of fences and the registration of livestock brands were discussed. (In the park adjacent to the town hall, Main Street West at Livingston Avenue (near the site of the first meeting), Grimsby)

Colonel Robert Nelles 1761-1842
A highly influential loyalist settler in the area of present-day Grimsby, Nelles came to Canada during the American Revolution. Here he became a prominent merchant, soldier, and legislator. His home, "The Manor", is one of the finest eighteenth-century houses remaining in the province. (On the grounds of his former home, 126 Main Street West, Grimsby)

St. Andrew's Anglican Church
The third church on this site, St. Andrew's was completed in 1825 by a congregation formed almost forty years earlier. The churchyard contains the graves of many early settlers at "The Forty", as Grimsby was originally called. (On the grounds of the church, Main Street West and St. Andrew's Avenue, Grimsby)

• JORDAN
The First Mennonite Settlement
The first Mennonites known to have settled in what is now Ontario took up land west of the mouth of Twenty Mile Creek in 1786. By the end of the century a settlement of some twenty-five families from Pennsylvania was established in the vicinity of present-day Vineland and Jordan where, in 1801, the first Mennonite congregation in Canada was organized. (Near the Jacob Fry House at the Museum of the Twenty, Main Street, Jordan)

- ## NIAGARA FALLS

Father Louis Hennepin

A native of Belgium, this adventurous Récollet priest travelled widely in Europe before setting sail for New France in 1675. Hennepin served as chaplain on La Salle's 1679 Mississippi expedition and later published an account of the voyage, which contains the first recorded description of Niagara Falls. (In Queen Victoria Park, along the footpath edging the gorge, Niagara Falls)

Sir Casimir S. Gzowski 1813-1898

Following the Polish uprising of 1830, Gzowski came to North America and in 1841 settled in Upper Canada. A highly skilled engineer, he organized the company that constructed the Grand Trunk Railway from Toronto to Sarnia between 1853 and 1857. From 1885 to 1893 he served as first chairman of the Niagara Falls Parks Commission. (On the grounds of the Niagara Parks Commission administration building, 7400 Portage Road South, Niagara Falls)

The Church of St. John the Evangelist

Begun in 1825, this Anglican church was constructed largely through the efforts of Lieutenant-Governor Sir Peregrine Maitland, and remained in regular use until 1957. Although it has been altered over the years, St. John's retains many of its original architectural features. (On the grounds of the church, 3428 Portage Road North, Niagara Falls)

"Stamford Park"

Preferring the quiet Niagara countryside to the social whirl of the capital at York (Toronto), Sir

---

In recognition of his achievements in the fields of engineering, defence, and education, Casimir Gzowski was made Knight Commander of the Most Distinguished Order of St. Michael and St. George in 1890. (Archives of Ontario S 17159)

Peregrine Maitland chose to live in Stamford Park, his luxurious 425-acre estate, during his term as lieutenant-governor of Upper Canada. His Regency-style mansion was sold in 1833, and shortly thereafter destroyed. (On the brow of the escarpment, near Mountain Road (near the site of the former estate), Niagara Falls)

- ## NIAGARA-ON-THE-LAKE
The Town of Niagara
Settled by loyalist refugees including members of Butler's Rangers in the 1780s, Newark, as the community was then known, was the scene of the first sessions of the Upper Canadian legislature. Captured and burned by American forces in 1813, the town was soon rebuilt, and served as the judicial and administrative centre for the district until 1866. (Opposite 6 Picton Street, on the boulevard, Niagara-on-the-Lake)

The First Provincial Parliament 1792
John Graves Simcoe, lieutenant-governor of Upper Canada, opened the first provincial parliament at Newark in September 1792, thus marking the introduction into this province of a form of representative government. (In front of the old court house building, 26 Queen Street, Niagara-on-the-Lake)

The Niagara Library
The first circulating library in Upper Canada, the Niagara Library was established in 1800 with a collection of some eighty books. The collection grew steadily and the library operated successfully until the 1812-14 war, when many volumes were lost. In 1820 the holdings were incorporated into a new subscription library that had opened two years previously. (At the old court house building, 26 Queen Street, Niagara-on-the-Lake)

Court House and Gaol 1817-1866

When the court house and jail complex for the Niagara District was erected at Newark in 1817 it was considered to be the finest public building in the province. The scene of Robert Gourlay's imprisonment in 1819 and a slave riot in 1837, the old structure ended its days as an orphanage. (At the site of the former complex, Rye and Cottage Streets, Niagara-on-the-Lake)

St. Andrew's

An outstanding example of Greek Revival ecclesiastical architecture, St. Andrew's was built in 1831 to replace an earlier Presbyterian church burned by American forces in 1813. The church still contains its original high pulpit and box pews, typical of the 1830s but rarely found in Ontario today. (On the grounds of the church, 323 Simcoe Street, Niagara-on-the-Lake)

The Niagara Agricultural Society

Founded by 1792, the Niagara Agricultural Society was the first organization in the province devoted to the advancement of agriculture. As well as distributing information on breeding and planting technologies, the society introduced several varieties of fruit into the Niagara peninsula. (In Simcoe Park, Picton and King Streets, Niagara-on-the-Lake)

The First Newspaper 1793

The first newspaper to be published in Ontario, the *Upper Canada Gazette*, was produced at Newark (Niagara-on-the-Lake) for five years before being moved to York (Toronto). A semi-official and then official organ of the government, the paper continued in publication under various names until 1845. (In Queen's Royal Park, opposite 84 King Street, Niagara-on-the-Lake)

The Canada Constellation 1799-1800

The first independent newspaper in Upper Canada, the *Canada Constellation* was published at Newark by the Tiffany brothers, Gideon and Silvester. Lack of government aid and a paucity of subscribers doomed the enterprise in its first year of operation. (On the grounds of the Niagara Historical Society Museum, 43 Castlereagh Street, Niagara-on-the-Lake)

Janet Carnochan 1839-1926

A teacher in Niagara-on-the-Lake for many years, Janet Carnochan founded the Niagara Historical Society in 1895. The author and editor of numerous works on the history of the Niagara peninsula, Carnochan worked with great zeal to preserve and protect the region's cultural and heritage resources. (On the grounds of the Niagara Historical Society Museum, 43 Castlereagh Street, Niagara-on-the-Lake)

Memorial Hall 1906

The first building in Ontario to be constructed specifically for use as a historical museum, Memorial Hall was built for the Niagara Historical Society largely through the efforts of its indefatigable founder and president, Janet Carnochan. (On the grounds of the museum, 43 Castlereagh Street, Niagara-on-the-Lake)

The Law Society of Upper Canada 1797

The Law Society of Upper Canada was founded in 1797 at a meeting held at Wilson's Hotel in Newark to regulate the activities and responsibilities of the legal profession. In 1832 it moved to new quarters in Osgoode Hall in York (Toronto), where it is still housed. (Opposite 142 Queen Street (near the site of the former Wilson's Hotel), Niagara-on-the-Lake)

Lieutenant-Colonel John Butler 1725-1796
By the end of the American Revolution John Butler's loyalist corps, supported by British regulars and Indian allies, had effectively contributed to the establishment of British control in the Great Lakes region. After the disbanding of Butler's Rangers in 1784, many of the men, including Butler himself, settled in the Niagara peninsula. (At Butler's Burying Ground, at the south end of Butler Street, Niagara-on-the-Lake)

St. Mark's Church
St. Mark's Anglican Church was constructed between 1804 and 1810, and numbered among its congregation Sir Isaac Brock and other important provincial figures. During the 1812-14 war the church was used as a hospital by the British and as a barracks by the Americans. (On the grounds of the church, 41 Byron Street, Niagara-on-the-Lake)

William Kirby's Home
Born in England, William Kirby (1817-1906) came to Canada in 1839. He was editor of the *Niagara Mail* for many years and in 1877 gained international renown with the publication of the historical romance, *The Golden Dog*. From 1857 until his death he lived in a simple stucco structure which had been built in 1818. (On the grounds of his former home, 130 Front Street, Niagara-on-the-Lake)

The Negro Burial Ground 1830
A long tradition of tolerance in Upper Canada attracted numerous refugee slaves to the Niagara area prior to the American Civil War. In 1830 a church was constructed by the predominantly black Baptist congregation led by John Oakley, a former soldier in the British forces. (At the site of the former church and its burial ground, adjacent to 494 Mississauga Street, Niagara-on-the-Lake)

Joseph-Geneviève, Comte de Puisaye

A leader of royalist resistance in France, Puisaye (c.1755-1827) was outlawed and sought refuge in England for a time before coming to Upper Canada in 1798. He established a short-lived settlement north of present-day Toronto prior to settling in the Niagara area. (On the east side of the Niagara River Parkway (near the site of his former farm), about 3 km south of Niagara-on-the-Lake)

The Capture of Fort Niagara 1813

In the early hours of December 19, 1813 a combined British and Canadian force crossed the icy waters of the Niagara River in open bateaux and marched over frozen roads to storm Fort Niagara. A turning point in the 1812-14 war, the decisive attack was a model of British military strategy. (Niagara River Parkway at the East-West Line (near the site from which the force embarked), south of Niagara-on-the-Lake)

The McFarland House 1800

Built by James McFarland, this Georgian-style house was used as a hospital during the War of 1812 by both British and American forces. After 1814 the war-torn house was repaired, and remained in the possession of the McFarland family for several generations. (On the grounds of the house, Niagara River Parkway, just south of the East-West Line, south of Niagara-on-the-Lake)

The Field House

One of the oldest brick houses in Ontario, the Field House was built about 1800. It was occupied by the British during the War of 1812 but managed to withstand American bombardment. In 1968 the Georgian-style house was purchased by the Ontario Heritage Foundation to ensure its preservation; it has since been repaired and restored and is now in private ownership. (On the grounds of the house, Niagara River Parkway, between Niagara-on-the-Lake and Queenston)

- ## PORT COLBORNE
  ### The Founding of Port Colborne
  Chosen in 1831 as the site for the southern terminus of the Welland Canal, Port Colborne was named in honour of Lieutenant-Governor Sir John Colborne. The community was dependent initially on the canal for its economic survival, but subsequently prospered as a railway junction and industrial centre. (At the city hall, 239 King Street, Port Colborne)

- ## PORT ROBINSON
  ### The Founding of Port Robinson
  Port Robinson flourished in the 1830s and '40s as the Welland Canal brought increased trade and industry to the region. Subsequent extensions to the canal deflected commerce elsewhere, however, and in the 1870s the shipyard and dry docks at Port Robinson were forced to close. (In Port Robinson Park, adjacent to the canal, Port Robinson)

- ## QUEENSTON
  ### The Colonial Advocate
  An influential journal of radical reform, the *Colonial Advocate* was published by William Lyon Mackenzie from his home in Queenston briefly in 1824 before he moved his press to Toronto. Because of its anti-government stand, the paper was in constant financial trouble but continued to be published, somewhat irregularly, for ten years. (At Mackenzie House, 1 Queenston Street, Queenston)

  ### Laura Ingersoll Secord 1775-1868
  In June 1813 Laura Secord set out from her home at Queenston on a trek of nineteen miles to

Beaverdams to warn the British commander of an impending American attack. Her courage, tenacity and patriotism have made her Ontario's best-known heroine. (At her former home, now the Laura Secord Homestead Museum, 29 Queenston Street, Queenston)

The Founding of Queenston
Following the loss of the east bank of the Niagara River to the Americans after the Revolution, a new portage was established around the falls in the 1780s with Queenston as its northern terminus. The village prospered as a trans-shipment point until the Welland Canal began to redirect commerce elsewhere after 1829. (On the grounds of the community centre, 32 Queenston Street, Queenston)

The Queenston Baptist Church
Built between 1842 and 1845 by a Baptist congregation dating back to 1808, this limestone church was used for religious services until 1918. Owned for a time by a Women's Institute, the building was given to the Town of Niagara-on-the-Lake in 1970 and two years later opened as the Queenston Library and Community Centre. (At the former church, 32 Queenston Street, Queenston)

Major John Richardson 1796-1852
As a professional soldier in the British Army, Major Richardson, who was born in Queenston, served in Upper Canada and the West Indies. After relinquishing his sword for a pen in 1818 he published the epic poem *Tecumseh* and the historical novel *Wacousta*, works that immediately established his literary reputation. (In front of Laura Secord Public School, Walnut and Queen Streets, Queenston)

"Willowbank"
Built in the 1830s for Alexander Hamilton, sheriff

of the Niagara District, Willowbank is a fine example of Classical Revival architecture. The formal elegance of its classic proportions is enhanced by its setting in spacious grounds. (On the grounds of the house, Queen Street and Dee Road, Queenston)

The Niagara Escarpment
A land formation of intriguing geological complexity, the escarpment stretches from central New York State to Manitoulin Island. It has had a significant influence on the pattern of settlement and the development of communications systems in Ontario. (On the road off Merritton Road to Queenston Memorial Park, Queenston)

Sir Roger Hale Sheaffe 1763-1851
A veteran of the American Revolution and the Napoleonic Wars, Sheaffe was second-in-command to Major-General Sir Isaac Brock in 1812. Following the latter's death on October 13, Sheaffe rallied his forces and successfully drove the invading American forces from Queenston Heights. (Near the Brock Monument in Queenston Memorial Park, Queenston)

• ST. CATHARINES
The Founding of St. Catharines
Capitalizing on the convenience of intersecting Indian trails, enterprising settlers widened the pathways for wagon traffic and by 1798 a crossroads community was in evidence at the future site of St. Catharines. Construction of the Welland Canal some thirty years later stimulated economic development and by mid-century St. Catharines had become a significant milling and ship-building centre. (At the municipal building, 50 Church Street, St. Catharines)

The First Welland Canal 1824-1833

Constructed under the charge of William Hamilton Merritt, the first Welland Canal – a narrow channel with forty small, wooden locks – ran from Port Dalhousie to Port Colborne. When completed it enabled vessels to pass directly between Lake Ontario and Lake Erie. (Near the site of former Lock #6, in Centennial Gardens Park (enter via Gale Crescent or Oakdale Avenue), St. Catharines)

Richard Pierpoint c.1774-c.1838

One of the first black settlers in the Niagara region, Pierpoint had been the slave of a British officer. During the American Revolution he enlisted in the British forces and thereby gained his freedom. A member of Butler's Rangers, "Captain Dick" settled in the vicinity of present-day St. Catharines after the rangers were disbanded in 1784. (In Centennial Gardens, Oakdale Avenue (near the site where he settled), St. Catharines)

William Hamilton Merritt 1793-1862

A prominent early settler in the St. Catharines area, Merritt was largely responsible for the construction of the first Welland Canal. During his long tenure in the legislative assembly he continued to promote various transportation projects. (In Memorial Park, St. Paul Street West, St. Catharines)

Lance-Corporal Fred Fisher, V.C. 1894-1915

A native of St. Catharines, Fisher enlisted with the Canadian Expeditionary Force in 1914. For his exceptional courage and skill in leading his machine-gun detachment at the second battle of Ypres in April 1915 he was awarded, posthumously, the Victoria Cross. (In Memorial Park, St. Paul Street West, St. Catharines)

Louis Shickluna 1808-1880

Reputedly a ship's carpenter in his native Malta,

Shickluna worked in several North American shipyards before coming to St. Catharines in 1838. The extensive ship-building operations he developed there contributed significantly to navigation on the Great Lakes as well as to the economic prosperity of the town. (Opposite CKTB Radio Station, Yates Street near St. Paul Street West, St. Catharines)

The Reverend Anthony Burns 1834-1862
Born a slave in Virginia, Anthony Burns escaped at the age of twenty. Arrested, returned to his owner and then sold, he was subsequently ransomed by a Baptist minister from Boston. Burns himself became a minister in the Baptist Church and from 1860 until his death led a congregation in St. Catharines. (At the entrance to Victoria Lawn Cemetery (where his grave is located), Queenston Street, St. Catharines)

The Mack Centre of Nursing Education
In 1874 Dr. Theophilus Mack established the St. Catharines Training School for Nurses. The school endorsed the Florence Nightingale system of training based on a sound knowledge of hygiene and medicine, and was the first school of its kind in Canada. (At the site of the school, now the Leonard Nurses' Home, 178 Queenston Street, St. Catharines)

The Royal Canadian Henley Regatta
Competitive rowing became popular in Canada in the 1860s, and in 1880 the first Royal Canadian Henley Regatta for international oarsmen was held in Toronto. In 1903 a section of the old Welland Canal at Port Dalhousie was chosen as the permanent site for this popular sporting competition. (At the entrance to the Henley Regatta Course Grandstand, Main Street, St. Catharines)

Ridley College
A renowned boarding school, Ridley College was

established in 1889 by Anglican churchmen determined to provide boys with sound academic, athletic and religious instruction. The college has expanded steadily over the years, and since 1973 has been co-educational. (At the front gates of the college, Ridley Road and Henrietta Street, St. Catharines)

Brock University

Chartered by a provincial Act in March 1964, Brock University began classes later that year in St. Paul Street United Church. In 1967, the year of the institution's first convocation, the DeCew campus was opened. (Beneath the podium at the end of Thistle Corridor, Brock University, Glenridge Avenue, St. Catharines)

• ST. DAVIDS

The Burning of St. Davids 1814

On July 8, 1814, during the final campaign of the 1812-14 war on the Niagara frontier, an American detachment commanded by Isaac Stone looted and burned the village of St. Davids. The excessive destruction of private property caused outrage on both sides of the frontier, and Stone was summarily dismissed from the United States Army. (On the grounds of St. Davids Public School, 1824 York Road, St. Davids)

Christian Warner 1754-1833

After serving in Butler's Rangers in the American Revolution, Warner settled in the vicinity of present-day St. Davids where he became the leader of one of the earliest Methodist congregations in Upper Canada. Services were held in his house until a simple frame church was built on his property in 1801, the first Methodist church west of the Bay of Quinte. (At the Warner Burying Ground (where his grave is located), Warner Road, about 3 km west of St. Davids)

• THOROLD

The Beaverdams Church 1832
One of the oldest remaining Methodist chapels in Ontario, the Beaverdams Church was built in 1832 by a congregation that had formed in the area in the 1790s. The simple frame church, modest and unadorned in true Methodist spirit, served its community until about 1890. (On the grounds of the church, Marlatts Road, in the former village of Beaverdams, now part of Thorold)

The Founding of Thorold
One of the first businessmen to exploit the water power offered by the Welland Canal was George Keefer, Sr. who, in 1828, built a large stone flour mill on the future site of Thorold. Other mills soon followed and by the 1840s Thorold had become a major mill-centre in the province. (In the Battle of Beaverdams Historic Park, Sullivan Avenue, Thorold)

The Welland Mills
Reputedly one of the largest flour-milling operations in Upper Canada, the Welland Mills were erected in the 1840s by Jacob Keefer, who capitalized on both the water power and transport facilities offered by the Welland Canal. (At the former mill building, Pine Street, Thorold)

The First Cotton Factory
The first cotton factory in the province was a joint-stock company founded by local citizens in Thorold in 1847. Twenty water-powered looms produced sheeting, scrim and batting in an operation that heralded the establishment of what was to become an important provincial industry. (In Centennial Park, Albert Street West (near the site of the former factory), Thorold)

- VINELAND
Ball's Grist-Mill
Powered by the current of Twelve Mile Creek, the Ball brothers' four-storey mill, which had been built by about 1809, was the only grist-mill in the area for many years. By the 1840s a small industrial complex had developed around the mill which, under varying economic conditions, remained in operation until 1910. (At the mill in Ball's Falls Conservation Area, Regional Road 24, just south of Vineland)

- BEAR ISLAND
Temagami Post 1834
Established to safeguard the Hudson's Bay Company's fur trading territory from competitors, the small post on Lake Timagami (now Temagami) was essentially an outpost of the company's major depot on Lake Timiskaming. (Near the site of the former post, Bear Island, Lake Temagami)

- BRENT
The Brent Crater
First noted in aerial photographs in 1951, the Brent Crater is a circular depression approximately three kilometres in diameter, and is thought to have been formed as the result of the high-speed impact of a giant meteorite some 450 million years ago. (At a lookout tower on the eastern rim of the crater, Brent Road, approximately 6 km northeast of the village of Brent – near the northern edge of Algonquin Park, about 32 km south of Highway 17)

- MATTAWA
The Canoe Route to the West
The Mattawa River formed an important link in the historic canoe route from Montreal to the upper Great Lakes. For more than 200 years explorers, fur traders, missionaries and *coureurs de bois* travelled the route – among them: Samuel de Champlain, Jean de Brébeuf, Sir Alexander Mackenzie, Simon Fraser and David Thompson. (In Legion Memorial Park, Main and Mattawa Streets, Mattawa)

Mattawa House 1837
Situated at the junction of major canoe routes, Mattawa House was established by the Hudson's Bay Company primarily to discourage lumbermen from

encroaching on the company's fur trading monopoly. The post profited more from the trans-shipment of supplies than from furs, however, and actually owed its continued existence to business with the lumber companies. (At the site of the former post, Explorers' Point, Highway 533, just north of Mattawa)

- ## NORTH BAY

Jean Nicolet

Born in France, Nicolet (c.1598-1642) came to Canada in 1618. He lived for a number of years with the Nipissing Indians, adopting their lifestyle and thereby helping to strengthen their alliance with the French. An intrepid explorer, Nicolet is gener-ally credited with the discovery of Lake Michigan, which he partially explored in 1634. (In Lee Park, Memorial Drive, North Bay)

The Ontario Northland Railway

Begun at North Bay in 1902, the Temiskaming and Northern Ontario Railway (renamed Ontario Northland in 1946) was completed to Moosonee on James Bay thirty years later. With spur lines connecting mining communities and isolated settle-ments to the main line, the railway effectively stimulated the economic development of northeast-ern Ontario. (In front of the tourist information centre at Regina and Main Streets, North Bay)

The Reverend Silas Huntington 1829-1905

A zealous Methodist missionary, Huntington trav-elled extensively throughout northeastern Ontario visiting outlying communities and CPR work-camps as far west as Schreiber. He was a man of magnetic personality and great physical strength, and became the hero of many local legends. (On the grounds of Trinity United Church (a congre-gation he established), McIntyre and Ferguson Streets, North Bay)

La Vase Portages

The three La Vase (Mud) portages, connecting Trout Lake with the La Vase River and hence Lake Nipissing, formed part of the historic canoe route to the west. Apparently true to their name, they were described by one despondent traveller as "an abominable marsh . . . knee-deep in mud and tree-roots". (Highway 17 (near the pond where the former portages began), about 4 km east of North Bay)

- ## STURGEON FALLS

The Founding of Sturgeon Falls

The development of Sturgeon Falls began in 1881 with the arrival of CPR construction crews. Lum-

On July 15, 1932 the "last spike" of the Ontario Northland railway was officially driven in at Moosonee amid much ceremony and celebration. (Archives of Ontario S 11320)

bering and the establishment of pulp and paper industries accelerated the village's growth and attracted many French-Canadian settlers to the area. (At the Champlain Bridge lookout, Front Street (Highway 17), Sturgeon Falls)

• TEMAGAMI
Grey Owl 1888-1938
Archibald Belaney came to Canada from England in 1906 and lived as a trapper and guide in the Temagami and Biscotasing areas. After joining an Ojibwa band he adopted the name Grey Owl. Alarmed at the rapid despoliation of the wilderness, the trapper turned conservationist and spent the last ten years of his life writing and lecturing on wildlife

In his books and lectures Grey Owl pleaded for recognition of the "natural brotherhood between man and animals" and for protection of the wilderness. He is shown here calling moose. (Archives of Ontario S 14248)

preservation. (At Finlayson Point Provincial Park, off Highway 11, about 1.5 km south of Temagami)

- VERNER
The Reverend Charles Alfred Marie Paradis
1848-1926

An Oblate missionary from Quebec, Paradis was posted to Lake Timiskaming in 1881. During his years in the region he did much to encourage agricultural settlement, particularly in the area around Verner, and took up farming himself. Paradis was an enterprising man of many talents: he prospected for gold, wrote meditative works, and painted in watercolour. (On the grounds of St. John the Baptist Roman Catholic Church, 38 Main Street, Verner)

NORTHUMBERLAND COUNTY

- BRIGHTON
  ### The Loss of the Speedy
  The schooner *Speedy* sailed from York (Toronto) on October 7, 1804 carrying members of the circuit court to attend a murder trial in the Newcastle District. All on board – including the lawyers, witnesses and the accused – were drowned when the ship foundered off Presqu'ile Point and sank. (On the grounds of the museum in Presqu'ile Provincial Park, south of Brighton, off Highway 2)

- CAMPBELLFORD
  ### The Founders of Campbellford
  The large land holdings in Seymour Township that were granted to Robert and David Campbell in 1831 included a ford on the Trent River, which in due time gave the village that grew there its name. Although David Campbell moved to Cobourg, he continued to promote the development of Campbellford. (Beside the Trent Canal, off Queen Street, Campbellford)

- COBOURG
  ### The Founding of Cobourg
  With the completion of the Kingston Road by 1817, and harbour facilities in 1832, the small milling community of Cobourg became a significant shipping centre and port of entry on Lake Ontario. (Near the Cobourg Marina, at the foot of Third Street on the harbour, Cobourg)

  ### William Weller 1799-1863
  A prominent resident of Cobourg for many years, Weller operated a stagecoach line from Toronto to Montreal which gained a reputation for fast, efficient service – no mean feat in the 1830s. (At the north end of Victoria Park, King Street, Cobourg)

The Honourable James Cockburn 1819-1883

A Father of Confederation, Cockburn, who practised law in Cobourg and represented the area in the legislature, was one of the delegates from Canada West at the Quebec Conference in 1864. Three years later he became the first speaker of the new federal House of Commons. (In Centennial Park, William Street, Cobourg)

Victoria College

Opened by the Wesleyan Methodists as the Upper Canada Academy in 1836, Victoria College obtained a provincial charter and became a degree-granting institution five years later. In 1890 the college federated with the University of Toronto. After 1892 the old college building was used for some time as a mental hospital. (In front of the former college building, 100 University Avenue, Cobourg)

The Cobourg and Peterborough Railway 1852-1898

Largely financed by the citizens and town of Cobourg, the Cobourg and Peterborough Railway was, like many small railway ventures in the 1850s, a financial and engineering disaster which left its promoters and investors heavily in debt. (At University Avenue and Spring Street (near the site where the first sod was turned for the line), Cobourg)

The Church of St. Peter

Constructed over and around an earlier wooden building, St. Peter's Anglican Church was built between 1851 and 1854 to the combined designs of noted architects Henry Bowyer Lane and Kivas Tully. Despite extensive alterations, especially to its interior, St. Peter's remains a fine example of early Gothic Revival architecture. (On the grounds of the church, 240 College Street, Cobourg)

Victoria Hall

One of the most elegant public buildings in Canada, Victoria Hall was completed in 1860 and for almost 100 years served as the Cobourg town hall and the Northumberland county court house. Following an extensive restoration program the building was re-opened for public use in 1983, and serves as a splendid example of nineteenth-century artistry and twentieth-century restoration technology. (On the grounds of the building, 55 King Street West, Cobourg)

Marie Dressler 1868-1934

Born in Cobourg, Leila Maria Koerber joined a touring stock company when she was about fifteen years old and, as Marie Dressler, soon gained popularity as a character actress on both stage and screen. She is probably best remembered for her feisty portrayal of Tugboat Annie. (At Dressler House (the cottage believed to be her birthplace, now a restaurant), 212 King Street West, Cobourg)

• COLBORNE

The Founding of Colborne

After Joseph Keeler opened a store on the site of present-day Colborne about 1819, other small businessmen followed suit and a community was soon in evidence. With the opening of harbour facilities and the arrival of the railway in the 1840s and '50s, Colborne became an important service centre for the region. (In Victoria Park, opposite the municipal building, 1 Toronto Street, Colborne)

Old St. Andrew's Church

One of the oldest surviving Presbyterian churches in Ontario, St. Andrew's was constructed in the early 1830s. Renovations later in the century altered the classical Georgian lines of the structure, giving it a distinctly Italianate character. (On the grounds of the church, at the intersection of King Street East, Victoria Lane and Church Street, Colborne)

- GORES LANDING
Gore's Landing
Named after a prominent early settler, Gore's Landing prospered briefly in the 1840s as the northern terminus of a plank road from Cobourg to Rice Lake. Constructed to facilitate stagecoach travel, the wooden road could not withstand the harsh Upper Canadian winters and with its inevitable disintegration the community suffered economic decline. (In Pioneer Park, Front and Kelly Streets, Gores Landing)

- GRAFTON
Barnum House
An excellent example of Neoclassical domestic architecture, Barnum House was constructed about 1819 by Eliakim Barnum to replace his previous home which had been destroyed during the War of 1812. In the first historic house restoration undertaken in the province, the structure was refurbished by the Architectural Conservancy of Ontario in 1940. It is now owned by the Ontario Heritage Foundation. (On the grounds of the house, Highway 2 at the western approach to Grafton)

- HARWOOD
Harwood
Following the opening of the Cobourg and Peterborough Railway in 1854, the community of Harwood began to develop at the northern terminus of the line. Competition from other rail lines was fierce, however, and to Harwood's disadvantage the Cobourg-Harwood line ceased operation in 1895. (At the community hall, Front Street, Harwood)

- HASTINGS
The Founding of Hastings
A small settlement known as Crooks Rapids began to develop on the Trent River when a lock and dam were completed in 1842 as part of the government's canalization project. Mills became the mainstay of the community, which early in the 1850s was renamed Hastings. (In the park on the north bank of the Trent River, between Hope and New Streets, Hastings)

- PORT HOPE
The Founding of Port Hope
The first permanent settlers in the vicinity of Smith's Creek were loyalist refugees brought to the area in 1793. Mills and a town plot were in evidence by the turn of the century. Despite pressure to name the community Toronto, the more appropriate name of Port Hope was officially adopted in 1818. (On the grounds of the town hall, 56 Queen Street, Port Hope)

Bluestone House 1834
A handsome limestone structure, the Bluestone House – originally painted blue – was built by John David Smith, a prosperous merchant and local justice of the peace. Designed in the Greek Revival style, the house has survived with remarkably little alteration. (On the grounds of the house, 117 King Street, Port Hope)

St. Mark's Church 1822
Originally consecrated to St. John the Evangelist, this pioneer Anglican church was closed for a few years and then re-dedicated in 1873 to St. Mark. The church has been carefully repaired, although frequent alterations over the years have left little of the original 1822 structure visible. (On the grounds of the church, 53 King Street, Port Hope)

The Eldorado Refinery

A pioneering operation in the development of nuclear energy, the Eldorado refinery was established in 1933 by the LaBine brothers to extract radium from ore mined in the Northwest Territories. The Canadian government acquired Eldorado in 1942 for uranium production during the war, and in 1944 made it a crown corporation. (At Eldorado Resources Limited, 1 Eldorado Place, Port Hope)

• WARKWORTH
J.D. Kelly 1862-1958

John David Kelly spent most of his boyhood in Percy Township before entering art school in Toronto. A highly skilled draftsman, he executed many paintings which depict in carefully researched detail significant moments in Canadian history. His works have been reproduced in school texts and are familiar, if his name is not, to anyone educated in the Ontario school system. (In Percy Township Centennial Park, Mill Street and Old Hastings Road, Warkworth)

OTTAWA-CARLETON REGIONAL MUNICIPALITY

- CARP
Christ Church 1838
Built to serve the combined Anglican parishes of March and Huntley, this solid stone church has undergone numerous renovations and alterations since its construction. In 1953 a handsome memorial window was installed depicting Holman Hunt's famous painting "Light of the World". (On the grounds of the church, Carp Road and McGee Side Road, about 5 km from Carp)

- MANOTICK
The Long Island Mill
Driven by water-powered turbines, the Long Island grist-mill began operation in 1860 and soon became the nucleus around which the village of Manotick developed. The mill has been restored to working order by the Rideau Valley Conservation Authority and is open to the public. (At the mill (now called Watson's Mill), Mill Street, Manotick)

- OTTAWA
The Commissariat Building 1827
Distinguished by skilful masonry and solid construction, the Commissariat building provides an excellent example of the workmanship of the Scottish stonemasons employed by Colonel By to work on the Rideau Canal. Used as a storehouse during the canal's construction, the building now houses the collections of the Bytown Museum. (In the lobby of the museum, beside the third lock of the head-locks of the canal, between Parliament Hill and the Chateau Laurier, off Elgin Street, Ottawa)

Lady Aberdeen 1857-1939
Widely respected for her organizational skills and strong commitment to public service, Lady Aber-

deen served as president of the International Council of Women from 1893 to 1939. During the Earl of Aberdeen's term as governor-general she helped to form the National Council of Women of Canada. (On the grounds of Rideau Hall, 1 Sussex Drive, Ottawa)

Charlotte Elizabeth Whitton, O.C., C.B.E. 1896-1975
A controversial fighter for social reform, Charlotte Whitton served on the Canadian Council on Child Welfare (later the Canadian Welfare Council) and on the League of Nations Social Questions Committee. In 1951 she was elected mayor of Ottawa. (In the council chambers, city hall, 111 Sussex Drive, Ottawa)

Brigadier-General Ernest Alexander Cruikshank 1853-1939
A noted authority on the history of Ontario, Cruikshank became the first director of the Historical Section of the Adjutant-General's Branch of the General Staff in 1918. From 1919 until his death he served as the first chairman of the Historic Sites and Monuments Board of Canada. (On the grounds of the Canadian War Museum, 330 Sussex Drive, Ottawa)

Thomas McKay 1792 1855
Master mason, entrepreneur, and founder of the community of New Edinburgh, McKay was responsible for the construction of a number of locks along the Rideau Canal. The McKay family home, Rideau Hall, was purchased by the government in 1868 to serve as the official residence of the country's governors-general. (In the park at the corner of Sussex Drive and John Street (near the site of his former New Edinburgh industrial complex), Ottawa)

Philip Dansken Ross 1858-1949

A distinguished journalist widely admired for his candour of expression and depth of knowledge, P.D. Ross was publisher-owner of the *Ottawa Journal* and one of the founders of the Canadian Press. (At the Journal Towers, Kent Street between Laurier and Slater, Ottawa)

The University of Ottawa

Established in 1848 and placed under the direction of the Oblate fathers, this bilingual institution received university status in 1866 and in 1889 was decreed a pontifical university by Pope Leo XIII. (Beside Tabaret Hall, 550 Cumberland Street, University of Ottawa campus, Ottawa)

Carleton University

Opened in 1942 as a small, private college offering evening courses in introductory university subjects, Carleton received a provincial charter in 1952 and five years later became a university in both name and status. (On a convocation podium, west of the administration building, University Drive, Carleton University campus, Ottawa)

L'École Guigues and Regulation 17

L'École Guigues became the centre for minority-rights agitation in Ontario when in 1912 the provincial government issued a directive, commonly called Regulation 17, restricting French-language education. Mounting protests forced the government to moderate its policy and in 1927 bilingual schools were officially recognized. (In front of the former school building, 159 Murray Street, Ottawa)

The Nile Voyageurs 1884-85

In 1884 the British government sent a military expedition up the Nile River to rescue Major-General Charles Gordon who was under siege at

Khartoum. On the recommendation of Lord Wolseley a number of Canadian voyageurs, many from the Ottawa valley area, were recruited to navigate the expedition through the river's long and treacherous cataracts. (At Kitchissippi Lookout, Island Park Drive, just west of the Champlain Bridge, Ottawa)

The Honourable Hamnet Kirks Pinhey 1784-1857
On land granted to him for service in the Napoleonic Wars, Pinhey built a substantial estate comprising several log and stone structures. Later he became prominent in local affairs and held a number of public offices. (At Horaceville, Pinhey's former estate beside the Ottawa River, Regional Road 21 north of Road 49, near South March – about 20 km from downtown Ottawa)

• RICHMOND
The Richmond Military Settlement 1818
The first large-scale community in what is now the Ottawa-Carleton region, the Richmond Military Settlement contained some 400 veterans and civilians by late 1818. Most of the inhabitants were discharged members of the 99th Regiment, a corps which had distinguished itself in the Peninsular campaigns under Lord Wellington and in the War of 1812. (At the agricultural fair grounds, Perth Street and Regional Road 10 (in the vicinity of the former military settlement), Richmond)

St. John's Anglican Parish
Formed shortly after the establishment in 1818 of the Richmond Military Settlement, the parish of St. John was served by itinerant missionaries for several years. The present church, the second on the site, was built in 1859-60 of quarried stone, and remains largely unaltered. (On the grounds of the church, 72 Fowler Street, Richmond)

- VERNON
Alexander Cameron Rutherford 1857-1941
A native of Osgoode Township, Rutherford became premier, provincial treasurer, and minister of education in the first Alberta government following that province's formation in 1905. After his retirement from politics he served as chancellor of the University of Alberta from 1927 until his death. (On the grounds of the Osgoode Township Museum, Highway 31, Vernon)

OXFORD COUNTY

• EMBRO
Henry John Cody 1868-1951
A native of Embro, Cody gained distinction as both a churchman and an educator. Rector of St. Paul's Anglican Church in Toronto for more than thirty years, he also played a vital administrative role at the Unversity of Toronto, serving as that institution's president (1932-45) and chancellor (1944-47). (In Memorial Park, St. Andrew and Argyle Streets, Embro)

• INGERSOLL
The Founders of Ingersoll
Promised 80,000 acres in present-day Oxford County in 1793, Major Thomas Ingersoll, a native of Massachusetts, brought a number of American settlers to this area before the end of the century. The major eventually settled at the mouth of the Credit River, but his son Charles returned to Oxford and became a leading citizen in the community bearing the family name. (Just south of the Thames Street bridge, Ingersoll)

Ingersoll Town Hall 1856
Constructed to replace an earlier building destroyed by fire, the town hall at Ingersoll contained a commodious auditorium which was often used for public meetings by such prominent figures as Sir John A. Macdonald, George Brown, and Alexander Mackenzie. The hall's Italianate design is quite characteristic of public buildings in the province at that time. (At the old town hall, 34 King Street West, Ingersoll)

The Big Cheese 1866
To draw world-wide attention to the excellent cheese produced in Oxford County local manufac-

turers co-operated, in June 1866, in producing a gigantic, 7,300-pound cheese which was exhibited to much acclaim at fairs in New York State and England. (Highway 19 (near the site of the factory at which the cheese was produced), just south of Ingersoll)

• NORWICH
The Norwich Quaker Settlement
In 1810 brothers-in-law Peter Lossing and Peter De Long purchased 15,000 acres in Norwich Township. The following year nine families from Dutchess County, New York joined the Lossings and the De Longs to form the nucleus of one of the most successful Quaker settlements in Upper Canada. (At the Quaker Pioneer Cemetery, Quaker Street and Concession Road 3, Norwich)

Emily Howard Jennings Stowe, M.D. 1831-1903
Born in Norwich Township to Quaker parents, Emily Stowe became the first female physician to practise medicine in Canada. A passionate advocate for social reform, she campaigned vigorously for female suffrage while still maintaining her medical practice. (On the grounds of the Norwich and District Historical Museum and Archives, Highway 59, Norwich)

• OTTERVILLE
Harold Adams Innis 1894-1952
A native of Oxford County, Innis became an economic historian whose books – in particular *The Fur Trade in Canada* – profoundly influenced

---

Refused entry to Canadian all-male medical schools, Emily Stowe earned her degree at the New York Medical College for Women in 1867. She opened a practice in Toronto that same year, but was not officially registered by the Ontario College of Physicians and Surgeons until 1879. (Archives of Ontario S 17839)

interpretive historical writing in Canada. His later studies dealt with the effects of communications technology on cultural and social values. (At his birthplace, Innisfree Farm, County Road 19, about 3 km west of Otterville)

- PRINCETON
Colonel Thomas Hornor 1767-1834
A native of New Jersey, Hornor settled in Blenheim Township in 1795 and built the first sawmill in present-day Oxford County. He held several local offices and in 1820 was elected to the provincial legislature. (At Princeton Cemetery, Highway 2 (near the site of his former mill), just west of Princeton)

- TILLSONBURG
George Tillson 1782-1864
A native of Massachusetts, Tillson operated the Normandale Iron Foundry in Norfolk County before moving to Oxford County in 1825. The sawmill and forge that he established in partnership with Benjamin Van Norman formed the nucleus of the future village of Tillsonburg. (In front of the public library, 2 Library Lane, Tillsonburg)

- WOLVERTON
Wolverton Hall
Designed in the Regency style with some Gothic flourishes, Wolverton Hall was built about 1855 by Enos Wolverton, a native of New York who, in 1851, registered a village plot on his land and became the community of Wolverton's first postmaster. (On the grounds of the house, 88 Wolverton Street, Wolverton)

- WOODSTOCK
The Old Stage Road
Following in part the Indian trail known as the

Detroit Path, the Old Stage Road was part of a series
of linked roads from Ancaster to Detroit, and during
the War of 1812 was the main route used by both
American and British troops. Sections of the old
route can still be travelled in Oxford East and West
Townships. (On the grounds of Sweaburg Central
School, Stage Road and County Road 14, southeast
of Woodstock)

Captain Andrew Drew, R.N. 1792-1878
A co-founder of Woodstock, Captain Drew is
probably best known for commanding the Canadian
force that destroyed the American steamer *Caroline*
during the 1837 rebellion. (On the grounds of his
former residence, 735 Rathbourne Avenue,
Woodstock)

St. Paul's Church 1834
Financed and built through the efforts of Woodstock's two founders, Admiral Henry Vansittart and
Captain Andrew Drew, St. Paul's Anglican Church
played a dual role in the history of the community
by serving as a temporary jail for rebel captives
during the 1837 rebellion. (On the grounds of the
church, Dundas Street east of Wilson Street,
Woodstock)

Woodstock College 1857 1926
Sponsored by the Baptist Church, the Canadian
Literary Institute (later renamed Woodstock College) opened in 1860 as a co-educational institution
offering courses in theology and the arts. During
the 1880s the theology faculty was transferred to
the Toronto Baptist College and the women's
department to Moulton College. The college then
operated as a boys' prep school until it closed in
1926. (At the site of the former college, Wilson
Street and College Avenue, Woodstock)

The Reverend Newton Wolverton 1846-1932

A man of multiple talents, Wolverton was a noted expert on meteorology, a teacher of mathematics, a Baptist minister, and from 1881 to 1886 principal of Woodstock College where he set up the first manual-training department in Canada. (In front of College Avenue Secondary School (near the site of the former Woodstock College), Wilson Street and College Avenue, Woodstock)

Thomas "Carbide" Willson 1860-1915

His discovery in 1892 of a commercial process for producing calcium carbide, a chemical compound used in the manufacture of acetylene gas, earned Tom Willson the nickname "Carbide". (On the grounds of his former home, now St. Joseph's Academy of Music, 210 Vansittart Avenue, Woodstock)

Lieutenant-Colonel Joseph Whiteside Boyle, D.S.O. 1867-1923

Known for many years as "Klondike Joe", Boyle was a prospector in the Yukon where he invested in timber and electric power operations as well as gold dredging. His daring exploits during the Second World War, especially on behalf of the people of Rumania, are legendary. (At the Presbyterian Cemetery (where his grave is located), Vansittart Avenue, Woodstock)

PARRY SOUND DISTRICT

- BURKS FALLS
Magnetawan River Steam Navigation
In 1879 the aptly named *Pioneer* was launched on the Magnetawan River, the first in a series of steamboats that for the next fifty years provided the only efficient means of transportation between the railhead at Burks Falls and the fledgling settlements along the river. (Near the boat-launching ramp in Burks Falls Park, Highway 520, Burks Falls)

- CALLANDER
Lake Nipissing
When the glacial ice began to retreat about 9000 BC, the Nipissing Basin formed an eastern extension of Georgian Bay and drained into the Ottawa and Mattawa Rivers. With the gradual tilting of the land, the lake began to drain westward some 7,000 years later, thereby creating the French River. (At the lookout over the lake, Highway 11, about 1.5 km south of Callander)

- COMMANDA
The Commanda General Store
Built about 1885, during Commanda's "boom" years, the general store played a significant role in the economic development of the community and its surrounds. The building is a rare example, especially in this part of Ontario, of High Victorian commercial architecture and is now operated as a public museum by the Gurd and Area Historical Corporation. (At the Commanda General Store Museum, Highway 522, Commanda)

- FRENCH RIVER
The Canoe Route to the West
The turbulent waters of the French River formed a vital link in the historic canoe route from Montreal

to the upper Great Lakes. For more than 200 years explorers, fur traders, missionaries, and *coureurs de bois* travelled the route – among them: Etienne Brûlé, Samuel de Champlain, Jean de Brébeuf, Sir Alexander Mackenzie, and Simon Fraser. (In French River Park, just off Highway 69 beside the southern approach to the French River bridge)

- MAGNETAWAN

The Rosseau-Nipissing Road
In an attempt to encourage settlement in what is now Parry Sound District, the government authorized construction of the Rosseau-Nipissing Road in 1864. By 1873 the road was open for winter traffic between the communities of Rousseau (now Rosseau) and Nipissing. The road is still used by local traffic through much of its course. (Sparks Street (part of the original route), Magnetawan)

The Magnetawan Lock
Built by the provincial government in the 1880s, and subsequently replaced in 1911, the lock at Magnetawan enabled boat traffic to circumvent the rapids at the village, thereby extending steamship service on the river as far as Ahmic Harbour. (Near the lock, Highway 520, Magnetawan)

Elise von Koerber and Swiss Settlement
The establishment of a Swiss settlement in the Parry Sound region was the result of an immigration policy adopted in 1872 which offered subsidized steamship fares and free inland transportation to European settlers. Elise von Koerber was one of several special agents appointed by the government, and by 1877 she had brought several hundred Swiss to Canada. (In Centennial Park (in the vicinity of the former Swiss settlement), off Highway 520, Magnetawan)

• NIPISSING

The Rosseau-Nipissing Road

In an attempt to encourage settlement in what is now Parry Sound District the government authorized construction of the Rosseau-Nipissing Road in 1864. By 1873 the road was open for winter traffic between the communities of Rousseau (now Rosseau) and Nipissing. The road is still used by local traffic through much of its course. (At the Nipissing Township Museum, Highway 654 and Beatty Street, Nipissing)

• PARRY SOUND

The Founding of Parry Sound

Named in honour of the noted Arctic explorer Sir William Edward Parry, the community of Parry Sound was founded by the enterprising Beatty family. After laying out a town plot in the 1860s, William Beatty and his two sons built a store and a church, constructed roads, and operated a stagecoach service to Bracebridge. (On the grounds of the municipal building, 52 Seguin Street, Parry Sound)

Parry Sound District Court House

The court house at Parry Sound was the first in a series of district court houses built in northern Ontario under the direction of the provincial department of public works. The modest frame building designed in 1871 by the department's chief architect, Kivas Tully, still forms the core of the present court house complex. (On the grounds of the court house, 101 James Street, Parry Sound)

The Sinking of the Waubuno 1879

During the era when the shipping trade was flourishing on the upper Great Lakes, the 200-ton *Waubuno* was one of many side-wheelers carrying freight and passengers between ports on Lake Huron and Georgian Bay. On a routine voyage from Collingwood to Parry Sound on November 22, 1879 the ship encountered a violent storm and sank with loss of all on board. (Beside the anchor from the *Waubuno*, Market Square Park, bordered by Gibson, Mary, and McMurray Streets, Parry Sound)

- ROSSEAU
  ### *The Rosseau-Nipissing Road*
  In an attempt to encourage settlement in what is now Parry Sound District the government authorized construction of the Rosseau-Nipissing Road in 1864. By 1873 the road was open for winter traffic between the communities of Rousseau (now Rosseau) and Nipissing. The road is still used by local traffic through much of its course. (At the community hall, Highway 141 and Victoria Street, Rosseau)

PEEL REGIONAL MUNICIPALITY

• BOLTON
The Founding of Bolton
James Bolton and his nephew George erected a grist-mill on the Humber River in 1823 which over the next few years became the centre of a small settlement known as Bolton's Mills. Other industries joined the mills and by 1871, with the arrival of railway service, Bolton was a thriving industrial centre. (Queen Street North, Bolton)

• BRAMPTON
The Founding of Brampton
Two early entrepreneurs at the crossroads hamlet of Buffy's Corners hailed from Brampton, England and were evidently successful in renaming the community when it was incorporated in 1853. Later in the century Harry Dale's horticultural business attracted thousands of visitors to its annual floral displays and earned Brampton the additional name of "Flower Town". (At the Pioneer Cemetery, 345 Main Street North, Brampton)

Peel County Court House
Built in 1865-66 to serve the newly created County of Peel, this buff brick court house was designed by the noted Toronto architect William Kauffmann in a charming, eclectic style that has been described as "Venetian Gothic". The court house served as the judicial and administrative centre for the county until 1973 when new facilities were built. (On the grounds of the former court house, 3 Wellington Street East, Brampton)

• MISSISSAUGA
Canada's First Aerodrome
The first aerodrome and flying school in Canada was established at Long Branch in 1915 and for a

time the first flying units of the Royal Flying Corps, Canada were based there. Muddy terrain numbered Long Branch's days as a flying school, however, and after June 1917 the school provided cadets with ground training only. (At the site of the former aerodrome, Lakeshore Boulevard West just west of Dixie Road, Mississauga)

Dixie Union Chapel
Also known as the Stone Chapel, this building is a rare example of a multi-denominational or "union" chapel from the settlement period of Upper Canada. The construction of chapels of this nature was necessitated by the small size and financial need

---

The Curtiss JN-4 ("Jenny") was one of several two-seater Curtiss biplanes that were used to train combat pilots at the Long Branch flying school during 1915-1917. (Archives of Ontario S 6759)

of many early religious congregations. (At the chapel, Cawthra Road and Dundas Street East, Mississauga)

The Honourable Thomas Laird Kennedy 1878-1959

During his forty years in provincial politics, Kennedy represented the riding of Peel for all but one term, serving as minister of agriculture in three administrations, and briefly (1948-49) as premier. He earned the respect of all parties and was known affectionately to many as "Old Man Ontario". (At Dixie Public School, 1120 Flagship Drive (once part of the former Kennedy family farm), Mississauga)

Sir William Pearce Howland 1811-1907

A native of New York State, Howland came to Upper Canada in 1830 and settled in Cooksville (now part of Mississauga). He took an active part in politics, and in 1866 was one of three representatives from Canada West at the London Conference. (In Confederation Square, near the former Toronto Township offices, Dundas Street, Mississauga)

Credit Indian Village 1826

Between 1826 and 1847 a band of Mississauga who had converted to Christianity formed a settlement on the Credit River and with government assistance constructed log houses, a sawmill, school, and chapel. By 1840 some 500 acres were under cultivation and the village contained about fifty houses. (Near the entrance to the Mississauga Golf Club, 1725 Mississauga Road (in the vicinity of the former Indian village), Mississauga)

The Reverend James Magrath at St. Peter's

Appointed to the Credit River area by the Society for the Propagation of the Gospel, Magrath served at St. Peter's Anglican Church from 1827 until his death in 1851 at the age of eighty-two. The original frame church was replaced in 1887 by the present stone structure. (On the grounds of St. Peter's, Mississauga Road and Dundas Street West, Mississauga)

Charlotte Schreiber 1834-1922

The first woman elected to the Royal Academy of Arts, Schreiber came to Ontario in 1875 from England where she had trained as an artist. Primarily a figure painter, she rendered her subjects in realistic, warm-toned detail. Her work signifies an important contribution to realistic painting in Canada. (On the grounds of the University of Toronto Erindale Campus (near the site of her former home), Mississauga)

• PORT CREDIT
Government Inn 1798-1861

In 1798 the government of Upper Canada built a post-house on the banks of the Credit River. The square-timbered inn served as a hostelry for people travelling between York (Toronto) and Niagara, and as a trading post for dealers in furs and salmon. The building was demolished in 1861. (In Memorial Park (near the site of the former inn), Lakeshore Road, Port Credit)

• STREETSVILLE
Streetsville

Named after Timothy Street, an early settler and entrepreneur, Streetsville was the largest village in the Home District by 1837. Mills and a variety of light industries sustained the village economically even though it was without railway connections until 1879. (At the Pioneer Cemetery, Queen Street, Streetsville)

PERTH COUNTY

- KIRKTON
Timothy Eaton 1834-1907
A pioneer in the art of retail merchandising, Eaton operated dry-goods stores in Kirkton and St. Marys before moving to Toronto in 1868. There he opened a store that grew in time into a nation-wide retail and mail-order business. (In the roadside park, Highway 23 (near the site of his former store), just north of Kirkton)

- LISTOWEL
The Founding of Listowel
The last section of Perth County to be opened for settlement was Wallace Township. It was not surveyed until 1852, but eager settlers had located in the area nonetheless. By 1856 the enterprising village of Listowel boasted a population of 200. (At the municipal building, 330 Wallace Avenue North, Listowel)

Andrew Edward McKeever 1895-1919
During a seven-month period in the First World War McKeever, with his attendant gunners, shot down some thirty enemy aircraft from the controls of his two-seater Bristol Fighter. His skill and gallantry earned the Listowel native the Military Cross and Bar, and the Distinguished Service Order (In Cenotaph Park, Wallace Avenue North and Elizabeth Street East, Listowel)

- MILVERTON
The Founding of Milverton
The hamlet that developed around the hotel Andrew West had opened by 1851 was known for many years as West's Corners before it was renamed Milverton. With the advent of rail service in 1877 the small agricultural village became a thriving commercial

centre. (At the public library, 27 Main Street South, Milverton)

• MITCHELL
The Founding of Mitchell
Settlement proceeded slowly at first on the town plot laid out by the Canada Company in 1836 at the junction of Whirl Creek and the Thames River. The opening of the Mitchell-Blanshard Road in 1845 encouraged light industries to locate in Mitchell, and with the arrival of rail service twelve years later economic growth was assured. (In Centennial Park, Huron and Blanchard Streets, Mitchell)

"Howie" Morenz 1902-1937
One of Canada's finest and most popular hockey players, Morenz was born in Mitchell and began his career with the Mitchell Juveniles in 1916. During his twelve years with the Montreal Canadiens he distinguished himself as an exceptionally fast skater and a player of intense concentration. (In Howie Morenz Memorial Gardens, Blanchard and Huron Streets, Mitchell)

• ST. MARYS
The Founding of St. Marys
The sawmill and grist-mill constructed by Thomas Ingersoll at the "Little Falls" on the Thames in the early 1840s formed the nucleus of the community of St. Marys. By the time railway connections were extended to the village some two decades later, St. Marys had become the centre of lumber and quarry activity in the region. (At the town hall, 175 Queen Street East, St. Marys)

The Right Honourable Arthur Meighen 1874-1960
Born near St. Marys, Meighen moved to Manitoba in 1902 where he practised law before entering federal politics. He held three portfolios under

Robert Borden, whom he succeeded as prime minister in 1920. Meighen served a second brief term as prime minister in 1926. (Concession Roads 2 and 3, west off County Road 18 (near the farm where he was born), northwest of St. Marys)

- ## SHAKESPEARE
Fryfogel's Inn
Built about 1845, Fryfogel's Inn was a favourite stopping place for travellers on the Huron Road and for settlers taking up land in the Huron Tract. The inn is one of very few remaining examples of Neoclassical architecture in this part of the province. (At the inn, Highway 7/8, about 3 km east of Shakespeare)

- ## STRATFORD
The Founding of Stratford
Despite activity by the Canada Company, the market centre of "Little Thames" was slow to develop at first. In the 1850s, with its designation as the administrative seat of Perth County and with the advent of railway connections to Goderich and Sarnia, the town – by now called Stratford – became a thriving commercial centre. (In the park near the Huron Street stone bridge, Stratford)

Sir John Cunningham McLennan 1867-1935
A distinguished Canadian scientist, McLennan achieved world-wide recognition for his work in spectroscopy and low-temperature research. During his long career at the University of Toronto, he developed the physics laboratory, which now bears his name, into a first-rate teaching and research institution. (On the Avon River footpath, behind 203 William Street (the former McLennan family home), Stratford)

PETERBOROUGH COUNTY

• BAILIEBORO
Joseph Medlicott Scriven 1819-1886
The author of the well known hymn *What a Friend We Have in Jesus*, Scriven was a native of County Down, Ireland and a graduate of Trinity College, Dublin. After coming to Upper Canada in 1847 he was engaged by Captain Robert Pengelley as tutor to his children, and lived in the Rice Lake area. (At the Pengelley Burying Ground (where his grave is located), south off Lakeview Road, about 4 km east of Bailieboro)

• KEENE
The Serpent Mounds
The serpentine-shaped, prehistoric burial mounds near the north shore of Rice Lake are the only ones of this type known to exist in Canada. It has been estimated that the mounds, which were built while the region was occupied by Indians of the Point Peninsula culture, date from the second century A.D. (In Serpent Mounds Provincial Park, County Road 34, Rice Lake – south of Keene)

The Lang Mill
The Allandale Flour Mill was built in 1846 by Thomas Short, and by 1858 had become one of the largest mills in the region. Renamed the Lang Mill in the 1870s, it continued in operation until 1965 when it was purchased by the Otonabee Region Conservation Authority. (At the restored mill, Century Village Museum Complex, County Road 34, about 3 km north of Keene)

• LAKEFIELD
Catharine Parr Traill 1802-1899
A member of the literary Strickland family, Catharine Parr Traill came to Upper Canada in 1832 and

with her husband took up farming in the Peterborough hinterland. Of her many published works, *The Backwoods of Canada* is probably the best known. In it she describes, with candour and insight, her experiences as a pioneer settler. (At her former home, 16 Smith Street, Lakefield)

Susanna Moodie 1803-1885

The youngest of the Strickland sisters, Susanna Moodie, with her husband, settled on a wilderness property in the Lakefield area in 1834. After six years of unsuccessful farming, she and her family moved to Belleville where she concentrated on literary work. Her poems, articles, stories, and

Susanna Moodie (left) and her sister Catharine Parr Traill (shown here with a niece in the 1880s) gained their initial readership by publishing stories in the Literary Garland, a monthly magazine which first appeared in 1838. (Archives of Ontario S 8364)

novels – most notably *Roughing It In The Bush* – gained her a wide readership. (In Cenotaph Park, Water Street, Lakefield)

Colonel Samuel Strickland 1804-1867

The first member of his family to come to Upper Canada, Strickland took up farming in Douro Township in 1831. He became a prominent citizen in the area, contributing to the erection of a church and school. Like his sisters, Catharine Parr Traill and Susanna Moodie, Strickland also published accounts of his experiences as a pioneer. (On the grounds of Christ Church (where his grave is located), 62 Queen Street, Lakefield)

• PETERBOROUGH

Scott's Mills 1820

The small community which developed around Adam Scott's sawmill and grist-mill was known briefly as Scott's Plains before being renamed Peterborough. The mills were a great boon to the Irish settlers brought to the area in 1825 by Peter Robinson. (In front of the Peterborough Canoe Company (near the site of the former mills), Water Street, Peterborough)

The Robinson Settlement 1825

In an effort to alleviate poverty and starvation in Ireland, the British government in 1825 sponsored a settlement of Irish families in the vicinity of present-day Peterborough. Under the supervision of Peter Robinson close to 2,000 people from County Cork were established in the region. (In Victoria Park, Water Street, Peterborough)

Thomas and Frances Stewart

Natives of Ireland, the Stewarts took up farming on the Otonabee River in 1823. As a justice of the peace and member of the legislative council,

Thomas Stewart played a significant role in the early development of Peterborough. Frances Stewart's published correspondence, *Our Forest Home*, provides a valuable record of pioneer life. (On the grounds of Thomas A. Stewart Secondary School, Armour Road, Peterborough)

District Court House and Jail

When the District of Colborne was established in 1838, Peterborough was selected as its judicial and administrative centre. The court house was completed within two years and the adjacent jail by 1842. Locally quarried stone from Jackson's Park was used in the construction of both buildings. (At the Peterborough county court house, overlooking Victoria Park between Brock and Murray Streets, Peterborough)

St. John's Church 1834

Designed in the Early English Gothic Revival style, St. John's Church is the oldest remaining church in Peterborough County. Prior to its construction, the local Anglican congregation had been holding services in a schoolhouse. (On the grounds of the church, 99 Hunter Street West, Peterborough)

The Cathedral of St. Peter-in-Chains

Constructed in 1837-38 to serve the large Irish-Catholic population of the Robinson Settlement, St. Peter's became a cathedral in 1882. It is one of the oldest Roman Catholic churches remaining in Ontario and despite renovations and additions has retained much of its original Gothic Revival elegance. (In front of the cathedral, 320 Hunter Street West, Peterborough)

The Hutchison House 1837

This handsome stone house belonged to Dr. John Hutchison, the first resident physician in Peterborough and a prominent citizen in the community. It is now operated as a historic house museum by the Peterborough Historical Society. (On the grounds of the house, 270 Brock Street, Peterborough)

The Grover-Nicholls House

A fine example of Greek Revival architecture modified in the Palladian manner, this house derived its name from two of its several owners, P.M. Grover and Robert Nicholls. The house has been owned by the Masonic Order since 1950. (On the grounds of the house, 415 Rubidge Street, Peterborough)

Sir Sandford Fleming, the inventor of Standard Time, was also responsible for designing the first Canadian postage stamp, the three-penny beaver issued in 1851. (Archives of Ontario S 426)

Sir Sandford Fleming 1827-1915

A pioneer in world communications, Fleming was born in Scotland where he trained as an engineer and surveyor before settling in the Peterborough area in 1845. Of his many achievements, he is probably best known as the inventor of Standard Time, the universal system for reckoning time which was adopted in 1884. (In Fleming Park, Aylmer Road and Brock Streets, Peterborough)

Trent University

Founded through the efforts of a citizens' committee interested in creating a university to serve the Trent valley, Trent University was established by provincial charter in 1963 as a degree-granting institution. Its first students were enrolled the following year. (At the driveway entrance to the Bata Library Building, Trent University campus, Peterborough)

PRESCOTT AND RUSSELL UNITED COUNTIES

- ## HAWKESBURY
Hawkesbury Mills
By 1850 the sawmilling operations begun early in the century by Thomas Mears and David Patee at present-day Hawkesbury had become, reportedly, the largest sawmilling establishment in Canada West and the most productive exporter of softwood planks to Britain. (In Confederation Park, John Street, Hawkesbury)

- ## L'ORIGNAL
The Seigneury of L'Orignal
A parcel of land along the Ottawa River which was granted to François Prévost in 1674 was the first seigneury in what is now Ontario. Perhaps because of its remoteness, the area was not developed for settlement until the end of the eighteenth century. By 1825, however, a thriving village was in evidence on the Pointe à l'Orignac seigneury. (In Centennial Park, 772 Front Street, L'Orignal)

The Founding of L'Orignal
Named after the moose that were so plentiful in the area, L'Orignal was developed primarily by Nathaniel Treadwell, a land speculator from New York State who acquired the Pointe à l'Orignac seigneury in 1796. (At St-Jean Baptiste School, 35 Longueuil Street, L'Orignal)

District Court House and Gaol 1825
The central portion of the present court house complex dates from 1825 and was built to hold the Ottawa District's courts of general quarter sessions, which at that time administered both judicial and municipal affairs. This Neoclassical structure is the oldest remaining court house in the province. (At

the county court house, 1023 Queen Street,
L'Orignal)

St. Andrew's Church 1832
The Presbyterian congregation at L'Orignal had
been in existence since 1822 but did not begin
construction of its church until ten years later when
Charles Treadwell, the current seigneur of Pointe
à l'Orignac, donated land for the structure. In 1925
the congregation voted to join The United Church
of Canada. (On the grounds of the church, 1008 King
Street, L'Orignal)

• ROCKLAND
William Cameron Edwards 1844-1921
A leading lumber producer in the Ottawa valley,
Edwards owned extensive mills in Rockland and
Ottawa. As the member of parliament for Russell
from 1887 to 1903 he vigorously promoted the
interests of lumbermen in the establishment of
provincial forestry policies. (At the site of the ruins
of his sawmill complex, Parc du Moulin, Edwards
Street, north of Highway 17, Rockland)

PRINCE EDWARD COUNTY

• CONSECON
The Kenté (Quinte) Mission
Established in 1668 by two Sulpician priests to serve the Iroquois bands migrating to the north shore of Lake Ontario, the Kenté mission became, for a time, a significant outpost of French influence in the lower Great Lakes region. The mission was abandoned in 1680 mainly as a result of the growth of Fort Frontenac. (In the park on County Road 29 (near the site of the former mission), just west of Highway 33, Consecon)

• PICTON
The Founding of Hallowell
In the secure harbour at the head of Picton Bay the community of Hallowell was well established early in the nineteenth century as a shipping and distribution centre for the peninsula. In 1837 it was amalgamated with the adjacent community of Picton. (In Queen Elizabeth Park, Hill and Bay Streets, Picton)

The Reverend William Macaulay 1794-1874
A prominent citizen and resident Anglican priest in Picton, Macaulay financed the construction of the Church of St. Mary Magdalene and donated the site of the Prince Edward District court house and jail. (On the grounds of the former Church of St. Mary Magdalene, now part of the Macaulay Heritage Park, Union and Church Streets, Picton)

District Court House and Gaol 1832
In 1831 Prince Edward County, which until then had been part of the Midland District, was declared a separate administrative district contingent upon the erection of a court house at Picton. The two-storey Greek Revival structure built between 1832

and 1834 is one of Ontario's oldest public buildings still in use. (On the grounds of the county court house, Union Street, Picton)

John A. Macdonald in Hallowell

Between 1833 and 1835 John A. Macdonald took over the law practice of an ailing cousin in Hallowell (later amalgamated with Picton). During this brief period he gained his first experience in public administration by serving as secretary of the district school board. (In front of the post office, Main Street, Picton)

The "Conference Church"

The Conference Church was a simple frame chapel that in 1824 was the site of the first Canada Conference of Methodist churchmen. This conference led to the official separation of the American and Canadian Methodist Churches four years later. Subsequent church buildings on the site have also been the scene of significant conferences. (On the grounds of Picton United Church, Chapel and Mary Streets, Picton)

Letitia Youmans 1827-1896

A school teacher and the devoted mother of a large household, Letitia Youmans became publicly active in temperance reform in 1874 when she organized a Women's Christian Temperance Union in Picton. She later served as the first president of the W.C.T.U. of Ontario, and of the federal organization. (At Glenwood Cemetery (where her grave is located), Grove Street, Picton)

West Lake Boarding School

The first seminary in Canada of the Society of Friends, the West Lake Boarding School was opened as a girls' school in 1841. A second building to house male students was completed the following year.

Remotely situated and inadequately supported, the institution was forced to close in 1865. (Near the former school building, now a private dwelling, Highway 33 just past Mallory Road, about 6 km west of Picton)

The White Chapel 1809
Known familiarly as the "Old Chapel", this simple frame church was built on land donated by Stephen Conger, a loyalist from New Jersey. It was the first Methodist church in Prince Edward and has been maintained as a place of worship longer than any other church of Methodist origin in Ontario. (At the church, Highway 49, about 3 km north of Picton)

Sir Rodmond P. Roblin 1853-1937
A native of Prince Edward County, Roblin moved to Winnipeg at the age of twenty-four and entered provincial politics. During his influential years as premier of Manitoba (1900-1915), he ardently promoted western grain trade and railway expansion, and made a significant contribution to that province's economic and social development. (At the former Roblin homestead, Bethesda Road, off County Road 15, about 16 km north of Picton)

• WAUPOOS
The Marysburgh Settlement
Among the early loyalist settlers in Marysburgh Township was a group of about forty disbanded German mercenaries who, by 1784, had begun to clear land and cultivate crops in the vicinity of Waupoos. This was one of the earliest German-speaking settlements in the province. (On the grounds of the Marysburgh Museum, Waupoos Road, off County Road 8, Waupoos)

RAINY RIVER DISTRICT

- ATIKOKAN
Steep Rock Iron Range
As early as 1897 it was thought that a substantial iron ore body lay beneath the waters of Steep Rock Lake, but it was not until 1938 that ore was actually discovered. Mining began six years later, and over the next twenty years more than 36 million tons of ore were mined. (At the civic centre, behind the post office at Burns and Main Streets, Atikokan)

- FORT FRANCES
Jacques de Noyon 1668-1745
Explorer, fur trader, and soldier, Noyon explored the Kaministiquia route to the Lake of the Woods in 1688, and was probably the first European to have travelled through this area. The report that he made after returning to Montreal was of great value to later explorers. (At Rainy Lake Lookout, Noden Causeway, about 6.5 km south of Fort Frances)

Sieur de La Vérendrye 1685-1749
Between 1727 and 1747, while searching for the illusive Western Sea, Pierre Gaultier de Varennes et de La Vérendrye explored much of present-day northwestern Ontario and southern Manitoba. He established several important fur trading posts which brought substantial prosperity to New France. (At Pither's Point (near the site of one of his former posts), off Mill Road, Fort Frances)

Fort Lac La Pluie
An important North West Company post situated between the Red River and Fort William, Fort Lac La Pluie (or Rainy Lake House) was the centre of much activity in the fur trade during the late eighteenth and early nineteenth centuries. It served as a meeting place for traders from Montreal in the

east and those from the Athabaska country to the west. (Faries Avenue, south of River Drive (near the site of the former fort), Fort Frances)

The Fort Frances Canal 1878

Providing unbroken passage between Rainy Lake and Lake of the Woods, the Fort Frances canal was constructed as part of a large-scale government plan to improve communication with the West. In 1908 it was incorporated into a dam and power development project. (In West End Park, Third Avenue West, Fort Frances)

At one point in its history the Hudson's Bay Company's post at Lac La Pluie appears to have served as a billboard for, among other things, cigars and grand opera. (Archives of Ontario S 6619)

- QUETICO PROVINCIAL PARK
The French Portage
This two-mile portage on the Kaministiquia canoe route was first travelled by a European, Jacques de Noyon, in 1688. Used extensively by French and British fur traders, it was later improved for wagon traffic and became a way-station on the Dawson Route. (In front of the visitors centre at the Dawson Trail Campground, off Highway 11 about 40 km east of Atikokan, in Quetico Provincial Park)

Quetico-Superior
A wilderness area co-operatively protected since the first part of this century by the governments of the United States, Minnesota, and Ontario, Quetico-Superior is one of the largest international nature sanctuaries in the world. (Near the park station on Basswood Lake, close to the international border, Quetico Provincial Park)

- RAINY RIVER
The Canadian Northern Railway
Incorporated in 1899, the Canadian Northern Railway proved a great boon to the development of northwestern Ontario and the Prairies. By 1915 it was operating from coast to coast. Eventually the line was integrated into the Canadian National system. (Beside CNR steam locomotive 4008, Highway 11 just east of the international border, Rainy River)

RENFREW COUNTY

• ARNPRIOR
The McNab Settlement
In 1824 some eighty Scottish Highlanders under the patriarchal rule of Archibald McNab established the first organized settlement along the Ottawa River in what later became McNab Township. (In Robert Simpson Park (in the vicinity of Archibald McNab's first house), at the foot of John Street, Arnprior)

Daniel McLachlin 1810-1872
An astute lumberman, McLachlin recognized the timber potential of the Madawaska watershed and in 1851 purchased a large tract of land at the site of Arnprior. Shortly thereafter he laid out a town plot and constructed large sawmills at the mouth of the river. (In Bell Park, Madawaska Street, Arnprior)

Timber Rafting on the Ottawa
The rafting of large cribs of square timber down the Ottawa River and then on to Quebec City was a highly lucrative trade throughout most of the nineteenth century, and was a significant factor in the economic development of the Ottawa valley. (In Robert Simpson Park, at the foot of John Street, Arnprior)

The Gillies Bros. Lumbering Firm
By the mid-1880s the four Gillies brothers had established their firm as one of the major lumber producers in the Ottawa valley, a position the company sustained well into the twentieth century. (In front of the Gillies Brothers and Company Mill, River Road, northwest of Arnprior)

• BARRYS BAY
The Opeongo Road
Part of a network of colonization roads constructed

by the government to open the hinterland for settlement, the Opeongo Road was completed as a winter road from Farrells Landing (Castleford) to Opeongo Lake by 1854. The offer of free, 100-acre lots along the road attracted many settlers to Renfrew County. (On the grounds of the post office, Highway 60 (which in this vicinity follows the former colonization route), Barrys Bay)

• CALABOGIE
The Black Donald Graphite Mine
The only large-scale graphite operation in Ontario, the Black Donald Graphite Mine was in almost continuous operation from 1895 to 1954. During a period of peak production following the First World

Daniel McLachlin's sawmilling complex at the junction of the Madawaska and Ottawa rivers was a thriving enterprise by 1855, the year in which this lithograph of Arnprior was printed. (Archives of Ontario S 13893)

War it was responsible for 90% of all graphite mined in Canada. (Near the site of the former mine, Black Donald Road (an extension of Highway 508) at Centennial Lake, near Calabogie)

• CASTLEFORD
Lieutenant Christopher James Bell, R.N. 1795-1836
One of the first lumbermen in the Ottawa valley, Bell came to Upper Canada about 1817 after receiving a grant of some 800 acres of land. The sawmill and timber slide he built at the first chute on the Bonnechère River became the centre of a

---

The offer of free land bordering a colonization road was an attractive prospect for many settlers despite the effort required to clear the land. This cabin was built on the Opeongo Road. (Archives of Ontario. Charles Macnamara Collection S 5056)

small milling community. (County Road 3 at the Bonnechère River (in the vicinity of his former sawmill and timber slide), about 2 km southeast of Castleford)

• CHALK RIVER
The ZEEP Reactor
A nuclear chain reaction was first initiated in Canada on September 5, 1945 when the ZEEP reactor went into operation at Chalk River. The small, experimental reactor was named Zero Energy Experimental Pile because it was developed to produce only one watt of heat. (In front of the public information centre at Chalk River Nuclear Laboratories, off Highway 17, about 8 km northwest of Chalk River)

• COBDEN
Champlain's Journey of 1613
On his first journey up the Ottawa River in search of the northern sea (Hudson Bay) Champlain stayed briefly at an Algonkian village near present-day Cobden. After learning that he had been misled as to the proximity of the illusive sea, Champlain proceeded down the Ottawa River from Lower Allumette Lake and returned to Quebec. (In Municipal Park, Highway 17, Cobden)

• DEUX RIVIÈRES
The Rapids of the Upper Ottawa
For over two centuries the canoe was the only means of transportation between the St. Lawrence settlements and the vast hinterland to the west and north. Four sets of dangerous rapids on the Ottawa River were the first of many obstacles to be negotiated by the intrepid explorers and adventurers in Canada's early years. (At the lookout point on Highway 17, about 3 km west of Deux Rivières)

- PEMBROKE
The Founder of Pembroke
Following naval service during the War of 1812, Scottish-born Peter White settled permanently in Upper Canada and entered the lumber trade. He made his headquarters at the wilderness site of present-day Pembroke and soon became a prominent businessman and public figure in the community that grew up around his enterprises. (On the grounds of the Champlain Trail Museum, 1032 Pembroke Street East, Pembroke)

The Pembroke and Mattawan Road
Constructed as a supply route to the lumber camps in the upper Ottawa valley, the Pembroke and Mattawan Road was begun in 1853 and completed to its full length over the next twenty years. Some sections have since been incorporated into Highway 17, but the original route can still be travelled between CFB Petawawa and Deep River. (At the tourist information booth in Riverside Park (in the vicinity of the former route), Highway 17, Pembroke)

- POINT ALEXANDER
Steamboating on the Upper Ottawa
Steam navigation began on the upper sections of the Ottawa River in 1833 and was instrumental in the early development of the region's lumber industry. Sight-seeing excursions also became popular. By the 1880s, however, most water traffic had been replaced by faster, more efficient rail service. (At the municipal building, Highway 17, Point Alexander)

- RENFREW
The Opeongo Road
Part of a network of colonization roads constructed by the government to open the hinterland for

settlement, the Opeongo Road was completed as a winter road from Farrells Landing (Castleford) to Opeongo Lake by 1854. The offer of free, 100-acre lots along the road attracted many settlers to Renfrew County. (In Hydro Park, Mutual and Raglin Streets, Renfrew)

The Founding of Renfrew
Attracted by the lumber activity in the upper Ottawa valley, settlers began moving into the area of present-day Renfrew in the 1830s, and soon a small community was in evidence. The opening of the Opeongo Road in 1854 ensured Renfrew's continued growth. (In Low's Square, Plaunt Street and Railway Avenue, Renfrew)

Sir Francis Hincks at Renfrew
A public figure of much prominence and influence in Upper Canada, Hincks purchased land north of the Bonnechère River in 1853. By subdividing his holdings into town lots and donating land for a public square he contributed substantially to the development of Renfrew as a community. (At Bruce and Albert Streets (the lot he donated for a public square), Renfrew)

- WILNO
Canada's First Polish Settlement
Leaving behind the adverse social and political conditions of their partitioned homeland, some 300 Polish immigrants came to Renfrew County in 1864 and rapidly established a thriving agricultural community. Wilno was augmented by a second wave of Polish immigration in the early 1900s and still retains much of its distinctive cultural heritage. (In Shrine Hill Park, near Our Lady Queen of Poland Roman Catholic Church, off Highway 60 about 1 km east of Wilno)

SIMCOE COUNTY

- ATHERLEY
Rama Indian Reserve
Pressure by land-hungry settlers in the vicinity of present-day Orillia forced the relocation in 1838-39 of a band of Ojibwa led by Chief William Yellowhead (Musquakie) to a new reserve in Rama Township. Over the years, as the residents made the transition from a nomadic to a settled life-style, more acreage was acquired and a thriving agricultural community emerged. (On the grounds of the United Church, Rama Road, Rama Indian Reserve, on the east shore of Lake Couchiching, north of Atherley)

- BARRIE
The Nine Mile Portage
A link in the line of communication between Lake Simcoe and Georgian Bay, this early portage ran west from the landing-place at the headwaters of Kempenfeldt Bay (today the site of Barrie) to Willow Creek. During the War of 1812 the portage was cleared and over the next decade was used as a supply route to the naval and military establishments at Penetanguishene. (In Memorial Park, Dunlop and Simcoe Streets (in the vicinity of the former portage), Barrie)

Hewitt Bernard 1825-1893
A native of Jamaica, Bernard settled in Barrie in 1851 where he opened a law practice. He accompanied John A. Macdonald to the Charlottetown Conference in 1864 and served as secretary of the Quebec and London Conferences at which the groundwork was laid for Confederation. (In Centennial Park, Lakeshore Drive, Barrie)

Simcoe County Court House and Gaol
Completed in 1842, the court house and jail complex

at Barrie served the region until 1976 when the court house was demolished. The jail, built of Lake Couchiching limestone in a radial design, still stands although additions and renovations have altered its original appearance significantly. (At the jail, 87 Mulcaster Street, Barrie)

Andrew Frederick Hunter 1863-1940

A native of Innisfil Township, Hunter was an active member of the Canadian Institute and the Ontario Historical Society. He undertook extensive research on the history and archaeology of Huronia, and his published writings did much to encourage the study of local history throughout the province. (On the grounds of the public library, 37 Mulcaster Street, Barrie)

William Edward Gallie, M.D. 1882-1959

A distinguished surgeon and teacher, Gallie was born in Barrie and educated at the University of Toronto. During his years as a surgeon at the Hospital for Sick Children in Toronto he devised revolutionary techniques in tissue transplant and bone repair that are now practised throughout the world. (In front of Royal Victoria Hospital, 76 Ross Street, Barrie)

Black Settlement in Oro Township

By 1831 nine black veterans of the War of 1812 had accepted land grants along Wilberforce Street, thus forming the only government-sponsored black settlement in Upper Canada. A community of about 100 settlers flourished briefly, but the poor soil and harsh climate ultimately brought discouragement and the settlement was gradually abandoned. (At the south end of former Wilberforce Street, County Road 20, between Barrie and Shanty Bay)

- BEETON
  ### David Allanson Jones 1836-1910
  The first commercial bee-keeper and breeder in Canada, Jones imported bees from Cyprus and Palestine (honey-bees are not native to North America) for the numerous apiaries on his farm at Clarksville. That community was renamed Beeton in 1874 in tribute to his flourishing enterprise. (In the community park at Prospect and Second Streets, Beeton)

- BOND HEAD
  ### Sir William Mulock 1843-1944
  A prominent lawyer and statesman, Mulock, who was born in Bond Head, served as postmaster-general and as minister of labour in Sir Wilfrid Laurier's cabinet. In 1924 he was appointed chancellor of the University of Toronto and for thirteen years served as chief justice of Ontario. (In Memorial Park, Highway 27, Bond Head)

  ### Sir William Osler 1849-1919
  A native of Bond Head, Osler graduated in medicine from McGill University in 1872. He was renowned as both teacher and physician at several distinguished medical schools, and in his lectures and published works did much to revolutionize methods of medical instruction. (On the grounds of the community centre, Highway 27, Bond Head)

- BRADFORD
  ### The Scotch Settlement 1819
  Disheartened by crop failures and the antagonism of North West Company agents, a group of Scottish settlers left Lord Selkirk's Red River settlement in 1815 and came to Upper Canada. By 1819 many of the Highlanders had taken up land in West Gwillimbury. (On the grounds of the *Auld Kirk* (the site of the Highlanders' original church building), Concession Road 6, Bradford)

• CFB BORDEN
Camp Borden
Established in 1916 as a training centre for Canadian
Expeditionary Force battalions, this military
reserve was soon occupied by some 32,000 troops.
The following year an air training program was
instituted under the Royal Flying Corps, Canada.
(Near Building T-47 (an original wash hut), Ortona
Road, CFB Borden)

• COLDWATER
Cowan's Trading Post
George Cowan, known to his French-Canadian
employees as Jean Baptiste Constant, established an
independent trading post on Matchedash Bay in the

*Camp Borden, comprising almost 18,000 acres in Simcoe County,
was officially opened on July 11, 1916 by Sir Sam Hughes, minister
of militia and defence. (Archives of Ontario S 1430)*

late 1770s. His fur-dealing territory probably included most of present-day Simcoe, Muskoka, and Haliburton. (On the east side of Matchedash Bay (near the site of the former trading post), Concession Road 12 near the Twin Oaks subdivision, about 11 km northwest of Coldwater)

The Coldwater Mill 1833

Taking advantage of the rapids at Coldwater, members of the Ojibwa band led by Chief Aisance constructed a grist-mill in 1833 to serve the residents of the Coldwater Reserve. Although the reserve was relinquished to European settlement in 1836, the mill remained in Indian ownership until 1849. It is

The size and splendour of the Northern Railway's terminal at Collingwood (shown here in 1880) reflects the prosperity experienced by the town as a result of active rail and steamship service. (Archives of Ontario S 1627)

believed that portions of the present mill date back to the original structure. (At the mill on Mill Street, just off Coldwater Road, Coldwater)

• COLLINGWOOD
The Northern Railway Company of Canada
Early in 1855 this pioneer railway company had completed a "portage" line from Toronto to Collingwood, thus linking ports on the Atlantic and Lake Ontario with the upper Great Lakes. Later in the century the Northern was absorbed by the Grand Trunk Railway Company. (On the grounds of the Collingwood Museum (a former railway station), St. Paul Street, Collingwood)

The Associated Country Women of the World
A non-sectarian, non-political, international organization, the Associated Country Women of the World was formed in 1933 largely through the efforts of Margaret Watt, a native of Collingwood, who was elected the association's first president. (On the grounds of the Collingwood Museum, St. Paul Street, Collingwood)

• CROWN HILL
The Honourable Ernest Charles Drury
A graduate of the Ontario Agricultural College, Drury (1878-1968) became the first president of the United Farmers of Ontario in 1914. That organization formed the provincial government from 1919 to 1923, during which time Drury served as prime minister. (On the grounds of his former farm, Highway 93, Crown Hill – about 8 km northeast of Barrie)

• MIDLAND
The Gateway to Huronia
During the seventeenth century the shore of Matchedash Bay marked the terminus of the historic

canoe route connecting New France with Huronia. Missionaries, soldiers, explorers, and fur traders ascended the Ottawa and Mattawa Rivers, crossed Lake Nipissing, descended the French River, and entered Huronia via Matchedash Bay. (Overlooking the bay and the Martyrs' Shrine, Highway 12, east of Midland)

Sainte-Marie Among the Hurons
Established in 1639 as a headquarters for Jesuit missions throughout Huronia, Sainte-Marie was a fortified post which comprised a hospital, chapels, living quarters, and farm buildings. Following the devastation of the Huron nation by the Iroquois in 1649, Sainte-Marie was burned by the Jesuits and abandoned. (Near the orientation centre at Sainte-Marie-Among-the-Hurons (a re-creation of the former post), Highway 12, east of Midland)

The Penetanguishene Road
Constructed in 1814 under the supervision of William "Tiger" Dunlop, the Penetanguishene Road was intended as a military route between Kempenfeldt Bay and Penetanguishene. The route also served as a colonization road during the 1820s when 200-acre lots were laid out along its length to stimulate settlement of the region. (On Hugel Avenue (a section of the old Penetanguishene Road), just off Highway 93, Midland)

The Founding of Midland
In 1871 the spot known as Mundy's Bay was chosen as the northern terminus of the Midland Railway, which at that time ran from Port Hope to Beaverton. A town site was surveyed the following year and settlers, attracted by the convenience of rail service, soon began to move into the area. (On the grounds of the public library, 320 King Street, Midland)

- MINESING
  ### Willow Creek Depot
  An important storage depot for supplies and trade goods during the War of 1812, "Fort Willow" was situated near the end of the Nine Mile Portage which connected the landing-place at the head-waters of Kempenfeldt Bay (today the site of Barrie) to Willow Creek. (At the site of the former depot, in an isolated clearing overlooking Minesing Swamp, Concession XI, Vespra Township, about 8 km south of Minesing)

- NEWTON ROBINSON
  ### The Honourable William Earl Rowe 1894-1984
  In 1963, after a distinguished forty-year career in provincial and federal politics, Rowe was appointed lieutenant-governor of Ontario, a position he held until his retirement from public life in 1968. (In front of his former home, "Rowelands", just off Highway 27, Newton Robinson – south of Cookstown)

- ORILLIA
  ### Chief William Yellowhead
  Chief of the Deer tribe of the Ojibwa, Yellowhead (c.1769-1864) established his band at the site of present-day Orillia in 1830 in accordance with the government's plan of settling nomadic tribes on designated reserves. In 1838 the highly respected chief (also known as Musquakie) relocated his people to a reserve in Rama Township. (In Couchiching Beach Park, Tecumseth Street, Orillia)

  ### "Jake" Gaudaur 1858-1937
  A lifelong resident of Orillia, Gaudaur began competitive rowing at the age of seventeen. Over the next twenty-five years he established a world's record and won several world championship races in Canada, the United States, and England. (At the Atherley Road bridge, Orillia)

Franklin Carmichael 1890-1945

A native of Orillia, Carmichael studied painting and design in Toronto and in Europe. He was a founding member of the Group of Seven and participated in all the Group's exhibitions. His paintings can be seen today in major galleries throughout Canada. (On the grounds of the public library, 36 Mississauga Street West, Orillia)

The Huron Fish Weirs

Constructed in the narrows connecting Lakes Simcoe and Couchiching, the weirs consisted of a network of stakes driven into the lake bed, with openings at which nets were placed to trap fish. The weirs were noted by Champlain in 1615 when he led a Huron war party through the area. (At the marina, 674 Atherley Road, near the Atherley Narrows (the site of the former weirs), Orillia)

The Founding of Orillia

The site of an Ojibwa reserve from 1830 to 1838, Orillia subsequently prospered as an agricultural and lumbering community. Transportation links with Toronto and Georgian Bay stimulated Orillia's development as a commercial centre and summer resort. (Beside the Orillia Opera House, Mississauga and West Streets, Orillia)

• PENETANGUISHENE

Captain James Keating, R.A.

A native of Ireland, Keating (c.1786-1849) joined the Royal Artillery at a young age and came to Canada in 1812. He saw action at many points and as the first adjutant of the military establishment at Penetanguishene figured prominently in that community's early years. (On the grounds of the Historic Naval and Military Establishments, Church Street, Penetanguishene)

Henry Wolsey Bayfield 1795-1885
A naval officer and self-taught nautical surveyor, Bayfield was stationed in Upper Canada in 1816. By the time he retired forty years later he had completed surveys of Lakes Erie, Huron, and Superior, using Penetanguishene as his headquarters; he also charted the coasts of Prince Edward Island and Nova Scotia, and the shore of the lower St. Lawrence. (In Bayfield Park, Penetanguishene)

The Founding of Penetanguishene
The village plot of Penetanguishene had been surveyed as early as 1811 but there were no civilian settlers on the site until troops and fur traders from Drummond Island began to relocate there in the 1820s. The nearby naval and military establishments helped to sustain the community during its early years. (In the Chamber of Commerce Park, Main Street, Penetanguishene)

Captain John Moberly, R.N. 1789-1848
Commandant of the naval establishment at Penetanguishene from 1834 to 1844, Moberly was an influential figure in the area. He was largely responsible for the building of the first Protestant church in the vicinity, St. James-on-the-Lines. (In the town of Penetanguishene)

St. James-on-the-Lines 1836
Built largely through the efforts of Captain John Moberly, St. James' was originally intended to serve the naval and military personnel in residence at the Penetanguishene establishments. Until the 1870s, however, it was the only Protestant church in the vicinity and consequently was attended by the civilian population as well. (On the grounds of the church, 215 Church Street North, Penetanguishene)

- SHANTY BAY
St. Thomas' Church 1838
St. Thomas' Church on Lake Simcoe was built by local parishioners using a construction technique known as "rammed earth". Wet clay mixed with straw was compacted into wooden moulds and left to harden. When completely dry, the mud walls were reinforced with a coating of plaster to protect them from the elements. (On the grounds of the church, Church Street, Shanty Bay)

- STAYNER
The Founding of Stayner
Early settlement on the site of Stayner coincided with the construction between 1851 and 1855 of a railway line from Toronto to Collingwood. Originally called Nottawasaga Station, the community of Stayner developed into a significant agricultural and lumbering centre. (At the centennial fountain, Main and Oak Streets, Stayner)

- WASAGA BEACH
"Schooner Town"
The Royal Navy's base of operations for vessels on Lake Huron was located at the foot of navigation on the Nottawasaga River between 1815 and 1817. Operations were then transferred to Penetanguishene which afforded better anchorage. (In Schoonertown Parkette (near the site of the former base), River Road West and Oxbow Park Road, Wasaga Beach Provincial Park)

- WASHAGO
Wasdell Falls Hydro-Electric Development 1914
Officially opened by Sir Adam Beck on October 16, 1914, the Wasdell Falls plant was the first generating station constructed by the Hydro-Electric Power Commission of Ontario. It continued to serve the region until 1955, by which time much

larger hydro-electric systems were in operation throughout the province. (Beside the former plant, Wasdell Falls Road, about 5 km northwest of Washago)

• WYEBRIDGE
Franz Johnston 1888-1949
After working as a commercial artist for some years, Johnston served as an official war artist with the Royal Flying Corps during the First World War. In 1920 he participated in the first exhibition of paintings by the Group of Seven. (On the grounds of his former home and studio, Highway 93 and Mill Street, Wyebridge – just south of Midland)

STORMONT, DUNDAS AND GLENGARRY UNITED COUNTIES

• ALEXANDRIA
The MacLeod Settlement
Some forty families from various Highland clans emigrated from Scotland under the leadership of Alexander MacLeod and took up land in Glengarry in 1794. One of the earliest Presbyterian parishes in Upper Canada was subsequently established in Lochiel Township. (At a MacLeod farm on Dalkeith Road, near Alexandria)

• CORNWALL
The Founding of Cornwall
During the 1780s disbanded loyalist soldiers and their families began to settle at the site of Cornwall, then called New Johnstown. The construction of the Cornwall Canal between 1834 and 1842 accelerated the community's development into a significant industrial centre. (In L'Ameurieux Park, at the foot of Augustus Street, Cornwall)

Captain Samuel Anderson 1736-1836
A veteran of the Seven Years War and the American Revolution, Anderson was one of the earliest settlers at the site of present-day Cornwall. In Upper Canada he served as a justice of the peace and as the first judge of the Eastern District. (On the grounds of Glen-Stor-Dun Lodge (within the vicinity of his land grant), 1900 Montreal Road, Cornwall)

The Reverend John Strachan in Cornwall
A renowned clergyman and teacher, Strachan (1778-1867) came to Upper Canada from Scotland in 1799. He was appointed a missionary at Cornwall where he built the first Anglican church in that community and established a school for boys. In 1812 he moved

to York (Toronto). (On the grounds of Trinity Church (a building dedicated to his memory), 105 Second Street West, Cornwall)

The Glengarry Fencibles
Raised from among the Highland settlers in the Cornwall area, the Fencibles distinguished themselves in many hard-fought engagements during the 1812-14 war, including battles at Ogdensburg, Lundy's Lane, and Fort Erie. (In front of the armouries, 515 Fourth Street East, Cornwall)

District Court House and Gaol 1833
The centre block of this court house complex was constructed in 1833 as the judicial headquarters of the Eastern District. The building replaced an earlier frame structure which had been built about 1802. Renovations have significantly altered the appearance of the court house over the years. (On the grounds of the court house, Pitt and Water Streets, Cornwall)

The Submerged Communities of the St. Lawrence
The construction of the St. Lawrence Seaway and the creation of Lake St. Lawrence necessitated the flooding of several villages along the river front in 1958. Some buildings were relocated and new communities such as Long Sault and Ingleside were established. (In Lakeside Park, Highway 2, just west of Cornwall)

• LONG SAULT
Holstein Friesian Cattle in Ontario
In 1881 Michael Cook, a prosperous farmer, imported the first Holstein Friesian cattle into Ontario. The breed quickly proved its worth and in 1886 was officially recognized by the Dairymen's Association of Eastern Ontario as the leading milk-producing breed. (At the site of the former Cook

farm, Aultsville Road, about 1.5 km southeast of Highway 2, west of Long Sault)

• MAXVILLE
The Glengarry Congregational Church 1837
The oldest remaining chapel in Ontario built by Congregationalists, this log church served the region for some seventy-five years. It is now owned by a nearby Presbyterian church. (On the grounds of the church, in the community of St. Elmo – north of Maxville on County Road 20)

The Reverend Charles W. Gordon 1860-1937
A Presbyterian minister and missionary of Highland ancestry, Gordon was born in St. Elmo. He spent much of his life in western Canada, and under the pen-name of Ralph Connor wrote some thirty popular novels, some of which were based on his memories of growing up in Glengarry County. (On the grounds of the Gordon Presbyterian Church in St. Elmo – north of Maxville on County Road 20)

• MORRISBURG
The Battle of Crysler's Farm 1813
On November 11, 1813 an American contingent of 4,000 troops was forced to withdraw after a battle with a combined force of some 800 Canadian militia, British regulars, and Indian supporters at John Crysler's farm. This hard-fought engagement was a decisive event in the defence of Upper Canada. (At the entrance to the former Crysler farm, now Crysler's Farm Battlefield Park, Highway 2, east of Morrisburg)

The Reverend Johann Samuel Schwerdtfeger 1734-1803
Born in Bavaria, Schwerdtfeger emigrated first to the United States and then, in 1791, to Upper Canada. He was the first resident Lutheran pastor in the province and served a congregation of

German loyalists who had been established in Williamsburg Township since 1784. (At St. John's Lutheran Church, Riverside Heights (within the vicinity of his former parish), Highway 2, east of Morrisburg)

Sir James Pliny Whitney 1843-1914
Elected to the Ontario legislature in 1888, Whitney, who was born in Williamsburg Township, served as leader of the opposition for nine years. With the Liberal defeat in 1905 he became Ontario's sixth prime minister, a post he held until his death. (On the grounds of Holy Trinity Church, Riverside Heights, Highway 2, east of Morrisburg)

• NORTH LANCASTER
Claude J.P. Nunney, V.C. 1892-1918
For his gallant conduct during the bitter campaigns in France in 1917 and 1918 Nunney, who had spent much of his childhood in Lancaster Township, was awarded the Distinguished Conduct Medal, the Military Medal, and, posthumously, the Victoria Cross. (At the municipal building, County Roads 18 and 26, North Lancaster)

• ST. ANDREWS
St. Andrew's Church
The oldest remaining stone structure in the province erected as a church, this building was constructed about 1801 and served its Roman Catholic congregation until 1860 when the adjacent church was built. During the War of 1812 St. Andrew's was used as a hospital. (On the grounds of the former church, now the parish hall, County Road 18 and Highway 138, St. Andrews)

Captain Miles Macdonell
After serving with the British forces during the American Revolution, Macdonell (c.1767-1828) took up farming in the Cornwall area. As Lord Selkirk's

agent he led the first band of settlers to the Red River colony in present-day Manitoba. He subsequently returned to eastern Ontario. (On the grounds of the former St. Andrew's Roman Catholic Church building (which was erected with the assistance of the Macdonell family), County Road 18 and Highway 138, St. Andrews)

Simon Fraser 1776-1862

A major figure in the history of Canadian exploration and the fur trade, Fraser joined the North West Company in 1792 and for twelve years was in charge of all operations west of the Rocky Mountains. Following his retirement from the company in 1817 he moved to eastern Ontario where he farmed and operated mills. (At the site of his former mills, County Road 18 and Concession Road 6, St. Andrews)

• ST. RAPHAELS

The Glengarry Emigration of 1786

Some 500 Scots, the majority of them Macdonells, left their native Highlands under the leadership of their parish priest, the Reverend Alexander Macdonell (of the family of Scotus), and arrived in Canada in 1786. (At the ruins of St. Raphael's Roman Catholic Church (which had served the settlers' congregation), King's Road, St. Raphaels)

The Parish of St. Raphael

Begun as a mission for Roman Catholic settlers on the Raisin River by the Reverend Alexander Macdonell (Scotus), St. Raphael's was officially recognized as a parish in 1802 and for a time served as the administrative centre of the Roman Catholic Church in Upper Canada. The handsome stone structure, built in the 1820s, was gutted by fire in 1970. (At the ruins of the church, King's Road, St. Raphaels)

The College of Iona

Established by the indefatigable Reverend Alexander Macdonell (later Bishop of Kingston), Iona College was the first seminary in Upper Canada. In addition to training young men for the priesthood, it offered a general academic program to prepare boys for secular vocations. (At Iona Academy, across from the ruins of St. Raphael's Church, King's Road, St. Raphaels)

The Honourable John Sandfield Macdonald 1812-1872

Born at St. Raphaels, Macdonald was elected to the

As Dr. Mahlon Locke's fame as a healer of arthritic pain spread to many parts of the world, huge crowds gathered daily outside his clinic in Williamsburg throughout the 1930s. (Archives of Ontario ACC 13441-4)

legislative assembly in 1841 and served in several administrations prior to 1867. Being an independent thinker, he originally opposed the idea of confederation, but later co-operated with Sir John A. Macdonald. He became the first prime minister of Ontario. (Near his birthplace, King's Road, St. Raphaels)

- SUMMERSTOWN
"Cariboo" Cameron 1820-1888
A descendant of one of Glengarry's pioneer families, John Angus Cameron spent many years in the Cariboo fields of British Columbia prospecting for gold. His exploits and adventures have made him something of a folk hero in his native county. (On the grounds of his former home, "Fairfield", which now houses Juvénat de Sacré-Coeur, Highway 2 and County Road 27, west of Summerstown)

- WILLIAMSBURG
Dr. Mahlon W. Locke 1880-1942
Locke's reputedly successful massage treatments for rheumatic and arthritic pain attracted thousands of patients to Williamsburg, which provided the region with welcome prosperity during the depression years. (In front of the house which served as his office, County Road 18 just east of Highway 31, Williamsburg)

- WILLIAMSTOWN
Sir John Johnson's Mills
Johnson's loyalist sympathies during the American Revolution led him to settle in Upper Canada at the close of that war. He built a sawmill and gristmill on the banks of the Raisin River about 1790

St. Andrew's Presbyterian Church in Williamstown is one of the oldest remaining churches in the province. Construction began in 1812. (Archives of Ontario S 1848)

around which the community of Williamstown developed. (At the site of the former mills, John Street, Williamstown)

The MacMillan Emigration 1802
Over 400 Highlanders, many of them MacMillans from Invernesshire, emigrated to Canada under the leadership of two cousins, Archibald and Alan MacMillan. These hardy clansmen settled in Argenteuil County, Lower Canada and in Glengarry and Stormont Counties, Upper Canada. (On the grounds of St. Andrew's Presbyterian Church (which served the Highlanders), Church Street West, Williamstown)

St. Andrew's Church 1812
St. Andrew's was built to house the province's first Presbyterian congregation, which had been formed in Williamstown in 1787. Sir Alexander Mackenzie, the intrepid explorer of the Canadian West, donated a bell for the church and persuaded friends in Scotland to provide a communion service. (On the grounds of the church, Church Street West, Williamstown)

The North West Company
Although its eastern headquarters were at Montreal and its inland depots at Grand Portage and later Fort William, the North West Company's roots were in Glengarry County: many employees were recruited from the county's Scottish settlements and several senior partners made their homes in Williamstown. (On the grounds of the Nor'Westers and Loyalist Museum, John Street, Williamstown)

Substantially built of stone and finished throughout in black walnut, Alexander Fraser's country estate "Fraserfield" was one of the finest country residences of its day. (Archives of Ontario S 17165)

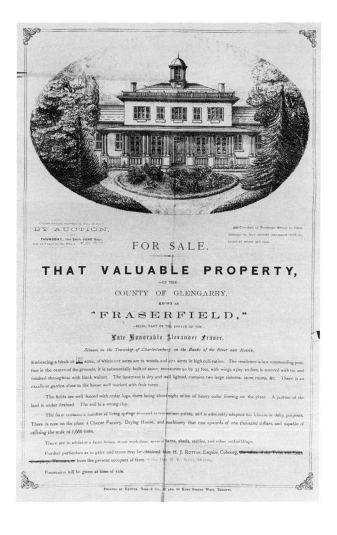

Duncan Cameron

A prominent member of the North West Company, Cameron (c.1764-1848) commanded the Red River area during the company's years of fierce rivalry with the Hudson's Bay Company. In 1820 he returned to live in Williamstown. (On the grounds of St. Andrew's Presbyterian Church, Church Street West, Williamstown)

The Williamstown Fair

Held regularly since 1808, the Williamstown Fair continues to operate on the twelve-acre site donated by Sir John Johnson in 1814. Over the years the fair has become a highly competitive showcase for livestock and farm produce. (At the entrance to the fair grounds, John Street North, Williamstown)

"Fraserfield"

This handsome country house was constructed about 1812 by Alexander Fraser, a prominent military and political figure in the Eastern District. (At the house, County Road 17, about 5 km west of Williamstown)

SUDBURY DISTRICT

• CHAPLEAU
Louis Hémon 1880-1913
The author of the highly acclaimed novel *Maria Chapdelaine*, Hémon was born in France and came to Quebec in 1911. His fictional treatment of life in the backwoods of French Canada has been enjoyed by generations of readers. Hémon was killed by a train near Chapleau and is buried in a local cemetery. (In Centennial Park, opposite the CPR station, Chapleau)

• NAUGHTON
Whitefish Lake Post
The Hudson's Bay Company constructed a trading post at Whitefish Lake about 1824 to discourage independent traders from infiltrating the area north of the French River. In 1887 the post was moved to Naughton to facilitate rail shipments. (At the site of the former post, Regional Road 55, Naughton – about 17 km southwest of Sudbury)

Salter's Meridian 1856
While surveying a meridian line north from Whitefish Lake in 1856 Albert Salter first noted the presence of mineral deposits in this remote region. In 1900 the Creighton Mine went into production at the site of Salter's original discovery and for the next thirty years was the world's leading nickel producer. (Regional Road 55 (near the site of the meridian line), Naughton – about 17 km southwest of Sudbury)

• SUDBURY
The Sudbury Basin
A geological formation of great complexity, the Sudbury basin is a roughly oval-shaped depression some sixty kilometres long containing vast ore deposits. One respected scientific theory attributes

the origin of the basin to the impact of a gigantic meteorite. (In Bell Park, Elizabeth Street, Sudbury)

The Founding of Sudbury
The establishment of a CPR work camp in 1883 marked the beginning of Sudbury. Located on the rim of the Sudbury basin, in a region rich in natural resources, the frontier community was soon flourishing as a service centre for logging and mining operations in the vicinity. (In Civic Square, Brady Street, Sudbury)

Sainte-Anne des Pins
Established as a mission by the Jesuits in 1883, Sainte-Anne des Pins played a prominent role in the development of Franco-Ontarian culture in the region. Until 1917 it was the only Roman Catholic congregation in Sudbury. (On the grounds of the church, 40 Beech Street, Sudbury)

Laurentian University of Sudbury
Higher education in northern Ontario had its origins with the founding of Sacred Heart College in 1913, which later became the University of Sudbury. In 1960 Laurentian University was incorporated and the University of Sudbury, Huntingdon University, and subsequently Thorneloe University were federated with the new bilingual institution. (At the entrance to the R.D. Parker Building, University Drive, Laurentian University campus, Sudbury)

The Discovery of the Sudbury Basin
In 1883 CPR construction crews inadvertently discovered what proved to be nickel-copper sulphides along the railway's right-of-way. The interest stimulated by this discovery eventually led to intensive mining of the rich mineral holdings of the geological formation known as the Sudbury basin. (Near the site of the Murray Mine, Highway 144, about 3 km northwest of Sudbury)

THUNDER BAY DISTRICT

- DOG LAKE
  Great Dog Portage
  Part of the Kaministiquia canoe route between Lake
  Superior and the West, Great Dog Portage was first
  recorded by Jacques de Noyon in 1688. The arduous
  route, which connected Dog Lake and Little Dog
  Lake, required travellers to ascend almost 150
  metres over a trek of three kilometres. (At the south
  end of Dog Lake, Fowler Township – northwest of
  Thunder Bay)

- GERALDTON
  The Geraldton Gold Camp
  The discovery of gold in the vicinity of Lake
  Kenogamisis in the early 1930s led directly to the
  founding of Geraldton. During peak production
  twelve mines were in operation and by 1971, when
  all mining ceased, gold valued at more than $156
  million had been produced. (At the public library,
  405 Second Street West, Geraldton)

- HYMERS
  **The Port Arthur, Duluth and Western Railway
  Company**
  This northern railway was built to serve the silver-
  mining region southwest of the Lakehead and to
  tap the iron ore deposits in northern Minnesota. The
  collapse of the silver boom ended the company's
  brief career and in 1899 it was purchased by the
  Canadian Northern Railway. (At the site of the
  former railway station in Hymers – Highway 595
  southwest of Thunder Bay)

- KAKABEKA FALLS PROVINCIAL PARK
  The Mountain Portage
  "Breakfasted near a very fine waterfall which is
  formed by the River running over a high perpen-

dicular Rock...." So wrote Nicholas Garry of the portage around Kakabeka Falls in 1821 en route to the Red River settlement. The portage is one of several overland links in the Kaministiquia canoe route to the West. (In Kakabeka Falls Provincial Park, Highway 11/17, west of Thunder Bay)

- LONGLAC
Long Lake Posts
The Hudson's Bay Company and the North West Company operated separate trading posts a short distance apart on Long Lake in bitter competition with each other from 1814 until the merger of the arch rivals in 1821. (In Centennial Park (in the

The Hudson's Bay Company's post on Long Lake served as a significant communications depot for over a century. In 1921 it was relocated to a site near the railway. (Archives of Ontario S 7641)

vicinity of the sites of the former posts), Forestry Road and York Street, Longlac)

• MARATHON
The Pic Fur Trading Post
In operation for almost a century, the fur trading post on the Pic River was run by several independent traders before being taken over by the North West Company. From 1821 until 1888 it was operated by the Hudson's Bay Company. (Near St. Xavier Church, off Park Road, Pic River Indian Reserve, near Marathon)

• MIDDLE FALLS PROVINCIAL PARK
The Grand Portage
Circumventing numerous falls and rapids, this portage of fifteen kilometres ran from Lake Superior to a point on the Pigeon River. In 1783 the portage fell within American territory and henceforth Canadian fur traders and explorers had to travel the more tortuous Kaministiquia canoe route. (In Middle Falls Provincial Park (across the river from the site of the former portage), Highways 593 and 61 – southwest of Thunder Bay)

The "Outlaw" Bridge
Completed in 1917, this was the first bridge to span the Pigeon River. It was financed primarily by the Rotary Clubs of Port Arthur-Fort William and Duluth, and became known locally as the "Outlaw" Bridge because it had been built without a formal international agreement. (At the bridge, Middle Falls Provincial Park, Highways 593 and 61 – southwest of Thunder Bay)

• MURILLO
The Founding of Oliver Township
Following the survey of Oliver Township in 1873 free land grants were offered to encourage farmers

to develop the agricultural potential of the area. Within five years about seventy families had settled in the township. (In front of the municipal building, Oliver Road, Murillo)

• NIPIGON

The Mission to the Nipissings 1667
At the Nipigon River on May 29, 1667 Father Claude Allouez, S.J. celebrated mass for members of the Nipissing tribe who had fled north and westward after being persecuted by the Iroquois some years earlier. Allouez spent some weeks in the area before returning to his headquarters in present-day Wisconsin. (At the Nipigon River lookout, Highway 11/17, Nipigon)

Kama Hill Mesa
This ancient geological feature began to form when the region was covered by an extensive sea. Over thousands of years layers of various sediments were deposited onto the bedrock of the Precambrian Shield. Erosion by wind, water, and ice later sculpted the rock into its present formation. (At the Mozakama Bay lookout, Highway 17, about 20 km east of Nipigon)

Prehistoric Copper Mining
Six to seven thousand years ago the first known surface mining of copper in the Americas was being conducted throughout much of the Lake Superior basin. The copper was traded extensively and used for tool-making by native peoples in the region until the introduction of iron by European traders. (At the Kama Bay lookout on Highway 17, about 27 km east of Nipigon)

The Nipigon Canoe Route
The Nipigon River formed part of the historic canoe route connecting Lake Superior with James Bay via

Lake Nipigon and the Albany River. During the seventeenth and eighteenth centuries several French fur traders built trading posts along the route in order to divert trade from the British establishments on James Bay. (In Lake Helen Park, near the river, Highway 11, about 10 km north of Nipigon)

• ORIENT BAY
The Palisades of the Pijitawabik
The pillar-like features of the sheer-rising cliffs at several points along the Lake Nipigon shoreline are the dramatic result of erosional and glacial activity that began more than a thousand million years ago. (At the scenic lookout on Highway 11 near Orient Bay, within sight of the formations – about 38 km north of Nipigon)

• PASS LAKE
The Aqua-Plano Indians of the Upper Great Lakes
In 1950 archaeologists uncovered evidence of a workshop used by the earliest known inhabitants of the upper Great Lakes basin. It is likely that these people appeared about 9,000 years ago following the retreat of glaciers and the northward spread of plant and animal life. (At Boegh Park, a picnic area on Highway 587 near Pass Lake – about 32 km east of Thunder Bay)

Silver Islet 1868
On a tiny barren rock thrusting no more than 2.5 metres above water level one of the richest sources of silver in North America was discovered in 1868. Despite the difficulties presented by such a restricted and isolated site, the Silver Islet mine produced silver worth more than $3 million during its years of operation. (In Sibley Provincial Park, within view of the former mine site, Highway 587, south of Pass Lake)

- RAITH
The Arctic Watershed
Winding an erratic course of some 2,240 kilometres across Ontario, the height of land, or watershed, figured prominently in several boundary disputes during the nineteenth century. (Highway 17 (where the watershed crosses the thoroughfare), near Raith – northwest of Thunder Bay)

The Savanne Portage
Part of the historic Kaministiquia canoe route to the West, the Savanne Portage connected Lac du Milieu with the Savanne River. Paul Kane travelled the route in 1846 and left this graphic description: "... poor fellows had sometimes to wade up to their middle in mud and water". (In the Ministry of Transportation Park, Highway 17, about 11 km northwest of Raith)

- RED ROCK
Red Rock
A striking geological structure, the Red Rock cuesta is composed of layers of rock formed deep in the earth during the Precambrian era. Millions of years of erosion and probable gouging by Pleistocene glaciers have exposed the rock to view. (Near the cuesta, Highway 11/17, just west of Red Rock)

- ROSSPORT
The Precambrian Shield
The shield is one of the oldest rock formations in the earth's crust and covers about two-thirds of the surface area of Ontario. Although the shield was not suitable for agricultural settlement, its lakes,

---

Despite the restrictions imposed by such a small mining site, the shaft of the Silver Islet mine (shown here about 1880) extended some 366 metres below the surface of Lake Superior. (Archives of Ontario ST 1232)

forests, and mineral resources proved to be the foundation of the province's economic development. (At Cavers Lookout, Highway 17, about 16 km west of Rossport)

- SCHREIBER
Sir Collingwood Schreiber 1831-1918
Schreiber's training in England as a civil engineer enabled him to play a prominent role in Canada during the country's years of railway expansion. He was associated with both the Northern and Inter-colonial Railways prior to succeeding Sandford Fleming as engineer-in-chief of the CPR in 1880. In 1885 the community of Isbester's Landing was renamed in his honour. (In front of the old town hall, 302 Scotia Street, Schreiber)

The Lake Superior Trek 1885
At the outbreak of the North-West Rebellion military forces were immediately dispatched to the West. The CPR was then under construction and the troops had to negotiate four treacherous gaps in the railway line north of Lake Superior over rocky terrain and lake ice. (At the scenic lookout at Selim (in the vicinity of one of the gaps), Highway 17, about 10 km west of Schreiber)

- SHEBANDOWAN
The Dawson Wagon Road
The 72-kilometre Dawson Road ran from the shore of Thunder Bay to Lake Shebandowan and formed part of the extensive land and water route maintained by the Canadian government to secure the territory west of Lake Superior. The road was travelled by thousands of soldiers and settlers between 1868, when construction began, and 1876 when it was abandoned in favour of railway travel. (Highway 11 (which follows the route of the former wagon road), Shebandowan)

- ## STANLEY
  ### Oliver Daunais 1836-1916
  Daunais' discovery and promotion of several short-lived but prosperous silver-mining ventures in the Thunder Bay area during the 1880s earned him the name "Silver King". Daunais also played a leading role in the early development of the town of Port Arthur. (Highway 588 and River Road (near the site of his first important discovery), Stanley – south of Highway 11/17, west of Thunder Bay)

- ## TERRACE BAY
  ### The Glacial Terraces
  As glacial melt-waters created new drainage patterns in the Lake Superior basin some 20,000 years ago and the level of the lake was gradually lowered, new shorelines were established and a succession of flat terraces separated by escarpments and cliffs resulted. The prominence of such geological formations gave Terrace Bay its name. (In Centennial Park, Highway 17, Terrace Bay)

- ## THUNDER BAY
  ### The Founding of Shuniah
  As a result of the discovery and development of significant silver deposits along the north shore of Lake Superior during the 1860s, a number of townships were surveyed back from the shoreline. In 1873 eight townships, including the town sites of Prince Arthur's Landing (Port Arthur) and Fort William, were incorporated into the municipality of Shuniah. This was the first organized municipality in north-western Ontario. (Near the entrance to Wild Goose Park, Lakeshore Drive, Thunder Bay)

  ### The Lakehead's First Grain Elevator 1883
  To ensure traffic on its recently completed line to Winnipeg and to facilitate the movement of grain from the West, the CPR began construction of the

first grain elevator at the Lakehead in 1883. Eventually thirty storage elevators were built. (At the Manitoba Pool Elevator 2, off Cumberland Street, Thunder Bay)

Sir William C. Van Horne 1843-1915
After a brilliant career with a number of railway companies in the United States, Van Horne became the general manager of the CPR in 1881. Despite physical difficulties the transcontinental line was rapidly extended westward under his supervision, and with its completion in 1885 Canadian unity was ensured. (In the municipal park opposite the public utilities building, off Cumberland Street, Thunder Bay)

The Reverend Richard Baxter, S.J. 1821-1904
After arriving at Fort William in 1872 Baxter spent twenty years ministering to miners, settlers, and construction workers along the CPR line and the Dawson Road. Tales of his heroism and stamina are legion throughout the area. (On the grounds of St. Andrew's Roman Catholic Church (a church he established), 292 Algoma Street, Thunder Bay)

Simon James Dawson 1820-1902
As a member of the Gladman-Hind expedition Dawson surveyed a road line from the Lakehead to Fort Garry and extensively explored the hinterland northwest of Superior. His report helped to stimulate government interest in developing the western regions for settlement. (In Hillcrest Park, High Street, Thunder Bay)

The Western Route of the CPR
The first sod on the rail line west from the Lakehead was turned in June 1875 at Fort William (now Thunder Bay). Ten years later the transcontinental route was completed to British Columbia and the

last spike driven in at Craigellachie in Eagle Pass on November 7, 1885. (Ridgeway Street and Syndicate Avenue, Thunder Bay)

Lakehead University
In response to a brief outlining the need for an institution of higher education in northwestern Ontario, Lakehead Technical Institute was established in 1946. This body became part of the new Lakehead College in 1957 which, eight years later, was granted university status. (At the Centennial Building, Oliver Road, Lakehead University campus, Thunder Bay)

Daniel Greysolon, Sieur Dulhut 1636-1710
A famous French-born explorer, Dulhut settled in Canada in 1675 and four years later built the first post at the mouth of the Kaministiquia River on the site of present-day Thunder Bay. He annexed the area that now comprises Ontario and northern Minnesota to France, and did much to further the westward expansion of New France. (In Vickers Park, Arthur Street, Thunder Bay)

Fort Kaministiquia 1717
A small fort built on the Kaministiquia River in 1717 by a French officer, Zacharie de la Nouë, was in use until the conquest of New France in 1760. A second Fort Kaministiquia, built by the North West Company a short distance down river from the earlier post, was renamed Fort William in 1807. (At the city hall, 500 Donald Street East, Thunder Bay)

William McGillivray 1764-1825
McGillivray joined the North West Company as a clerk in 1784 and in 1804 became its principal director. The company's wilderness headquarters, Fort Kaministiquia, was renamed Fort William in

his honour. (In front of the city hall, 500 Donald Street East, Thunder Bay)

The Capture of Fort William 1816
In retaliation for the violent opposition encountered from fur traders to his Scottish settlement in the Red River valley, Lord Selkirk attacked and seized the North West Company's headquarters at Fort William in 1816. In his capacity as a justice of the peace, Selkirk arrested several of the company's senior partners. (In Paterson Park, May Street, Thunder Bay)

The Gladman-Hind Expedition 1857
The Canadian government's objective in organizing this exploratory expedition was to establish a strong communications link between Lake Superior and the Red River region, thereby discouraging American annexation of the vast lands to the west and north. The findings of the expedition figured prominently in the establishment of the province of Manitoba in 1870. (In Marina Park, at the foot of Arthur Street (in the vicinity of the expedition's former base depot), Thunder Bay)

Colonel Elizabeth Smellie 1884-1968
A native of Port Arthur (now Thunder Bay), Elizabeth Smellie became the first woman to attain the rank of colonel in the Canadian Armed Forces. In the First World War she served with the Royal Canadian Army Medical Corps in France and England, and in 1941 organized the Canadian Women's Army Corps. (In front of McKellar General Hospital, Archibald Street, Thunder Bay)

The Mission of the Immaculate Conception 1849
This mission was established by two priests of the Society of Jesus on the shores of the Kaministiquia River and included a church, a day-school, an

orphanage, and numerous outbuildings. It served the area from this location until 1908 when it was moved to the Fort William Band Reserve. (In front of the administration building, Mission Road, Fort William Band Reserve #52, Thunder Bay)

The Pigeon River Road
Completed in 1874, this sixty-kilometre road facilitated the transportation of mail between Thunder Bay and Duluth, Michigan during the winter when Lake Superior was closed to navigation. It was used by mail couriers until 1882 when railway service reached the Lakehead. (On the grounds of the Correctional Centre, Highway 61 (which replaced the old road as the route to the border), Thunder Bay)

The Robinson Superior Treaty
Under this treaty, which was concluded in 1850, the Ojibwa surrendered territory extending some 640 kilometres along the shore of Lake Superior and northward to the height of land. In return they received three reserves, including the Fort William reserve, a cash settlement, and a small annual stipend. (In Chippewa Park, City Road adjacent to the Indian Reserve, at the southern approach to Thunder Bay)

The Union of the North West and Hudson's Bay Companies 1821
This union ended the long-standing rivalry between the fur-trading interests of the St. Lawrence and Hudson Bay, the two great waterways giving access to the interior of North America. A joint committee administered trade until 1824 when control was assumed solely by the Hudson's Bay Company. (Near the information centre at Old Fort William (a re-creation of the inland headquarters of the North West Company), south of Broadway Avenue, Thunder Bay)

- COBALT

The Timiskaming Mission

The Roman Catholic mission originally established at Fort Timiskaming on the eastern shore of Lake Timiskaming in present-day Quebec was relocated to the Ontario shore of the lake in 1863. Here the mission comprised a presbytery for the Oblate fathers, a small hospital operated by two Grey Sisters of the Cross, and eventually a frame church. (At the site of the former mission, Mission Point, at the foot of Old Mission Road, east off Highway 567 about 20 km south of North Cobalt)

A shipment of silver about to leave the station was a common sight in Cobalt following the chance discovery of vast ore deposits in the area in 1903. (Archives of Ontario S 13661)

The Cobalt Mining Camp
The initial discovery of silver deposits in this area was made in 1903 by lumbermen searching for timber for railroad ties, and led to one of the most intensive mining rushes in Ontario history. In the 1930s the demand for cobalt assured the economic stability of the mining camp despite a sharp reduction in the price of silver. (Opposite the Cobalt Northern Ontario Mining Museum, 26 Silver Street (near the site of the initial discovery), Cobalt)

William Henry Drummond 1854-1907
Characterized by humour and pathos, the *habitant* verses of Dr. William Drummond appealed to readers of many cultures and earned their author international recognition. In 1905 Drummond joined his brothers in a silver-mining venture at Kerr Lake on the outskirts of Cobalt where, two years later, he died. (In Drummond Park, Silver Street and Prospect Avenue, Cobalt)

• KENOGAMI LAKE
The Arctic Watershed
Winding an erratic course of some 2,240 kilometres across Ontario, the height of land, or watershed, figured prominently in several boundary disputes during the nineteenth century. (Highway 11 (where the watershed crosses the thoroughfare), about 14 km northwest of Kenogami Lake)

• KIRKLAND LAKE
The Kirkland Lake Gold Camp
The discovery of gold in the vicinity of Kirkland Lake in 1911 led to the development of a highly lucrative mining industry in this part of northeastern Ontario. During peak-production years in the late 1930s some 5,000 men were employed by mines in the region yielding an annual output valued at more than $30 million. (Near the Toburn Vault (the

remains of the original Tough-Oakes mine buildings), Highway 66, at the eastern approach to Kirkland Lake)

- LATCHFORD
The Ferguson Highway
This 415-kilometre trunk road from North Bay to Cochrane was built in 1925-27 to link the developing mining and agricultural communities of "New Ontario" with the province's southern regions. Named after the Honourable Howard G. Ferguson, a strong promoter of northern development, the road now forms parts of the Trans-Canada Highway. (In the picnic area south of the Montreal River bridge, Highway 11 (formerly the Ferguson Highway), Latchford)

- SWASTIKA
Swastika
A small community of hopeful mining families formed around the railway stop at Swastika during the gold rush era of the early 1900s. When the Swastika mines failed, the community became an active trade centre for the prosperous gold fields at Kirkland Lake. (In Fireman's Park, Riverside Drive, Swastika)

- THORNLOE
The Great Fire of 1922
In early October 1922 scattered bush fires burning north of Haileybury were united by high winds into a mammoth forest fire that swept eighteen townships. Several communities were destroyed and more than 5,000 people left homeless. Snow and rain finally brought the blaze under control. (In a roadside park, Highway 11, about 3 km south of the Earlton Overpass, Thornloe)

TORONTO REGIONAL MUNICIPALITY

• CITY OF TORONTO
Toronto Island

The sand-bar that comprises Toronto Island began to form about 8,000 years ago as sand from the eroding bluffs situated to the east was washed westward. The long, curving peninsula that resulted created a large natural harbour for the future city of Toronto. (Near the ferry dock at Wards Island, Toronto Islands)

The Royal Canadian Yacht Club

Formed in 1852 to promote yachting and naval interests, the Toronto Boat Club was the first sailing association in the province. Two years later it became the Royal Canadian Yacht Club. (In front of the entrance to the club's summer quarters, Chippewa Avenue, Toronto Islands)

The Lake Light

The lighthouse at Gibraltar Point (now Hanlans Point) dates from 1808 and was one of the first to be built on the Great Lakes. In 1832 the tower was heightened and its stationary whale-oil lamp replaced by a revolving light. (At the lighthouse, Hanlans Point, Toronto Islands)

Gibraltar Point

The site of fortifications to guard the harbour of York during the early years of the nineteenth century, Gibraltar Point was renamed Hanlans Point after the family of the world-championship rower, Ned Hanlan. (Near the ferry dock, Hanlans Point, Toronto Islands)

"Ned" Hanlan 1855-1908

A native of Toronto, Hanlan took up rowing as a child after his family moved to a house on Gibraltar

Point. After winning several amateur rowing events, Hanlan turned professional in 1876. For four years he held the world single sculls championship. (Near the ferry dock, Hanlans Point, Toronto Islands)

The Battle of York 1813

On April 27, 1813 a large American contingent landed just west of York and after a fierce battle forced the defending militia to retire. During the five days of occupation the invaders burned much of the town, including the parliament buildings. (At the entrance to Fort York, Lakeshore Boulevard West, at the eastern end of Exhibition Place, Toronto)

The first Canadian athlete to gain international recognition, Ned Hanlan (shown here in Toronto Bay) brought much fame to his native city during his years as a championship rower. (Archives of Ontario S 14176)

The Second Invasion of York 1813

In July 1813, just three months after an earlier invasion, American troops landed at York and briefly took possession of the town. They raided the largely unoccupied fort, set fire to the barracks and storehouses, and two days later departed. (Near the entrance to Coronation Park, Exhibition Place (in the vicinity of the invaders' landing site), Lakeshore Boulevard West, Toronto)

The Princes' Gates

An outstanding example of monumental architecture in the Beaux-Arts style, the gates were constructed to commemorate the Diamond Jubilee of Confederation. They were opened on August 30, 1927 by Their Royal Highnesses, the Prince of Wales and Prince George. (Near the gates, at the Strachan Avenue entrance to Exhibition Place, Toronto)

Stanley Barracks 1841

The military establishment built at Toronto in 1840-41 to house additional British soldiers was commonly called "New Fort" until 1893 when the name was officially changed to Stanley Barracks. The only remaining building is the officers' quarters, which now houses the Marine Museum of Upper Canada. (On the grounds of the museum, Exhibition Place, Lakeshore Boulevard West, Toronto)

The Queen's Rangers

This corps was organized in 1791 under Lieutenant-Colonel John Graves Simcoe and was the first regiment raised specifically for service in Upper Canada. Among the Rangers' peace-time activities was the construction of two major thoroughfares: Dundas Street (Governor's Road) and Yonge Street. (Opposite the entrance to Ontario Place, Exhibition Place, Lakeshore Boulevard West, Toronto)

The Canadian National Exhibition

The exhibition held by the Industrial Exhibition Association of Toronto beginning in 1879 proved so successful that the annual event soon gained national stature. During its long history the CNE has provided a showcase for Canadian agriculture and industry, arts groups and sporting events. (At the entrance to Centennial Square, near the Dufferin Gate, Exhibition Place, Toronto)

Fort Rouillé

The last French post established in what is now southern Ontario, Fort Rouillé was built in 1750-51 to help strengthen French control of trade in the Great Lakes region. It was a palisaded fortification with four bastions and five main buildings. (At the Fort Rouillé Monument, near Scadding Cabin, Exhibition Place, Lakeshore Boulevard West, Toronto)

The Enoch Turner School 1848

This schoolhouse was built in 1848 by Enoch Turner, a wealthy Toronto brewer, as a "free school" for the Anglican parish of Trinity. It is the oldest remaining school building in Toronto. (At the schoolhouse, now the Enoch Turner Schoolhouse Museum, 106 Trinity Street, Toronto)

The Bishop's Palace 1818

The residence of John Strachan, the first Anglican Bishop of Toronto, the "Bishop's Palace" was a large two-storey house built in 1817-18 when Strachan was the incumbent at St. James' Church. It was also the place of assembly in 1837 for the loyalist forces that defeated Mackenzie's rebels

---

St. James' Anglican Cathedral was built between 1850 and 1874 on the site of the first church building constructed in the town of York. This photo, taken from Church Street, dates from about 1875. (Archives of Ontario S 15334)

at Montgomery's Tavern. (At the northwest corner of Front Street West and University Avenue (the site of the former house), Toronto)

Canada's First Victoria Cross

Alexander Dunn, a native of Toronto, served with the British Army during the Crimean War. The young hussar was awarded the Victoria Cross for saving the lives of two members of his regiment during the Charge of the Light Brigade at Balaclava on October 25, 1854. (In the small park at Clarence Square and Spadina Avenue (near his birthplace), Toronto)

St. James' Cathedral

The first church in Toronto (then called York) was begun on this site in 1803. The present St. James', which was begun in 1850 but not completed until 1874, is the second Anglican cathedral and the fourth religious structure on the site. (On the grounds of the cathedral, 106 King Street East at Church Street, Toronto)

St. Lawrence Hall 1850

Situated in the heart of the city, St. Lawrence Hall was the site of gala occasions and civic events throughout the 1850s and '60s. In the 1,000-seat recital hall Torontonians were offered a variety of entertainments – from the vocal artistry of Jenny Lind to the fiery oratory of George Brown. (In the main foyer of the hall, 157 King Street East at Jarvis Street, Toronto)

Little Trinity Church

Known colloquially as "The Poor Man's Church" because of the large percentage of industrial workers in its congregation, Little Trinity Anglican Church was begun in 1843 and opened for service the following year. It is the oldest remaining church in Toronto. (At the church, 425 King Street East, Toronto)

St. Andrew's Church
Built between 1874 and 1876 St. Andrew's was designed by the noted Toronto architect William Storm in the then-popular Romanesque Revival style. Under the vigorous leadership of the Reverend D.J. Macdonnell St. Andrew's became one of the most influential Presbyterian churches in Canada. (On the grounds of the church, King Street West at Simcoe Street, Toronto)

Ontario's First Mechanics' Institute
Modelled after similar organizations in Great Britain, the Mechanics' Institute was established in 1830. It had as its aim the education of all workingmen ("mechanics"), and to this end operated a lending library and offered classes in a wide range of subjects. (In front of The Bentley (the site of the former Mechanics' Institute building), 77 Church Street, Toronto)

The Birthplace of Standard Time
At a meeting of the Canadian Institute in Toronto in 1879 Sandford Fleming first presented his idea for a standardized, worldwide system for reckoning time. His proposal led to the International Prime Meridian Conference in Washington five years later at which the present system of Standard Time was adopted. (At 60 Richmond Street East (near the site of the former Canadian Institute building), Toronto)

The "Canada First" Movement
"Canada First" was the name and slogan of a patriotic movement which originated in Ottawa in 1868. By 1874 the group was based in Toronto and had founded the National Club as its promotional

headquarters. (At the entrance to the National Club, 303 Bay Street, Toronto)

Metropolitan United Church
Built between 1870 and 1872, Metropolitan United was designed by Henry Langley in the High Victorian Gothic style. The church has been the scene of many important events in the history of Methodism in Canada, including the World Ecumenical Methodist Conference in 1911 and the first General Council of the United Church in 1925. (On the grounds of the church, Queen Street East at Church Street, Toronto)

Woodbine Race Course
The oldest permanent racing establishment in Ontario, Woodbine was the site of the running of the Queen's Plate from 1883 to 1955. The track became "Old Woodbine" in 1956 when a new Woodbine was opened in Etobicoke. In 1963 it was renamed Greenwood. (At Greenwood Race Course, Queen Street East and Kingston Road, Toronto)

"Old" City Hall 1899-1965
Designed by E.J. Lennox in the Romanesque Revival style – an architectural style unique to North America – Toronto's third city hall was constructed of sandstone from the Credit River valley, grey stone from the Orangeville area, and brown stone from New Brunswick. The rugged, towering façade has often been described as cliff-like. (In front of the east wing of the building, 60 Queen Street West, Toronto)

William Lyon Mackenzie 1795-1861
Writer, publisher, and politician, Mackenzie was the first mayor of Toronto (1834) and the most famous radical reformer in Upper Canada. After the failure of the 1837 rebellion he took refuge in the United

States, but returned to Canada in 1849 and for several years served as a member of parliament. (At the west side of the city hall, 100 Queen Street West, Toronto)

Osgoode Hall

Constructed between 1829 and 1832 to house the provincial law courts and judicial offices, Osgoode Hall was named in honour of the province's first chief justice, William Osgoode. Rebuilt, extended, and renovated frequently during its long history, the building stands as one of the finest examples of Victorian architecture in Canada. (On the grounds of the hall, 130 Queen Street West at University Avenue, Toronto)

Walter Seymour Allward, R.C.A. 1876-1955

A native of Toronto, Allward had executed several notable public monuments by 1922 when he was commissioned to design the Canadian War Memorial at Vimy Ridge – a project to which he devoted fourteen years. His work can be found in the National Gallery in Ottawa and in public squares in several Canadian cities. (At the South African War Memorial (one of his works), University Avenue at Queen Street West, Toronto)

Sir William Campbell 1758-1834

Campbell served as chief justice of the King's Bench and as speaker of the legislative council in Upper Canada during the late 1820s. He was the first judge in the province to receive a knighthood. His former home, furnished in period style, is now a public museum. (On the grounds of Campbell House, 160 Queen Street West at University Avenue, Toronto)

Major-General The Honourable Aeneas Shaw

A loyalist who served in the Queen's Rangers during the American Revolution, Shaw (c.1740-1814) was one of the earliest settlers at the future site of York. He served as a member of both the legislative and executive councils, and held several public offices. (At the entrance to Trinity Bellwoods Park (near the site of his former home), Queen Street West opposite Strachan Avenue, Toronto)

The Church of the Holy Trinity 1847
This Gothic-style Anglican church was built in 1847 as the result of a donation of £5,000 from a Mrs. Swale of Yorkshire who stipulated that no pew rentals were to be charged to the church's parishioners. (On the exterior west wall of the church, 19 Trinity Square, off Bay Street behind the Eaton Centre, Toronto)

The Reverend Henry Scadding 1813-1901
The first rector of the Church of the Holy Trinity, Scadding was a noted historian as well as a religious scholar. He produced numerous works on the history of Toronto, and was instrumental in the formation of several historical societies in Ontario. (At Scadding House (his former home), 6 Trinity Square, off Bay Street behind the Eaton Centre, Toronto)

St. Michael's Cathedral
Built between 1845 and 1848, St. Michael's was designed by William Thomas in a style adapted from fourteenth-century English Gothic architecture. It is the principal church in the largest English-speaking Roman Catholic archdiocese in Canada. (At the west entrance to the cathedral, Bond and Shuter Streets, Toronto)

Dr. Henry Scadding was a prolific writer throughout his life. His best-known work is Toronto of Old (1873), an invaluable source of historical information, which is still in print. (Archives of Ontario S 677)

Colonel James Givins

After fighting with the British forces in the American Revolution, Givins (c.1759-1846) was commissioned in the Queen's Rangers and subsequently served in the Indian Department in Upper Canada. He was highly commended for his role in defending the town of York against invasion in 1813. (At Givins/Shaw Public School (on land he formerly owned), 49 Givins Street, Toronto)

Colborne Lodge 1836

This handsome house was built in 1836 by John Howard, an architect, engineer, and prominent Toronto citizen. Following Howard's death in 1890 the house and grounds became the property of the city. Colborne Lodge is now a public museum operated by the Toronto Historical Board. (Near the museum, Colborne Road, High Park, Toronto)

The First Unitarian Congregation in Canada West 1845

The Unitarian congregation led by the Reverend William Adam held services in an unused Wesleyan chapel until its own church building was completed in 1854. The Neo-Gothic structure designed by William Thomas has since been demolished. (At the site of the former church building, at the parking lot adjacent to 222 Jarvis Street, Toronto)

Mary Pickford

Born in Toronto in 1893, "America's Sweetheart" began her acting career on stage at the age of five. Eleven years later her first film was released. Pickford's golden curls and children's roles, which she played well into her adult life, endeared her to millions of cinema-goers. She died in 1979. (On the grounds of the Hospital for Sick Children (near her birthplace), 555 University Avenue, Toronto)

St. Anne's Anglican Church

Toronto architect Ford Howland designed St. Anne's

Church in the Byzantine style, a style rarely used in Ontario church architecture. Interior decoration includes wall and ceiling paintings executed by members of the Group of Seven. (In front of the church, 270 Gladstone Avenue, Toronto)

John Ross Robertson 1841-1918

Founder and publisher of the *Evening Telegram*, Robertson was a principal benefactor of the Hospital for Sick Children and served on its board of trustees for over thirty years. His vast collection of documents, maps, and paintings, dealing primarily with the history of Toronto, is now owned by

This building housed the Toronto Normal School from 1852 until 1941 when the school moved to a new site. In 1962-63 the structure was demolished, save for the façade which was incorporated into the new Ryerson Polytechnical Institute complex. (Archives of Ontario S 15343)

the Toronto Public Library. (On the grounds of his former home, 291 Sherbourne Street, Toronto)

Ryerson Polytechnical Institute
Named after the Reverend Egerton Ryerson, founder of the province's education system, the Ryerson Institute of Technology was established in 1948 to provide technological education for post-secondary students. It rapidly became a leading centre for technical education in Ontario and in 1971 was given degree-granting status. (Near the statue of Egerton Ryerson at the main entrance to the Institute, 40 Gould Street, Toronto)

Toronto Normal School
The first provincial institution for the systematic training of elementary-school teachers, the Toronto Normal School was established in 1847 through the initiative of the indefatigable Egerton Ryerson. (Near the statue of Ryerson at the main entrance to Ryerson Polytechnical Institute, 40 Gould Street, Toronto)

The Home of George Brown
One of the Fathers of Confederation, Brown was a political reformer and the publisher of the influential weekly, *The Globe*. His former home, a stately Victorian mansion, is now owned by the Ontario Heritage Foundation. (On the grounds of the house, 186 Beverley Street, Toronto)

The Toronto Horticultural Society
The first horticultural society in Upper Canada was established in Toronto in 1834 under the patronage of the lieutenant-governor. The donation of a five-acre plot of land by the Honourable George Allan enabled the society to develop extensive horticultural gardens which later became the Allan

Gardens. (In front of the greenhouse in Allan Gardens, Carlton and Jarvis Streets, Toronto)

Toronto General Hospital
The first general infirmary in Upper Canada, this institution began operation in 1829. In association with the University of Toronto, Connaught Laboratories, and other institutions, it has achieved international recognition in the fields of heart surgery, radiology, and the treatment of kidney and vascular disease. (At the entrance to the hospital's research centre, 101 College Street, Toronto)

St. Stephen-in-the-Fields Anglican Church
Reminiscent of an English parish church in its Gothic Revival design, St. Stephen's represents the work of two prominent Ontario architects, Thomas Fuller and Henry Langley. The church derived its name from its original rural setting. (At the church, 103 Bellevue Avenue, at College Street west of Spadina, Toronto)

The Archives of Ontario
In response to public demand the Ontario government established a provincial archives in 1903. Under the direction of Alexander Fraser, provincial archivist from 1903 to 1935, a comprehensive acquisition program was undertaken as well as the annual publication of government reports. (In front of the Archives building, 77 Grenville Street, Toronto)

Sir John Lefroy 1817-1890
An officer in the Royal Artillery, Lefroy was posted to Canada from 1842 to 1853. Here he conducted the first comprehensive magnetic and meteorological survey in British North America and served as director of the magnetic observatory at Toronto. (In front of the Sandford Fleming Building (the site of the former magnetic observatory), 10 King's College Road, University of Toronto campus)

The Discovery of Insulin 1921

A major medical discovery took place in Toronto during 1921 when Frederick Banting and Charles Best successfully proved the life-saving properties of insulin in the treatment of diabetes. (In front of the Medical Sciences Building (the site of the former building in which the discovery was announced), 1 King's College Circle, University of Toronto campus)

Maud Leonora Menten 1879-1960

A graduate in medicine from the University of Toronto, Dr. Menten gained international recognition in 1913 for the discovery, with Dr. Leonor

---

The circular opening in the west tower of the parliament buildings (shown here under construction in 1891) was designed to hold a chiming clock — but one was never installed. (Archives of Ontario S 2928)

Michaelis, of an equation now considered basic to all work in enzyme kinetics. (Near the entrance on Queen's Park Crescent West to the Medical Sciences Building, University of Toronto campus)

Queen's Park
Named in honour of Queen Victoria, this park was opened in 1860 by the Prince of Wales. Construction of the parliament buildings was begun in 1886, and on April 4, 1893 Sir Oliver Mowat opened the first legislative session in the new building. Over the years the name Queen's Park has become synonymous with both the legislature and the public park. (In front of the Legislative Building, Queen's Park Crescent, Toronto)

King's College
Chartered in 1827 through the efforts of the Reverend John Strachan, King's College was the first university in Upper Canada. It offered instruction in science, law, theology, medicine, and the arts, and in 1850 became – as a secularized institution – the University of Toronto. (Near the entrance to the East Block of the Legislative Building (the site of the former college building), Queen's Park Crescent East, Toronto)

Canada West's Fathers of Confederation
Conferences at Charlottetown and Quebec (1864) and London (1866) preceded proclamation of the British North America Act in 1867. The participation of seven statesmen from Canada West (present-day Ontario) in these meetings ranks them among the Fathers of Confederation. (On the ground floor of the Legislative Building, east wing corridor, Queen's Park, Toronto)

The Loyalists in Upper Canada
At the close of the American Revolution a large

number of refugees who had remained loyal to the Crown were awarded land in present-day Ontario. It is estimated that when Upper Canada was created in 1791 some 10,000 loyalists were resident in the new province. (Near the entrance to the Legislative Chambers, on the second floor of the Legislative Building, Queen's Park, Toronto)

Lieutenant-General John Graves Simcoe 1752-1806
During his five-year term as Upper Canada's first lieutenant-governor (1791-96), Simcoe was responsible for the opening of major communication routes throughout the new province. He encouraged immigration and was instrumental in the founding of the town of York (Toronto). (Near the entrance to the Legislative Chambers, on the second floor of the Legislative Building, Queen's Park, Toronto)

Frederic W. Cumberland 1820-1881
After training as an architect and civil engineer in his native England, Cumberland came to Toronto in 1847. St. James' Cathedral and University College are but two of the many notable buildings he designed in Ontario. In 1858 he became managing director of the Northern Railway and, not content with just two careers, in 1867 entered politics. (On the grounds of his former residence, now the International Students' Centre, 33 St. George Street, University of Toronto campus)

Edith Kathleen Russell 1886-1964
A distinguished nurse and educator, Kathleen Russell was the first director of the Department of Public Health Nursing at the University of Toronto. In 1949 she received the Florence Nightingale Medal for her outstanding contribution to nursing education. (In front of Cody Hall, Faculty of Nursing, 50 St. George Street, University of Toronto campus)

The Macdonald-Mowat House 1872

This Second-Empire-style house was owned by Canada's first prime minister, Sir John A. Macdonald, 1876 to 1886, and by Ontario's third prime minister, Oliver Mowat, 1888 to 1902. The building now houses the University of Toronto's School of Graduate Studies. (In front of the house, 63 St. George Street, University of Toronto campus)

St. Michael's College

Established in 1852 as a Roman Catholic boys' school, St. Michael's affiliated with the University of Toronto in 1881. In 1910 it formally became an arts college within the university. (On the grounds of the college, near the corner of Bay and St. Joseph Streets, University of Toronto campus)

Wycliffe College

Originally called the Protestant Episcopal Divinity School, this theological college was founded in 1877 to train young men of evangelical conviction for the Anglican ministry. The school was renamed Wycliffe College in 1885, and four years later was federated with the University of Toronto. (In front of the college, 5 Hoskin Avenue, just west of Queen's Park Crescent, University of Toronto campus)

St. John Ambulance in Ontario

Formed in England in 1877, the St. John Ambulance Association was introduced in Ontario in 1895 by George Ryerson, a military surgeon. Its extensive volunteer first-aid programs have made the association one of the most respected humanitarian organizations in the province. (At the St. John Ambulance (Ontario Council) building, 46 Wellesley Street East, Toronto)

Jarvis Collegiate Institute

One of the oldest public secondary schools in

Ontario, Jarvis Collegiate was established in 1807 as the Home District Grammar School. Under headmaster John Strachan the school gained wide recognition for its high academic standards and eminent graduates. (In front of the present school building, 495 Jarvis Street, Toronto)

The Honourable Herbert Alexander Bruce, M.D. 1868-1963

The founder of Toronto's Wellesley Hospital (originally a small private institution), Bruce combined a career as a medical practitioner with a life of active public service. He was appointed lieutenant-governor of Ontario in 1932 and during the 1940s represented Parkdale in the House of Commons. (On the grounds of The Wellesley Hospital, 160 Wellesley Street East, Toronto)

Moulton College

A girls' preparatory school founded by Susan Moulton McMaster, Moulton College opened in 1888 as part of McMaster University. The school was housed in the former McMaster residence and for sixty-six years provided classes for day and resident students from junior grades to university entrance. (In the main foyer of the Hudson's Bay Centre (near the site of the former college building), 2 Bloor Street East, Toronto)

Elizabeth Posthuma Simcoe 1766-1850

As the wife of the first lieutenant-governor of Upper Canada, Mrs. Simcoe travelled extensively during her years in Canada. Her diaries and water-colour sketches provide a valuable picture of life in this country during the late eighteenth century. (At the entrance to Castle Frank High School (near the site of the former Simcoe summer house), 711 Bloor Street East at Castle Frank Road, Toronto)

William Arthur Parks 1868-1936
The first director of the Royal Ontario Museum of
Palaeontology, Parks organized several expeditions
to the Canadian and American West between 1918
and 1935. Much of the material collected on these
trips formed the basis of the museum's renowned
dinosaur collection. (In front of the Royal Ontario
Museum, 100 Queen's Park, Toronto)

Charles Trick Currelly 1876-1957
The first director (1912-1946) of the Royal Ontario
Museum of Archaeology, one of the five component
museums of the Royal Ontario Museum, Currelly
was renowned as a teacher and author as well as
an archaeologist and administrator. His autobiography, *I Brought The Ages Home*, was published in
1956. (On the grounds of the Royal Ontario Museum,
on the Bloor Street side, just west of Queen's Park/
Avenue Road, Toronto)

McMaster Hall
After housing the Toronto Baptist College for six
years and McMaster University for more than forty,
McMaster Hall, erected in 1880-81, was purchased
by the University of Toronto in 1930. Since 1963
it has been the home of the Royal Conservatory
of Music. (In front of the building, 273 Bloor Street
West, Toronto)

Lionel Conacher 1900-1954
During his twenty-five-year career in competitive
sports, Conacher excelled in wrestling, boxing,
football, and hockey. In 1950 the "Big Train" was
voted the outstanding Canadian male athlete of the
half-century. (In Frank Stollery Parkette (near his
birthplace), Davenport Road and Yonge Street,
Toronto)

The Loring-Wyle Studio
The executors of many impressive public monu-

ments, Frances Loring and Florence Wyle were founding members of the Sculptors' Society of Canada. For many years their studio was an important meeting-place for students, artists, writers, and patrons of the arts. (On the grounds of their former studio, 110 Glenrose Avenue, just east of Mount Pleasant Road, Toronto)

Upper Canada College
From its inception in 1829 as a preparatory school for the proposed provincial university, Upper Canada College has offered a strong classical curriculum. It is one of the oldest and most prominent schools in Canada. (Beside the main entrance to the college grounds, Avenue Road and Lonsdale Road, Toronto)

The First Jewish Congregation in Canada West
With the arrival in 1856 of seventeen Jewish families from England and Europe, the first Canadian Jewish congregation west of Montreal was formed. The group became known as the Toronto Hebrew Congregation – Holy Blossom. (On the grounds of Holy Blossom Temple, 1950 Bathurst Street, Toronto)

The Honourable William McDougall 1822-1905
A prominent lawyer, newspaper publisher, and parliamentarian, McDougall was a leading member of the Reform party and a Father of Confederation. Following his retirement from politics in 1882 he resumed his legal career. (In Lawrence Park (in the vicinity of his birthplace), Lawrence Avenue East and Yonge Street, Toronto)

• BOROUGH OF EAST YORK
Todmorden Mills
In the 1790s the Skinner Brothers built a sawmill and grist-mill on the banks of the Don River. This

small complex was augmented over the years by other light industries as the nearby village of Todmorden began to develop. (On the grounds of Todmorden Mills Historic Site, 67 Pottery Road, East York)

Canada's First Air Mail Flight 1918
A JN-4 Curtiss aircraft from the RAF detachment at Leaside was chosen for the first air mail delivery in Canada. The plane took off from Montreal at 10:30 a.m., refueled at Kingston, and landed in Toronto with its cargo of 120 letters at 4:55 p.m. (At 970 Eglinton Avenue East (the site of the former Leaside flying field), East York)

• SCARBOROUGH
The Scarborough Bluffs
The fossil beds and alternating layers of sand and clay that form these bluffs provide a comprehensive record unique in North America of the last stages of the Great Ice Age. (At the bluffs, Scarborough Bluffs Park, Scarborough Crescent at Drake Crescent, Scarborough)

The Thomson Settlement
The first permanent resident in Scarborough Township was David Thomson who emigrated from Scotland in 1796. He and his two brothers built mills and a Presbyterian church which became the centre of this early rural settlement. (Near the Scarborough Historical Museum in Thomson Memorial Park, 1007 Brimley Road, just north of Lawrence Avenue East, Scarborough)

The Armadale Free Methodist Church 1880
Built largely by volunteer labour, this modest frame church is the oldest continuing Free Methodist place of worship in Canada. It serves the combined congregation of Ellesmere and Armadale. (In front

of the church, Passmore Avenue, west of Markham Road, Scarborough)

- ## BOROUGH OF YORK
William Hume Blake 1809-1870
A prominent lawyer and politician during the province's formative years, Blake was elected to the legislative assembly in 1847. During his years as solicitor-general and then chancellor of Canada West he made substantial contributions to the structuring and functioning of Ontario's legal system. (In Humewood Park (part of his former estate), Humewood Drive, one block north of St. Clair Avenue West, Borough of York)

The Founding of Weston
Rich timber resources and the water-power potential of the Humber River attracted settlers to this area as early as the 1790s. Traffic along the Weston Road and, after 1856, on the Grand Trunk Railway stimulated Weston's steady economic growth. (In Memorial Park, Lawrence Avenue West and Little Avenue, Weston)

Queen Mary Hospital
The first sanatorium in the world devoted solely to the treatment of children with tuberculosis, the Queen Mary Hospital was opened in 1913. Ten years later its expanded services included a school under the supervision of the Toronto Board of Education. (On the grounds of West Park Hospital (the site of the former Queen Mary Hospital), 82 Buttonwood Avenue, Borough of York)

- ## ETOBICOKE
Jean Baptiste Rousseaux 1758-1812
A French-Canadian fur trader known to his English colleagues as St. John, Rousseaux had built a post at the mouth of the Humber River as early as 1791.

His knowledge of the area and its native inhabitants proved indispensable to Upper Canada's early administrators. (In Etienne Brûlé Park (near the site of his former trading post), on the east side of the Humber River, at the foot of Riverside Drive, Etobicoke)

Flight Lieutenant David Ernest Hornell, V.C. 1910-1944

In command of an eight-man crew, Hornell attacked and, under heavy fire, destroyed an enemy submarine off the Shetland Islands on June 24, 1944. For his courage throughout the ordeal, which ultimately cost him his life, the Toronto-born Hornell was awarded the Victoria Cross. (At David Hornell Public School, 32 Victoria Street, Etobicoke)

Montgomery's Inn

Situated on Dundas Street, one of the principal highways in Upper Canada, Montgomery's Inn was erected about 1832. A favourite stopping-place for travellers throughout much of the nineteenth century, it is now a public museum operated by the Etobicoke Historical Board. (In front of the inn, 4709 Dundas Street West, Etobicoke)

Corporal Frederick George Topham, V.C. 1917-1974

Topham served as a medical orderly with the 1st Canadian Parachute Battalion during the Second World War. The Toronto native was awarded the Victoria Cross for the exceptional courage he displayed in treating the wounded following a parachute drop east of the Rhine near Wesel on March 24, 1945. (At the Etobicoke Civic Centre, Highway 427 and Burnhamthorpe Road, Etobicoke)

James Shaver Woodsworth 1874-1942

A parliamentarian, social reformer, and pacifist of firm conviction, Woodsworth was the principal

founder of the Co-operative Commonwealth Federation (CCF) in 1932 and served as that party's
president for eight years. (In front of "Applewood",
the former Woodsworth homestead, 450 The West
Mall, Etobicoke)

• NORTH YORK

York Mills   MISSING!

In the 1820s James Hogg's grist-mill on a branch
of the Don River became the centre of a small
settlement known as Hogg's Hollow. More mills
were built and when a post office was opened about
the middle of the century the community became
known as York Mills. (In York Mills Park (near the
site of Hogg's former mill), Yonge Street and York
Mills Road, North York)

C.W. Jefferys 1869-1951

Born in England, Jefferys came to Canada about
1880 and settled in Toronto where he worked as a
lithographer's apprentice while studying art. He
was a prolific illustrator and became widely
acclaimed for his drawings of events in Canadian
history and scenes of pioneer life. (On the grounds
of his former residence, 4111 Yonge Street, just north
of York Mills Road, North York)

David Gibson 1804-1864

A deputy land surveyor and Reform politician,
Gibson was an ardent supporter of William Lyon
Mackenzie. He sought refuge in the United States
after the failure of the 1837 rebellion, but returned
to Upper Canada in 1848 and resumed his work as
a surveyor. (On the grounds of his former home,
now Gibson House Museum, 5172 Yonge Street,
North York)

The Honourable George Stewart Henry 1871-1958

Henry began his political career as a councillor for

York Township in 1903 and then served as warden of York County. In 1913 he entered the provincial arena and during his thirty years in the Ontario legislature held a number of important portfolios, including that of prime minister from 1930 to 1934. (At St. Matthew the Apostle and The Church of the Covenant (the site of his former farm), 80 George Henry Boulevard, North York)

The Right Honourable Lester Bowles Pearson 1897-1972

After a brilliant career in the diplomatic service, Pearson entered politics and from 1963 to 1968 was the prime minister of Canada. He was the first Canadian to receive the Nobel Peace Prize, which was awarded for his peace-making role in the Suez Crisis of 1956. (On the grounds of the Newtonbrook United Church (near his birthplace), 53 Cummer Street, North York)

York University

Incorporated in 1959 in response to a petition from a group of professional educators and engineers, York University was affiliated with the University of Toronto for its first five years. In 1965 the 600-acre York Campus, now the principal seat of the institution, was opened. (Near the main entrance to York University, St Lawrence Boulevard, off Keele Street south of Steeles Avenue, North York)

VICTORIA COUNTY

• BOBCAYGEON
The Founding of Bobcaygeon
In 1833 the government began construction of a lock and canal at the narrows between Sturgeon and Pigeon Lakes. Soon a community began to develop around the lock and the two mills that Thomas Need built there. In the 1850s Mossom Boyd's lumbering business further stimulated Bobcaygeon's growth. (At the municipal building, 21 Canal Street East, Bobcaygeon)

• FENELON FALLS
John Langton 1808-1894
A native of England, Langton came to Upper Canada in 1833 and settled near present-day Fenelon Falls. He was one of the earliest settlers in the Otonabee region and his published correspondence is a valuable source of information about nine-teenth-century life in Victoria County. (At the Horticultural Society Gardens, Fenelon Falls)

James Wallis 1806-1893
An Irishman from Maryborough in County Cork, Wallis came to North America in 1832 and lived for a time at Montreal before settling in Upper Canada. In partnership with Robert Jameson he built a sawmill and grist-mill which formed the nucleus of the village of Fenelon Falls. (On the grounds of his former home, "Maryboro Lodge", now open to the public as the Fenelon Falls Museum, 50 Oak Street, Fenelon Falls)

After a distinguished career as a railway promoter, George Laidlaw took up farming in his retirement years and as a successful cattle-breeder became a strong advocate of farmers' rights. (Archives of Ontario S 474)

• KIRKFIELD

Sir William Mackenzie 1849-1923

In 1899 William Mackenzie and Donald Mann organized the Canadian Northern Railway which later became a transcontinental line. His involvement in railway and power-development projects in Europe, South America, and the Caribbean as well as in Canada earned Mackenzie international renown. (On the grounds of his former home, "Mackenzie House", Nelson Street, Kirkfield)

George Laidlaw 1828-1889

An important figure in the history of railway development in Ontario, Laidlaw came to Canada in 1855 after having spent several years in the merchant marine. Realizing the commercial potential of a systematic railway scheme, he strongly promoted the construction of rail lines radiating from the port at Toronto. (On the grounds of St. Thomas' Anglican Church (near his former Balsam Lake ranch), Highway 48, about 5 km east of Kirkfield)

The Portage Road

Generally following the route of the old Indian portage from Lake Simcoe to Balsam Lake – the route travelled by Champlain and his Huron allies in 1615 – the Portage Road was surveyed in 1834-35 by John Smith and did much to encourage settlement in the district. (At the intersection of Highways 46 and 48 (on a section of the former road), west of Kirkfield near Bolsover)

The Trent-Severn Waterway

The canalization of the water route from the Bay of Quinte to Lake Simcoe was begun in 1833 with the construction of a lock at Bobcaygeon. Since the completion of the system through to Georgian Bay in 1920, the Trent-Severn has become one of

Ontario's major recreational waterways. (Near the Kirkfield lift lock, Highway 503, about 3 km north of Kirkfield)

The Victoria Road

To encourage settlement on the southern edge of the Precambrian shield the government undertook construction of a network of colonization roads into the hinterland. The Victoria Road was built between 1859 and 1864, and ran from the present-day village of Glenarm north into Oakley Township to meet up with the Peterson Road. Highway 505 follows part of the former road. (At the intersection of Highways 503 and 505, in the community of Uphill – about 20 km north of Kirkfield)

- LINDSAY

The Scugog Route

Scugog Lake and the Scugog River formed a link in the long water route from the Kawarthas to Lake Ontario travelled by the country's native inhabitants. The route also proved useful to settlers in the nineteenth century. It now forms part of the Trent-Severn Waterway. (At Riverside Cemetery, Lindsay Street, Lindsay)

Purdy's Mills

The mills built on the Scugog River between 1828 and 1830 by William Purdy and his sons formed the nucleus of the developing community of Lindsay. The mills provoked some unrest among the residents because the mill-dam caused frequent flooding in the area. (In McDonnell Park, on the west bank of the Scugog River, between Wellington and Lindsay Streets, Lindsay)

Ernest Thompson Seton 1860-1946

An amateur naturalist and free-lance illustrator, Seton combined his two interests to produce some forty books of stories about North American wildlife. As a child he lived on a farm in the Lindsay area. (On the grounds of the Victoria County Historical Society Museum, 435 Kent Street West, Lindsay)

• OMEMEE
The Founding of Omemee
The community that grew up around William Cottingham's mills on the Pigeon River was first called Williamstown and then Metcalfe. In 1857 the inhabitants finally settled on the name Omemee, a Mississauga word meaning "pigeon". (At the municipal building, 1 King Street West, Omemee)

WATERLOO REGIONAL MUNICIPALITY

• BADEN
Sir Adam Beck's Birthplace
Born and raised in Baden, Adam Beck attended Dr. Tassie's renowned school in Galt, and in 1885 moved to London. In 1906, as a member of the Ontario legislature, he introduced a bill which established the Hydro-Electric Power Commission of Ontario. (In front of Baden Public School, 220 Snyder's Road East, Baden – west of Kitchener on Regional Road 6)

The First Amish Settlement
In the 1820s, with assistance from Mennonites already established in the area, Christian Nafziger arranged for a number of European Amish families to settle on a tract of land in what later became Wilmot Township. (At Steinman Mennonite Church (near the site of the Amish settlers' first meeting house), Regional Road 6, just west of Baden)

• CAMBRIDGE
The Founders of Galt
In 1816 William Dickson, a Niagara merchant and politician, purchased a large parcel of land on which his agent Absalom Shade built a sawmill and gristmill. The community that developed around these enterprises was originally called Shade's Mills, but was later renamed in honour of Dickson's friend, John Galt. (In High Park (also called Centennial Park), Main Street, Cambridge)

Galt City Hall
This attractive limestone building, which dates from 1857, was designed and built by a local architect, H.B. Sinclair, to serve as the community's town hall and market place. Various additions have been made to the structure over the years but its exterior

features have been little altered. (At the Market Square (west) side of the building, 46 Dickson Street, Cambridge)

Tassie's School
The Galt Grammar School, familiarly known as "Tassie's", gained widespread recognition for its high academic standards under William Tassie, headmaster from 1853 to 1881. The school was among the first in the province to be made a collegiate institute. (On the grounds of the school, now the Galt Collegiate and Vocational Institute, 244 Bridge Street North, Cambridge)

The Honourable James Young 1835-1913
A native of Galt, Young served in both the federal and provincial parliaments during his political career. He was also a noted local historian and published several books dealing with the history of Waterloo County. (On the grounds of Central Presbyterian Church (of which he was an active member), Queen's Square, Main Street, Cambridge)

The Founder of Preston
John Erb, a Mennonite from Pennsylvania, came to Upper Canada in 1805. He acquired a large tract of land from the German Land Company and within two years had built a sawmill and grist-mill. These mills formed the nucleus of the community of Preston. (In front of the former Preston town hall, King Street, Cambridge)

• KITCHENER
Bishop Benjamin Eby 1785-1853
A Mennonite from Pennsylvania, Eby came to Upper Canada in 1806 and purchased a large tract of land, part of which is now the site of Kitchener (originally called Ebytown). He constructed a log church and played a leading role in the early

religious and secular life of the community. (On the grounds of First Mennonite Church, 800 King Street East, Kitchener)

The Joseph Schneider House 1820

On land he had purchased in 1807 Joseph Schneider built a farm and sawmill, and cleared a road along present-day Queen Street. His home – the oldest remaining house in Kitchener – has been restored and is operated as a museum by the Regional Municipality of Waterloo. (On the grounds of the museum, 466 Queen Street South, Kitchener)

William Lyon Mackenzie King 1874-1950

A native of Kitchener, King began his public service career in 1900 as a specialist in labour relations. Eight years later he entered federal politics and as leader of the Liberal party became prime minister in 1921 – a position he held for more than twenty years. (On the grounds of the public library, 85 Queen Street North, Kitchener)

The Huron Road

By the early 1830s the Huron Road had been built from Guelph to Goderich by the Canada Company to promote the sale of company lands within the Huron Tract. Highways 8 and 24 follow, approximately, the original colonization route. (At the entrance to Doon Heritage Crossroads (on a section of the former road), Huron Road and Homer Watson Boulevard, Kitchener)

• NEW DUNDEE

William J. Wintemberg 1876-1941

A native of New Dundee, Wintemberg was an authority on Iroquoian and Algonkian prehistoric cultures. His systematic field work and scholarly reports greatly advanced the study of archaeology in Canada and gained him an international reputation. (Inside the entrance to Recreation Park, Bridge Street, New Dundee – southwest of Kitchener on Regional Road 12)

- ## NEW HAMBURG
The Founding of New Hamburg
A grist-mill built in the 1830s by Josiah Cushman formed the centre of a small settlement of Mennonites and German immigrants. Agricultural prosperity and, after 1856, railway service ensured the continued prosperity of the community. (On the grounds of the municipal building, 121 Huron Street, New Hamburg)

- ## WATERLOO
Abraham Erb 1772-1830
A younger brother of John Erb, the founder of Preston, Abraham Erb settled in 1806 on a 900-acre tract of bushland. The grist-mill he built ten years later became the business and social centre of the community of Waterloo. (In Waterloo Park, Young Street West, Waterloo)

The Evangelical United Brethren
A camp meeting held in Waterloo in 1839 resulted in the formation of the first Evangelical Church congregation in Upper Canada. In 1946 the Evangelical Church joined with the United Brethren in Christ to form the Evangelical United Brethren. (In Hillside Park (near the site of the founding camp meeting), Marsland Drive, Waterloo)

Waterloo Lutheran University
The first institution of higher education in Waterloo County, Waterloo Lutheran University (now Wilfrid Laurier University) had its origins in the Evangelical Lutheran Seminary of Canada. The seminary opened in 1911 in a house on the present campus. (At the Albert Street entrance to the

Central Teaching Building, Wilfrid Laurier University campus, Waterloo)

The University of Waterloo
This university was established in the 1950s in response to community demand for improved education facilities, particularly in technical and scientific fields of study. Renowned for the success of its co-operative education programs, it now has the largest engineering school in Canada. (At the entrance to South Campus Hall, University Avenue, Waterloo)

• WEST MONTROSE
The West Montrose Covered Bridge
The last remaining covered bridge in Ontario, the West Montrose bridge over the Grand River was built in 1881 by John and Benjamin Bear. The floor and sub-structure have since been rebuilt and reinforced to ensure the bridge's continued existence. (At the bridge, Township Road 50, just south of Regional Road 86, West Montrose)

WELLINGTON COUNTY

- ARTHUR
  ### The Founding of Arthur
  The town site of Arthur – named in honour of Arthur Wellesley, Duke of Wellington – was laid out at the southern end of the Garafraxa colonization road in 1846. The construction of mills attracted settlers to the site, and in time Arthur became a regional market centre for agricultural produce. (In MacPherson Park, Francis Street, Arthur)

- BALLINAFAD
  ### Early Settlement in Erin Township
  In 1818 the Crown purchased land now comprising Erin Township from the Mississauga Indians, an Ojibwa tribe, and within two years settlers had located near present-day Ballinafad. Small communities soon formed around the mills that were built at scattered sites throughout the tract. By 1850 the population of the township exceeded 3,000. (At the Ballinafad Cemetery (in the vicinity of the earliest settlement in the area), County Road 24, Ballinafad)

- CONN
  ### Lieutenant S. Lewis Honey, V.C., D.C.M., M.M. 1894-1918
  A native of Conn, Honey served with the Canadian Expeditionary Force in France during the First World War. For his conspicuous bravery on several occasions, particularly in the fierce fighting in the Bourlon Wood area in September 1918, he was awarded, posthumously, the Victoria Cross. (On the grounds of Westcott United Church, County Road 14, Conn – on Highway 89 east of Mount Forest)

• ELORA

The Founder of Elora

In 1832 William Gilkison, a Scotsman from Ayr-shire, purchased a tract of 14,000 acres in Nichol Township. At the falls of the Grand River he laid out a town site named Elora, and the following year established a sawmill and general store. (Near the cenotaph in Town Square, Geddes Street, Elora)

Charles Clarke 1826-1909

A long-time resident of Elora, Clarke was a prom-inent figure in the radical reform movement in Ontario. He played a leading role in drafting the Clear Grit platform in 1851 which included such policies as representation by population and the

A self-educated teacher and archaeologist, David Boyle was well known for his unconventional (and highly successful) teaching methods, his wit, and his humour. (Archives of Ontario S 385)

secret ballot. (In front of his former home, now the Graham A. Giddy Funeral Home, Geddes and Church Streets, Elora)

David Boyle 1842-1911
Boyle spent over fifteen years in Elora as a school teacher and principal prior to his appointment in 1886 as the first curator of the Provincial Archaeological Museum in Toronto. His work on the prehistory of Ontario earned him an international reputation as an archaeologist and anthropologist. (On the grounds of the public library (the forerunner of which, the Elora Mechanics' Institute Library, Boyle actively promoted), 144 Geddes Street, Elora)

• ERIN
The Founding of Erin
The abundant water power of the Credit River attracted millers to this area in the late 1820s. By 1850, with the addition of other small industries, Erin had become a significant milling and manufacturing centre for the region. (Near the Main Street bridge, opposite the cenotaph, Erin)

• FERGUS
The Founders of Fergus
In 1833 two Highlanders, Adam Fergusson and James Webster, purchased 7,000 acres of uncleared land in Nichol Township. They laid out a town site and Webster took up residence to supervise the early development of Fergus. (In front of the public library, 190 St. Andrew's Street West, Fergus)

St. Andrew's Presbyterian Church
The first church on this site was built in 1835 by a congregation of Scottish settlers who had held their first services in a local tavern. The present St. Andrew's dates from 1862, and despite some

structural changes retains much of its original Gothic Revival character. (On the grounds of the church, 325 St. George Street West, Fergus)

The Fergus Curling Club
Formed in 1834, the Fergus Curling Club has been in continuous operation longer than any other curling club in Ontario. The sport was played out-of-doors until 1879 when a covered rink was built which soon became the social centre of the area. (At the entrance to the club's present building, St. George Street West, Fergus)

• GUELPH
The Founding of Guelph
John Galt, the first superintendent of the Canada Company, established Guelph in 1827 to serve as the company's headquarters during the development of the Huron Tract. The town later came into its own as a prosperous railway and industrial centre. (In Exhibition Park, Exhibition Street and London Road, Guelph)

Guelph City Hall 1856
Designed in the Classical style by the noted Toronto architect William Thomas, the Guelph town hall was constructed from locally quarried stone. The building included an indoor market area, administrative offices, and a large assembly hall. (At the front entrance to the building, 59 Carden Street, Guelph)

Wellington County Court House
A rare example in Ontario of the castellated style of architecture, the court house erected at Guelph between 1842 and 1844 is reminiscent of a medieval fort. The limestone structure has been expanded and altered many times over the years. (At the former court house, now the Wellington County Administration Centre, 74 Woolwich Street, Guelph)

The Guelph Public Library

This library was established by the City of Guelph shortly after passage of the Free Libraries Act in 1882. It replaced a limited circulating library service that for several decades had been provided by the Farmers' and Mechanics' Institute. (In front of the present library building, 100 Norfolk Street, Guelph)

John Galt 1779-1839

A Scotsman of both literary and business talents, Galt was appointed the first superintendent of the Canada Company in 1826 and founded Guelph the following year as the company's headquarters. He proved more popular with the settlers he helped to locate in the Huron Tract than with his business colleagues, and in 1829 he was discharged. He returned to Britain and successfully pursued a literary career. (In Royal City Park, Gordon Street, Guelph)

The La Guayra Settlers

Named after their original destination in Venezuela, the La Guayra settlers were a group of Scottish emigrants who, unable to adapt to the tropical climate of South America, came to Upper Canada in 1827. John Galt, the superintendent of the Canada Company, helped them settle in and around Guelph. (In Royal City Park, Gordon Street, Guelph)

John McLean 1799-1890

During his time in the service of the Hudson's Bay Company McLean made several important voyages of exploration and discovery into the interior of Labrador. His book, *Notes of a Twenty-five Years' Service in the Hudson's Bay Territory*, is a classic work on the Canadian fur trade era. (In front of his former home, 21 Nottingham Street, Guelph)

Henry Langley 1836-1907

One of the most prolific architects working in Ontario in the nineteenth century, Langley designed some seventy churches throughout the province. He also produced numerous residential, commercial, and public buildings during his long career. (On the grounds of St. George's Anglican Church (a structure he designed), 99 Woolwich Street, Guelph)

Joseph Connolly 1840-1904

A specialist in Gothic Revival design, Connolly trained as an architect in his native Ireland before coming to North America. Although he produced some industrial and residential buildings, he is best known for the many splendid churches he built throughout Ontario, primarily for the Irish Roman Catholic community. (In front of The Church of Our Lady (a structure he designed), 28 Norfolk Street, Guelph)

Edward Johnson 1878-1959

Born and raised in Guelph, Johnson made his operatic debut in Italy in 1912 (billed as Eduardo di Giovanni). He sang leading tenor roles in major opera houses in Europe and North America, and from 1935 to 1950 was general manager of the Metropolitan Opera Association in New York. Throughout his life he worked to promote and encourage Canadian musicians. (In Riverside Park (near the site of his former home), Woolwich Street, Guelph)

The Ontario Agricultural College

Opened in a Guelph farmhouse in 1874 and originally called the Ontario School of Agriculture, this research and teaching institution was for many decades affiliated with the University of Toronto. In 1964 it was one of three provincial colleges which together formed the nucleus of the Universtiy of

Guelph. (Near the Johnston Arch (the portico of the farmhouse in which classes were first held), Gordon Street and College Avenue, University of Guelph campus)

The Ontario Veterinary College
Founded in Toronto in 1862 as the Upper Canada Veterinary School, this was the first institution in Canada to offer courses in veterinary medicine. Since 1922 the college has been located in Guelph. (In front of the Dean's residence, on the grounds of the college, Gordon Street and College Avenue, Guelph)

Prior to the opening of a railway station at the site of Palmerston in 1871, the area was little more than a farm settlement, as evidenced by this photograph taken in 1865. (Archives of Ontario ST 1005)

- HARRISTON
  The Founding of Harriston
  The mills built in the 1850s by Joshua and George
  Harrison formed the nucleus of a small industrial
  settlement on the Maitland River. Within two
  decades Harriston was a prosperous manufacturing
  centre with railway connections westward to Lake
  Huron. (In the park adjacent to the town hall, 68
  Elora Street, Harriston)

- MOUNT FOREST
  The Founding of Mount Forest
  Surrounded by rich agricultural land and stimulated
  by activity along the Garafraxa colonization road,
  Mount Forest quickly grew from a village plot in
  1853 to a community of 1,400 inhabitants by 1867.
  (In the Lion's Club Park, Main Street and Parkside
  Drive, Mount Forest)

  Captain Frederick W. Campbell, V.C. 1867-1915
  Born in Oxford County, Campbell grew up on a
  farm near Mount Forest. On June 15, 1915 in an ill-
  fated battle near Givenchy, France he was wounded
  while covering, with a single gun, the withdrawal
  of his two detachments. He died four days later and
  was posthumously awarded the Victoria Cross. (On
  the grounds of the Royal Canadian Legion Hall, 140
  King Street West, Mount Forest)

- PALMERSTON
  The Founding of Palmerston
  A station built on the main line of the Wellington,
  Grey and Bruce Railway in 1871 provided the
  nucleus around which Palmerston developed.
  Within three years lines were in operation to
  Southampton and Listowel, and the population of
  this burgeoning railway town had reached 1,400.
  (In the park at the corner of William and Bell
  Streets, Palmerston)

The Ontario Vaccine Farm
This vaccine farm was established in 1885 by a local physician, Dr. Alexander Stewart, and was the first institution in Ontario to produce smallpox vaccine. In 1916 the operation was transferred to the University of Toronto. (Near the former Stewart residence, 290 Main Street, Palmerston)

• PUSLINCH TOWNSHIP
The Settlement of Puslinch
Originally known as the "Church Lands" because of the extensive clergy reserves within its borders, Puslinch was surveyed as early as 1791 by Augustus Jones. Settlement did not begin, however, until 1828 when extensive surveys were instigated by John Galt. (At the Ellis Chapel, Accommodation Road (also called Givin Road), Puslinch Township – about 4 km east of Cambridge)

• ROCKWOOD
Rockwood Academy 1850
William Wetherald, a Quaker from England, established the Rockwood Academy in 1850. During its thirty-two years of operation this boys' boarding school was known for its high academic standards. The stone building dates from 1853-54 and for a time after 1882 was used as a woollen mill. It is now owned by the Ontario Heritage Foundation. (On the grounds of the former academy, Main Street South, Rockwood)

YORK REGIONAL MUNICIPALITY

• AURORA
Aurora Public School
In 1886, to accommodate an ever-growing student body, a two-storey white brick school was built in Aurora to replace the frame schoolhouse that had served the community until then. The new school was designed in the High Victorian manner with much detailing and decoration, and remains an excellent example of that architectural style. (At the former school building, now the Aurora Museum, 22 Church Street, Aurora)

The First Steam Train 1853
In May 1853 the first steam train to operate in Canada West began service between Toronto and Aurora, then called Machell's Corners. This was the first stage in a line being constructed through to Collingwood by the Ontario, Simcoe and Huron Union Railroad Company. (At the railway station, Wellington Street, Aurora)

• HOLLAND LANDING
Samuel Lount 1791-1838
A prosperous farmer at Holland Landing and a reform politician, Lount was in joint command of Mackenzie's rebel forces when they met defeat at Montgomery's Tavern in 1837. Lount was convicted of treason and executed at Toronto the following year. (In Anchor Park, Doane Road, Holland Landing Conservation Area)

• LLOYDTOWN
Lloydtown
Jesse Lloyd, a Pennsylvania Quaker, was instrumental in establishing the community of Lloydtown. He became a prominent figure in the 1837 rebellion and following the defeat of Mackenzie's rebel forces fled

to the United States where he died in exile. (Regional Road 16, about 2 km west of Highway 27 (in the vicinity of Lloyd's original land purchase), Lloydtown)

- MAPLE
St. Andrew's Church
Constructed in 1862 to serve a Church of Scotland congregation formed some thirty years earlier, St. Andrew's was built by a local contractor, John McDonald. The church is an excellent example of a style of architecture known as Carpenter's Gothic. (On the grounds of the church, 9860 Keele Street, Maple)

Lord Beaverbrook 1879-1964
Publisher, politician, and philanthropist, Lord Beaverbrook was born in Maple, the son of a Presbyterian minister, the Reverend William Aitken. Following a successful career in Canada as a financier, he went to England in 1910 and entered politics. In 1917 he was raised to the peerage. (At St. Andrew's Presbyterian Church (to which he donated a carillon), 9860 Keele Street, Maple)

Zion Evangelical Lutheran Church
One of the earliest Lutheran congregations in Upper Canada was formed in Vaughan Township in 1806 by a group of German-speaking settlers from Pennsylvania. The present church, which dates from 1860, was the site of the founding of the Canada Synod of the Lutheran Church in 1861. (On the grounds of the church, Keele Street, about 3 km south of Maple)

- MARKHAM
The Founding of Markham
By 1810, ten years after the arrival of the first settlers at the Rouge River, aptly-named Nicholas Miller

had erected mills around which a community known as Markham Mills gradually formed. Other small industries extended the village's economic base and by mid-century Markham was an active manufacturing centre. (At the Markham District Historical Museum, Highway 48, Markham)

• NEWMARKET

The Founding of Newmarket
A grist-mill built in 1801 by Joseph Hill marked the beginning of a small community on the banks of the Holland River. The arrival of the Ontario, Simcoe and Huron Union Railroad in 1853 strengthened Newmarket's position as a regional market centre. (In Wesley Brooks Memorial Park, Water and Main Streets, Newmarket)

Mazo de la Roche 1879-1961
The author of the ever-popular *Jalna* novels, Mazo de la Roche was born in Newmarket. Although she wrote numerous plays, poems, short stories, and articles, it was the chronicles of the Whiteoak family that earned her an international reputation. (In Wesley Brooks Memorial Park, Water and Main Streets, Newmarket)

The Meeting House of the Religious Society of Friends (Quakers) 1810
Members of the Society of Friends began to settle on an extensive land grant in this region in the first years of the nineteenth century. Their frame meeting house was the first permanent place of worship built in this part of the province. (At the meeting house, Yonge Street (Highway 11), Newmarket)

The Newmarket Radial Railway Arch
One of the first railway arches in Canada to be made of reinforced concrete, this graceful parabolic structure was built in 1909 to support part of a trestle

bridge over the Holland River. The bridge was demolished after the Toronto and York Radial Railway Company ceased operation in 1930. (Near the Recreation Works Building, Queen Street, Newmarket)

The Dutch Settlement of the Holland Marsh

In 1934 fifteen Dutch families settled on recently drained land in the Schomberg River valley, in present-day Ansnorveldt. Using skilled farming techniques and co-operative management they began to develop the Holland Marsh into one of the most important vegetable-growing districts in Ontario. (Near the old schoolhouse, Concession Road 3, Ansnorveldt – west of Newmarket)

• RICHMOND HILL

The de Puisaye Settlement 1799

Led by the Comte de Puisaye, some forty exiled French royalists attempted to form a settlement in uncleared townships along Yonge Street. The noblemen and their servants could not adapt to the rigours of pioneer life, however, and by 1806 most had returned to Europe. (On the grounds of St. John's Anglican Church (in the vicinity of the former settlement), Yonge Street (Highway 11), at the Jefferson Side Road, Richmond Hill)

The Founding of Richmond Hill

The extension of Yonge Street north to Holland Landing prompted the formation of small settlements along the route. The community of Mount Pleasant served as a popular way-station along the road, and in 1819 was renamed in honour of the Duke of Richmond who had stopped there for dinner on his way to Penetanguishene. (In front of the town hall, Yonge Street (Highway 11), Richmond Hill)

Lieutenant-Colonel Robert Moodie 1778-1837

A veteran of the Napoleonic Wars and the War of 1812, Moodie was fatally wounded on the night of December 4, 1837 when he attempted to warn government authorities in Toronto of an impending attack by William Lyon Mackenzie's rebel forces. (At Yonge Street (Highway 11) and Trayborne Drive (near the site of his former home), Richmond Hill)

• SHARON

Sharon Temple

The unique structure of Sharon Temple embodies, symbolically, the religious beliefs of David Willson, the founder of the Children of Peace. This small sect built the temple between 1825 and 1831 specifically for the celebration of special festivals. It is now operated as a museum by the York Pioneer and Historical Society and is the site of an annual summer music festival. (At the temple, Leslie Street, Sharon – north of Newmarket)

• SUTTON

Stephen Butler Leacock 1869-1944

Although Leacock wrote extensively on economics and history, and for many years headed the department of political science at McGill University, it is as a humorist that he is best known. Among other works, *Literary Lapses* and *Sunshine Sketches of a Little Town* continue to delight generations of readers. (At St. George's Anglican Church (where his grave is located), Sibbald Point Provincial Park Road and Lakeshore Road, about 5 km northeast of Sutton)

Eildon Hall

One of the oldest structures in the Lake Simcoe region, Eildon Hall was begun in 1830 by William Rains. The original Regency-style cottage was transformed by its subsequent owner, Susan Sibbald, into a grand rural manor. It is now operated as a museum by the Ontario Ministry of Natural Resources. (On the grounds of the museum, Sibbald Point Provincial Park, northeast of Sutton)

• THORNHILL
The Founding of Thornhill
Although a grist-mill and sawmill were in operation on the Don River by 1802, it was not until 1829 when Benjamin Thorne built a large flour mill, a tannery, and a store that a community of any size began to develop. Over the next decades Thornhill became a successful milling and agricultural centre. (On the grounds of the post office, 7751 Yonge Street, Thornhill)

J.E.H. MacDonald 1873-1932
A founding member of the Group of Seven artists, MacDonald lived and painted in Thornhill from 1913 until his death. "A Tangled Garden" is probably his best-known work and typifies the artist's strong sense of colour, deft brush work, and sure grasp of design. (At his former home, "Oakbank Pond", 121 Centre Street, Thornhill)

• UNIONVILLE
The Berczy Settlement 1794
The German settlers who were brought to this area in 1794 by William Berczy were the first residents in Markham Township. Despite sickness and famine these hardy pioneers laid the foundations for pros-perous agricultural development. (At Bethesda Lutheran Cemetery (in the vicinity of the former settlement), Kennedy Road, just north of Union-ville)

Bethesda Church and Burying Ground
One of the earliest Lutheran congregations in the province was formed near present-day Unionville

shortly after the arrival in 1794 of a group of German settlers led by William Berczy. Services were held in the home of Phillip Eckardt, a member of the community, who later donated land for a church and burying ground. (At Bethesda Lutheran Cemetery (near the site of the former church), Kennedy Road, just north of Unionville)

- ## WHITCHURCH-STOUFFVILLE
  ### *The Whitchurch Quaker Settlement*
  Among the early settlers in this area were a number of Quakers who, until 1816 when they established their own organization, had formed part of the Yonge Street Meeting. The Whitchurch Quaker group later split into several factions, but by 1900 they had come together to form Pine Orchard Union Church. (On the grounds of Pine Orchard Union Church, Vivian Road, Whitchurch-Stouffville)

  ### *The Founding of Stouffville*
  A sawmill and grist-mill built by Abraham Stouffer on the banks of Duffin's Creek in the 1820s marked the beginning of the community of Stouffville. The village grew steadily and by the 1860s contained many prosperous manufactories. (At the public library, 65 Main Street West, Whitchurch-Stouffville)

Index

Aberdeen, Lady, 196
Aberhart, William, 106
Actinolite, founding of, 93
Acton, founding of, 78
Addington Road, 148
ADOLPHUSTOWN, 143-144
Aerodrome, first in Canada, 211
Ailsa Craig, 153
Air mail flight, first in Canada, 301
AJAX, 28
Albert College, 94
ALEXANDRIA, 250
ALGOMA DISTRICT, 1-6
Allan, Ebenezer, 153
Allan Gardens. *See* Toronto Horticultural Society, 292
Allenford pow-wow, 17
"Alligator" tug, 72, *73*
Allward, Walter Seymour, 287
Alma College, 38
ALMONTE, 123-124
Alwington House. *See* Government House, 55
AMHERST ISLAND, 145
AMHERSTBURG, 42-44
AMHERSTVIEW, 145-146
Amish settlement, 311
ANCASTER, 83
Anderson, Samuel, 250
Anne, capture of, 44
Aqua-Plano Indians, 267
Archives of Ontario, 293
Arctic watershed, 268, 277
Arkona, founding of, 117
Armadale Free Methodist Church, Scarborough, 301
ARNPRIOR, 232, *233*
Arthur, founding of, 316
Associated Country Women of the World, 243
ATHERLEY, 238
ATIKOKAN, 229
Atkinson, Joseph E., 30
"Auchmar", 87
Auld Kirk, Almonte, 123

INDEX

Aurora Public School, 325
Aylesworth, Allen B., 149
Aylmer, founding of, 36

Baby, James, 47
Backhouse, John, mill, 71
Backus. *See* Backhouse
BADEN, 311
BAILIEBORO, 218
Baker, Edwin A., 146
BALA, 160
Baldoon settlement, 116
Baldwin homestead, 31
BALLINAFAD, 316
Ball's grist-mill, 184
Ballygiblin riots, 124
BANCROFT, 93
Baraga, Frederic, 2
Barber, John R., 80
Barnum House, 193
BARRIE, 238-239
BARRIEFIELD, 52
BARRYS BAY, 232
BATCHAWANA BAY, 1
BATH, 146-147
Baxter, Richard, 272
Bayfield, founding of, 100
Bayfield, Henry W., 247
BAYSVILLE, 160
BEAR ISLAND, 185
Beatty, Elizabeth Rabb, 135
Beautiful Joe, 65
Beaverbrook, Lord, 326
Beaverdams Church, 183
BEAVERTON, 28
Beck, Adam: 155; birthplace, 311
Becker, Abigail. *See* Heroine of Long Point, 71
Bedford Mills, 52
BEETON, 240
Belaney, Archibald ("Grey Owl"), 187, *189*
Bell, Christopher J., 234
Bell, William, 127
Belle River, founding of, 44
BELLEVILLE, 93-95
"Bellevue", 43
Berczy settlement, 330

Bernard, Hewitt, 238
Bethesda Church and burying ground, Unionville, 330
Bethune, Henry Norman, 164
Bible Christian Church, 29
Bishop, William (Billy), 66
Bishop's palace, Toronto, 282
Birthplace of standard time, 285
Black Donald graphite mine, 233
Black settlement, 239
Blackburn, Josiah, 154
Blackfriars Bridge, 157
Blake, Edward, 159
Blake, William Hume, 302
BLENHEIM, 112
Blockhouse: Chatham, 112; Merrickville, 137
Blockhouse Island, 130
"Bloody Assize", 83
Blue Church, 141
Bluestone House, 194
Blyth, founding of, 100
Bobcaygeon, founding of, 306
Bobcaygeon Road, 76
"BOB-LO" ISLAND, 44
Bois Blanc Island fortifications, 44
Bolton, founding of, 211
BOND HEAD, 240
Bonnycastle, Richard, 60
Bostwick, John, 36
Bothwell, founding of, 112
Boucher, René-Amable, 56
Boundaries: international, 121; Ontario-Manitoba, 109
Bowell, Mackenzie, 94, 95
BOWMANVILLE, 28
Boyle, David, 317, 318
Boyle, Joseph W., 206
BRACEBRIDGE, 161
BRADFORD, 240
BRAMPTON, 211
BRANT COUNTY, 7-16
Brant County court house, 7
Brant House, 78, 79
Brant, John, 14
Brant, Molly, 54
BRANTFORD, 7-12
Brent, Charles H., 30
Brent crater, 185

INDEX

BRIGHTON, 190

BRIGHTS GROVE, 117

British Commonwealth Air Training Plan, 105

British garrison, London, 156

Brock University, 181

BROCKVILLE, 130-131

Brockville, Westport and Sault Ste. Marie Railway, 142

Brown, A. Roy, 124

Brown, George: 12; home, 292

Brown, John, convention, 113

BRUCE COUNTY, 17-20

Bruce, Herbert A., 298

Bruce, William Blair, 86

Bruce Mines, 1

Brussels, founding of, 100

Brusso, Noah ("Tommy Burns"), 62

Buade, Louis de, Comte de Frontenac, 53

Buchanan, George, 124

Bucke, Richard Maurice, 154

Buell, William, Sr., 131

BURKS FALLS, 207

BURLINGTON, 78-80

Burlington glass works, 89

"Burlington Races", 85

Burns, Anthony, 181

Burns, Tommy, 62

BURRITTS RAPIDS, 132

Burwell, Mahlon, 36

Butler, John, 175

Buxton settlement, 115

By, John, 135

Bytown and Prescott Railway Co., 140

CAINSVILLE, 12

CALABOGIE, 233

Caldwell, William, 43

CALLANDER, 207

CAMBRIDGE, 311-312

CAMDEN EAST, 147

Cameron, "Cariboo", 256

Cameron, Duncan, 260

Cameron, Malcolm, 126

Camp Borden, 241

Campbell, Frederick W., 323

Campbell, William, 287

Campbell's raid, 70

INDEX

Campbellford, founders of, 190
CAMPBELLVILLE, 80
Canada Constellation, 174
"Canada First" movement, 285
Canada West's Fathers of Confederation, 295
Canada's pioneer airlines, 108
Canadian National Exhibition, 282
Canadian Northern Railway, 231
Canard River skirmishes, 42
CANNINGTON, 29
Canoe route to the west, 185, 207
Cantin, Narcisse M., 105
Capron, Hiram "King", 14
CARDINAL, 132
CARLETON PLACE, 124
Carleton University, 198
Carman, Albert, 95
Carmichael, Franklin, 246
Carnochan, Janet, 174
Caroline, destruction of, 167
CARP, 196
CASTLEFORD, 234
Cathedral of St. Peter-in-Chains, Peterborough, 221
Cavelier de La Salle, René-Robert, 56, 78
CAYUGA, 69
Central Presbyterian Church, Hamilton, 88
Chaffey, George, 131
Chaffey's Mills, 133
CHALK RIVER, 235
Champlain, Samuel de, 99, 235
CHAPLEAU, 261
CHATHAM, 112-113
CHATSWORTH, 61
CHEAPSIDE, 69
Cheese, "Big", 201
Chesley, founding of, 17
Chicora incident, 2, 4
CHIPPAWA, 166
Chisholm, William, 81
Christ Church, Amherstburg, 42
Christ Church, Burritts Rapids, 132
Christ Church, Carp, 196
Christ Church, Deseronto, 96
Christ's Church Cathedral, Hamilton, 88
Church of the Holy Trinity, Chippawa, 166
Church of the Holy Trinity, Toronto, 288

INDEX

Church of the Immaculate Conception, Formosa, 17
Church of St. John the Evangelist, Niagara Falls, 170
Church of St. Peter, Cobourg, 191
City hall: Belleville, 94; Galt, 311; Guelph, 319; Toronto, 286
"Claremont Lodge", 87
Clarke, Charles, 317
Clarke, Lionel B., 92
Clergy House, Minden, 77
CLINTON, 100-101
Coats, Robert H., 101
COBALT, 276-277
COBDEN, 235
COBOURG, 190
Cobourg and Peterborough Railway, 191
COCHRANE, 21-26
Cockburn, James, 191
Cody, Henry J., 201
COLBORNE, 192
Colborne Lodge, 290
COLDWATER, 241-242
College of Iona, 255
COLLINGWOOD, *242*, 243
Colonial Advocate, 177
Commanda general store, 207
Commissariat building, 196
Commune, first in Canada, 117
Conacher, Lionel, 299
Conant, Gordon D., 31
"Conference Church", Picton, 227
CONN, 316
CONNAUGHT, 21
Connolly, Joseph, 321
CONSECON, 226
CONWAY, 147
Co-operative Union of Canada, 89
Copper mining, prehistoric, 266
CORNWALL, 250-251
Cosens, Aubrey, 25
Cotton factory, 183
Court house: Brant County, 7; Dufferin County, 27; Kent
    County, 113; Norfolk County, 72; Peel County, 211; Simcoe
    County, 238; Wellington County, 319 (*See also* District
    court house and gaol)
COURTICE, 29
Covered bridge, West Montrose, 315
Cowan's trading post, 241

INDEX

CPR, western route of, 272
Craigleith shale oil works, 61
Crawford, Isabella V., 18
Crawford Lake Indian village, 80
Credit Indian village, 213
Credit River dynamo, 80
CROWN HILL, 243
Cruikshank, E.A., 197
Crysler's Farm, battle of, 252
CRYSTAL BEACH, 167
Cumberland, Frederic W., 296
Currelly, Charles T., 299
Currie, Arthur W., 159
Curtiss JN-4 ("Jenny"), *212*

Dafoe, John Wesley, 93
Dalhousie Library, 125
Daunais, Oliver, 271
Dawson, Simon James, 272
Dawson wagon road, 270
De La Roche, Mazo, 327
DELAWARE, 153
DELTA, 133
Denison, Merrill, 99
DESBARATS, 1
DESERONTO, 96
Desjardins Canal, 84
Detroit, siege of, 50
DEUX RIVIÈRES, 235
District capital, Vittoria, 73
District court house and gaol: Brockville, 130; Cornwall, 251;
    L'Orignal, 224; Niagara-on-the-Lake, 173; Parry Sound,
    209; Peterborough, 221; Perth, 127; Picton, 226; Windsor, 48
Dixie Union Chapel, 212
DOG LAKE, 263
DORSET, 76
Dreamer's Rock, 150, *151*
DRESDEN, 113
Dressler, Marie, 192
Drew, Andrew, 205
Drummond, William Henry, 277
Drury, Ernest Charles, 243
Duel, last fatal in Upper Canada, 126
Duff, Lyman Poore, 65
DUFFERIN COUNTY, 27
Dufferin County court house, 27

Dulhut, Daniel Greysolon, Sieur, 273
Dunbar, Charles D., 86
Duncan, Sara J., 11
Duncombe, Charles, 37
Duncombe's uprising, 15
DUNDAS, 83-85
DUNDAS COUNTY. *See* STORMONT, DUNDAS AND GLENGARRY
    UNITED COUNTIES, 250-260
Dundas Mills, 83
Dundurn Castle, 87
Dunlop, William "Tiger", *103*, 104
DURHAM (town), 62
DURHAM REGIONAL MUNICIPALITY, 28-35
Durham Road, 62
Dutch settlement, 328

EAST YORK, 300-301
Eaton, Timothy, 215
Eby, Benjamin, 312
École Guigues, 198
Edison homestead, 40
Edwards, William Cameron, 225
EGMONDVILLE, 101-102
Eildon Hall, 329
Eldon House, 154
ELDORADO, 97
Eldorado Refinery, 195
ELGIN COUNTY, 36-41
Elliot Lake mining camp, 1
Elliott, Matthew, 43
ELORA, 317-318
EMBRO, 201
Erb, Abraham, 314
Erin, founding of, 318
Erin Township, settlement of, 316
ESSEX COUNTY, 42-51
ETOBICOKE, 302-303
Evangelical United Brethren, 314
EXETER, 102
Explorers of Muskoka and Haliburton, 160

Fairfield House, 145
Fathers of Confederation, 295
FENELON FALLS, 306
FERGUS, 318-319
Ferguson, G. Howard, 135

Ferguson Highway, 278

Fetterly House. *See* Prescott Barracks, 139

Field House, 176

Fighting Island, 45

Fires: "Great" (1916), 24; Porcupine, *25*, 26; "Great" (1922), 278

Fisher, Fred, 180

Fleming, Sandford, *222*, 223

FONTHILL, 168

Forest, founding of, 117

Forestry station, first in Canada, 72

FORMOSA, 17

Forsyth's raid, 130

Fort Chippawa, 166

FORT ERIE, 168

FORT FRANCES, 229

Fort Frances Canal, 230

Fort Henry, 58

Fort Kaministiquia, 273

Fort Lac La Pluie, 229, *230*

Fort Niagara, capture of, 176

Fort Rouillé, 282

Fort Schlosser, raid on, 166

Fort William, capture of, 274

Forty-ninth parallel, 21

Forwarding trade at Prescott, 139

Fowler, Daniel, 145

FRANKTOWN, 124-125

FRANKVILLE, 133

Fraser, Simon, 254

"Fraserfield", *259*, 260

Frederick House, 21

French Portage, 231

FRENCH RIVER, 207

French settlement, south shore of Detroit River, 49

Frise, James L., 33

Frontenac, Comte de, 53

FRONTENAC COUNTY, 52-60

Frontenac Road, 60

Fryfogel's Inn, 217

Gallie, William E., 239

Galt, founders of, 311

Galt Grammar School. *See* Tassie's School, 312

Galt, John, 320

GANANOQUE, 133-134

INDEX

Garafraxa Road, 62
Gardiner, James G., 102
Gateway to Huronia, 243
Gaudaur, Jake, 245
GEORGETOWN, 80
Geraldton gold camp, 263
Gibraltar Point, 279
Gibson, David, 304
Gillies Bros. Lumbering Firm, 232
Givins, James, 290
Glacial terraces, 271
Gladman-Hind expedition, 274
Glengarry Congregational Church, 252
GLENGARRY COUNTY. *See* STORMONT, DUNDAS AND
    GLENGARRY UNITED COUNTIES, 250-260
Glengarry emigration, 254
Glengarry Fencibles, 251
GODERICH, 104-105
Gold mine, first in Ontario, 97
Good, William Charles, 12
Gordon, Charles W., 252
Gores Landing, 193
GOULAIS BAY, 2
Government House, Kingston, 55
Government Inn, 214
Gowan, Ogle R., 131
GRAFTON, 193
Grain elevator, first at Lakehead, 271
Grand Portage, 265
Grand River mission, 12
Grand River naval depot, 70
Grant, Alexander, 48
GRAVENHURST, 162-164
Great Dog portage, 263
Great Sauk Trail, 43
Great Western Railway, 49
Greene, Thomas, 79
GREENSVILLE, 85
GRENVILLE COUNTY. *See* LEEDS AND GRENVILLE UNITED
    COUNTIES, 130-142
GREY COUNTY, 61-68
Grey Owl, 188
Griffon, 118
GRIMSBY, 168-169
Grover-Nicholls house, 222
GUELPH, 319-322

INDEX

Gull River, 77
Gzowski, Casimir, 170, *171*

Haggart family, 127
Haines, Frederick S., 65
Haldimand Grant, 69
HALDIMAND-NORFOLK REGIONAL MUNICIPALITY, 69-75
Hale, Horatio E., 101
HALIBURTON, 76-77
Hallowell, founding of, 226
HALTON REGIONAL MUNICIPALITY, 78-82
HAMILTON, 85-89
Hamilton, George, 86
Hamilton Central Public School, 89
HAMILTON-WENTWORTH REGIONAL MUNICIPALITY, 83-92
Hanlan, Ned, 279, *280*
HANOVER, 62
Hardy, Arthur Sturgis, 7
Harris, Lawren, 8
Harriston, founding of, 323
HARTINGTON, 52
Harvey, John, 85
Harwood, 193
Hastings, founding of, 194
HASTINGS COUNTY, 93-99
Hastings Road, 98
Hawkesbury mills, 224
Hawley House, 146
Hay Bay Church, 144
Hearst, William H., 19
HEATHCOTE, 63
"Heathfield", 52
Hellmuth, Isaac, 155
Hémon, Louis, 261
Hennepin, Louis, 170
Henry, George S., 304
Henson, Josiah, house, 113
Hepburn, Mitchell F., 37
Heroine of Long Point, 71
"Hillcroft", 53
Hincks, Francis, 237
HOLLAND LANDING, 325
Holland Marsh, Dutch settlement of, 328
Holleford crater, 52
Holmes, Robert, 29
Holmes, Thomas W., 67

Holstein Friesian cattle, 251
Holy Trinity Church, Chippawa, 166
Holy Trinity Church, Toronto, 288
Honey, S. Lewis, 316
Hoodless, Adelaide Hunter, 15, *91*
HOPEVILLE, 63
Hornell, David E., 303
Hornings Mills, 27
Hornor, Thomas, 204
Howland, William P., 213
HUDSON, 108
Hudson, Henry, 24
Hudson's Bay Company: post at Little Current, 150; union
    with NWC, 275
Hull's Landing, 50
Hunter, Andrew F., 239
Huntington, Silas, 186
HUNTSVILLE, 164-165
Huron Church Reserve, 49
Huron College, 156
HURON COUNTY, 100-107
Huron fish weirs, 246
Huron mission, Windsor, 49
Huron Road, 313
Huronia, gateway to, 243
Hutchison House, 221
HYMERS, 263

Indian flint bed, 117
INGERSOLL, 201
Innis, Harold Adams, 202
Insulin, discovery of, 294
International boundary, 121
Iona College, 255
IPPERWASH PROVINCIAL PARK, 117
IROQUOIS FALLS, 22

James, Thomas, 25
Jameson, Anna, 4, *5*
Jane Miller, loss of, 68
Jarvis Collegiate Institute, 297
Jefferys, C.W., 304
Jessup, Edward, 140
Jesuit mission: Manitoulin, 150; Windsor, 49
Jewish congregation, 300
Johnson, E. Pauline, *13*, 14

INDEX

Johnson, Edward, 321
Johnson, John, mills, 256
Johnston, Donald A., 120
Johnston, Franz, 249
Johnston, "Pirate", 134
Johnstown, 135
Johnstown District court house and gaol, 130
Jones, Augustus, 7
Jones, David Allanson, 240
JONES FALLS, 135
Jones, Peter, 10, *11*
Jones, Solomon, 137
Jones, Thomas Mercer, 104
JORDAN, 169
Jumbo, 39

KAKABEKA FALLS PROVINCIAL PARK, 263
KALADAR, 148
Kama Hill mesa, 266
Kapuskasing, founding of, 22, 23
Keating, James, 246
KEENE, 218
Kelly, J.D., 195
KEMPTVILLE, 135
Kennedy, Thomas Laird, 213
KENOGAMI LAKE, 277
Kenogamissi post, 23
KENORA, 108-111
Kenora Thistles, 109
Kent, sinking of, 46
KENT COUNTY, 112-116
Kent County court house, 113
Kenté mission, 226
Kerr, Bobby, 87
Kerr, George F., 96
Killarney, founding of, 150
King, William Lyon Mackenzie, 313
King's College, 295
King's Royal Regiment of New York, 53
KINGSTON, 52-60
Kingston observatory, 56
KINGSVILLE, 44
KIRBY, 30
Kirby, William, home, 175
KIRKFIELD, 308
Kirkland Lake gold camp, 277

INDEX

KIRKTON, 215
KITCHENER, 312-313
Koerber, Elise von, 208

Lacombe, Albert, 108
La Guayra settlers, 320
Laidlaw, George, *307*, 308
Lake light, Toronto Islands, 279
Lake Nipissing, 207
Lake Superior, first shipyard, 2
Lake Superior trek, 270
LAKEFIELD, 218-220
Lakehead, first grain elevator, 271
Lakehead University, 273
LAMBTON COUNTY, 117-122
LANARK COUNTY, 123-129
Lanark settlement, 125
Lang Mill, 218
Langhorn, John, 146
Langley, Henry, 321
Langton, John, 306
LANSDOWNE, 135
LA SALLE (town), 45
La Salle, René-Robert Cavelier de, 56, 78
LATCHFORD, 278
Laurentian University of Sudbury, 262
La Vase portages, 187
La Vérendrye, Sieur de, 229
Law Society of Upper Canada, 174
Lawson site, 157
Leacock, Stephen B., 329
Leamington, founding of, 46
LEASKDALE, 30
Lee, James Paris, 116
LEEDS AND GRENVILLE UNITED COUNTIES, 130-142
Lefroy, John, 293
LEITH, 63
LENNOX AND ADDINGTON COUNTY, 143-149
LINDSAY, 309
LION'S HEAD, 17
LISTOWEL, 215
LITTLE CURRENT, 150
Little Trinity Church, Toronto, 284
Lloydtown, 325
Locke, Mahlon W., *255*, 256
LONDON, 153-156

INDEX

Long Island Mill, 196
Long Lake trading posts, 264
Long Point: heroine of, 71; portage, 69; settlement, 69
LONG SAULT, 251
Longboat, Tom, 14
LONGLAC, 264
L'ORIGNAL, 224-225
Loring-Wyle studio, 299
Lount, Samuel, 325
Loyalists: Adolphustown, 143; Cataraqui, 57; Upper Canada, 295
LUCAN, 157-158
Lyndhurst, founding of, 136

Macaulay, William, 226
McClung, Nellie, 61
McCullough, C.R., 28
MacDonald, J.E.H., 330
Macdonald, John A., 227
Macdonald, John Sandfield, 255
MacDonald, Wilson Pugsley, 69
Macdonald-Mowat House, 297
Macdonell, Alexander, 54
Macdonell, Miles, 253
McDougall, William, 300
McDowall, Robert J., 143
MacDowell, Thain Wendell, 136
McFarland House, 176
McGillivray, William, 273
Mack Centre of Nursing Education, 181
McKay, Thomas, 197
McKeever, Andrew E., 215
McKenzie, Robert Tait, 123
Mackenzie, Sir William, 308
Mackenzie, William Lyon, 168, 286
Mackenzie house and family, Sarnia, 121
McKinney, Louise C., 133
McLachlin, Daniel, 232, *233*
McLaughlin, R.S. "Sam", 32
McLaughlin, Robert, 33
McLean, John, 320
McLennan, John Cunningham, 217
MacLeod settlement, 250
McMartin House, 128
McMaster Hall, 299
McMaster University, 89

INDEX

MacMillan emigration, 258
McNab settlement, 232
MacPhail, Agnes Campbell, 63
Macpherson House, 148
Madill Church, 165
Madoc, founding of, 97
MAGNETAWAN, 208
Magnetawan River steam navigation, 207
Magrath, James, 213
MAITLAND, 136
Malcolm's Mills, battle of, 13
MALDEN CENTRE, 46
MANITOULIN DISTRICT, 150-152
Manitowaning Indian treaties, 152; mission, 152
MANOTICK, 196
MAPLE, 326
MAPLE LAKE, 76
MARATHON, 265
Markham, founding of, 326
Marmora ironworks, 97
Mary Ward, sinking of, 61
Marysburgh settlement, 228
Massey family, Newcastle, 31
MATHESON, 24
Mattawa House, 185
MAXVILLE, 252
MAYNOOTH, 97
MEAFORD, 63, 65
Mechanics' Institute, first in Ontario, 285
Meeting House, Newmarket, 327
Meighen, Arthur, 216
Memorial Hall, 174
Mennonite settlement, 169
Menten, Maud L., 294
MERRICKVILLE, 137
Merritt, William Hamilton, 180
Methodist Church (Canada, Newfoundland & Bermuda, 1884), 94
Metropolitan United Church, Toronto, 286
Michipicoten canoe route, 6
MIDDLE FALLS PROVINCIAL PARK, 265
MIDDLESEX COUNTY, 153-159
MIDLAND, 243-244
Militia garrison, Kingston, 56
Mill of Kintail, 123
Mills, David, 114

Milne, David, 18
MILTON, 80
Milverton, founding of, 215
MINDEN, 77
Miner, Harry G.B., 112
Miner, Jack, 44, *45*
MINESING, 245
Mission of the Immaculate Conception, Thunder Bay, 274
Mission to the Nipissings, 266
MISSISSAUGA, 211-214
MITCHELL, 216
Moberly, John, 247
Mohawk chapel, 9; Institute, 10; "village", 10
Monck Road, 93
Montgomery, Lucy Maud, 30
Montgomery's Inn, 303
MONTREAL RIVER HARBOUR, 2
Moodie, Robert, 329
Moodie, Susanna, 219
MOORETOWN, 118
Moose Factory, *23*, 24
MOOSONEE, 25
Morenz, Howie, 216
Morris, Alexander, 126
Morris, James, 131
MORRISBURG, 252
Moulton College, 298
MOUNT FOREST, 323
MOUNT HOPE, 90
MOUNT PLEASANT, 12
MOUNTAIN GROVE, 60
Mountain portage, 263
Mowat, Oliver, 54
Muir, John, 67
Mulock, William, 240
MURILLO, 265
MUSKOKA DISTRICT, 160-165
MUSKOKA FALLS, 165
Muskoka Road, 162

NAIRN, 158
Naismith, James, 124
NAPANEE, 148
NAUGHTON, 261
Negro burial ground, 175
Nelles, Robert, 169

Nelles settlement, 75
Neutral Indian burial ground, 168
New Credit Indian Reserve, 12
NEW DUNDEE, 313
New Fairfield, 115
New Hamburg, founding of, 314
Newash Indian village, 66
NEWBORO, 138
NEWBURGH, 148-149
Newbury, founding of, 158
NEWCASTLE, 30-31
NEWMARKET, 327-328
Newmarket radial railway arch, 327
Newspaper, first in Ontario, 173
NEWTON ROBINSON, 245
Niagara Agricultural Society, 173
Niagara escarpment, 89, 179
NIAGARA FALLS, 170
Niagara Library, 172
NIAGARA-ON-THE-LAKE, 172-176
NIAGARA REGIONAL MUNICIPALITY, 166-184
Niagara, Town of, 172
Nicolet, Jean, 186
Nile voyageurs, 198
Nine Mile portage, 238
NIPIGON, 266
Nipigon canoe route, 266
NIPISSING (community), 209
NIPISSING DISTRICT, 185-189
Nipissing mission, 266
Niven's meridian, 21
Nixon, Harry C., 15
Nodwell Indian village site, 18
Norfolk County court house, 72
NORTH BAY, 186-187
NORTH LANCASTER, 253
North West Company: 258; post at Sault Ste. Marie, 4; union
    with HBC, 275
NORTH YORK, 304-305
Northern Railway Company of Canada, *242*, 243
NORTHUMBERLAND COUNTY, 190-195
Northwest Passage, 24, 25
Norwich Quaker settlement, 202
Noyon, Jacques de, 229
Nunney, Claude J.P., 253

INDEX

OAKLAND, 13

OAKVILLE, 81

Octagonal house. *See* Woodchester Villa, *161*, 162

Ogdensburg, capture of, 139

Ohio, capture of, 167

OHSWEKEN, 14

Oil refining industry, 121

"Old" city hall, Toronto, 286

Old Mail Road, 63

Old St. Andrew's Church, Colborne, 192

Old Stage Road, 204

Old Stone Church. *See* St. Andrew's Church, Beaverton, 28

Old Trinity Church, Mooretown, 118

Oliver Township, founding of, 265

Omemee, founding of, 310

ONONDAGA, 14

Ontario Agricultural College, 321

Ontario boundary dispute, 109

Ontario Ladies' College, 35

Ontario Northland Railway, 186, *187*

Ontario School for the Blind, *8*, 9

Ontario School for the Deaf, 95

Ontario Vaccine Farm, 324

Ontario Veterinary College, 322

Opeongo Road, 232, *234*, 236

ORANGEVILLE, 27

ORIENT BAY, 267

ORILLIA, 245-246

ORMSBY, 98

Oro Township, Black settlement, 239

Oronhyatekha, 96

Osgoode Hall, 287

OSHAWA, 31-32

Osler, William, 240

Osnaburgh House, *109*, 110

OTTAWA, 196-199

Ottawa River: rapids, 235; steamboating, 236; timber rafting, 232

OTTAWA-CARLETON REGIONAL MUNICIPALITY, 196-200

OTTERVILLE, 202

Outlaw Bridge, 265

OWEN SOUND, 66-67

OXFORD COUNTY, 201-206

P.L. Robertson Manufacturing Co., 80

Pain Court, 114

INDEX

PAISLEY, 18
Palisades of the Pijitawabik, 267
PALMERSTON, *322*, 323-324
PALMYRA, 114
Paper mill, 85
Paradis, Charles Alfred Marie, 189
PARIS, 14-15
Paris Plains Church, 15
Parish of St. Raphael, 254
Parker, Gilbert, 147
Parkhill, founding of, 158
Parks, William Arthur, 299
PARRY SOUND, 207-210
PASS LAKE, 267
Pearson, John, 17
Pearson, Lester Bowles, 305
Peel County court house, 211
Peel, Paul, 155
PEEL REGIONAL MUNICIPALITY, 211-214
Pelee Island, battle of, 46
PEMBROKE, 236
Pembroke and Mattawan Road, 236
PENETANGUISHENE, 246-247
Penetanguishene Road, 244
PERTH (town), 126-128
PERTH COUNTY, 215-217
Perth military settlement, 126
Perth Road, 142
PETERBOROUGH, 218-223
Peterson Road, 97, 165
Petrolia, founding of, 118, *119*
Philips, James, 139
PHILLIPSVILLE, 139
Philo Parsons incident, 46
Pic fur trading post, 265
Pickering, founding of, 28
Pickford, Mary, 290
PICTON, 226-228
Pierce, Lorne, 133
Pierpoint, Richard, 180
Pigeon River Road, 275
Pijitawabik, palisades of, 267
Pinhey, Hamnet Kirks, 199
POINT ALEXANDER, 236
POINT EDWARD, 118, 120
Point Frederick, 57

INDEX

POINT PELEE NATIONAL PARK, 46
POINTE AUX PINS, 2
Polish settlement, 237
Pope, William, 71
Porcupine fire, 26
Porcupine mining area, 26
PORQUIS JUNCTION, 25
Port Arthur, Duluth and Western Railway Company, 263
PORT BURWELL, 36
Port Carling, 165
Port Colborne, founding of, 177
PORT CREDIT, 214
PORT DOVER, 70
PORT ELGIN, 18
PORT HOPE, 194-195
PORT MAITLAND, 70
Port Robinson, founding of, 177
PORT ROWAN, 71
PORT RYERSE, 71
PORT STANLEY, 36
Portage Road, 308
Potier, Pierre, 48
Precambrian shield, 160, 268
Precious Blood Cathedral, Sault Ste. Marie, 5
Prehistoric copper mining, 266
PRESCOTT, 139-141
PRESCOTT AND RUSSELL UNITED COUNTIES, 224-225
Preston, founder of, 312
Prince, John, 4
PRINCE EDWARD COUNTY, 226-228
Princes' Gates, 281
PRINCETON, 204
Proudfoot, William, 154
Provincial parliament, first, 172
Puisaye, Joseph-Geneviève, Comte de, 176
Puisaye settlement, 328
Purdy's mills, 309
Puslinch Township, settlement of, 324

Quaker meeting house: Newmarket, 327; Uxbridge, *34*, 35
Quaker settlement: Adolphustown, 144; Norwich, 202;
    Whitchurch, 331
Queen Mary Hospital, 302
Queen's Park, *294*, 295
Queen's Plate, 81
Queen's Rangers, 281

INDEX

Queen's University, 57
QUEENSTON, 177–179
QUETICO PROVINCIAL PARK, 231
Quetico-Superior, 231
Quinte mission. *See* Kenté mission, 226

Radial railways, 81
Raid: on Fort Schlosser, 166; on Gananoque, 133; on Sault Ste. Marie, 4
Railway arch, Newmarket, 327
Rainy Lake House. *See* Fort Lac La Pluie, 229, *230*
RAINY RIVER, 229–231
RAITH, 268
Rama Indian Reserve, 238
Rankin, Arthur, 50
Rankin, Charles, 67
Rapelje, Daniel, 38
Rapids of the Upper Ottawa, 235
Rat Portage post, 108
RCAF Technical Training School, 39
Reade, Herbert T., 127
Rectory of Beckwith, 125
Red Lake House, 110
Red Lake mining district, 110
Red Rock, 268
Regiopolis College, 55
Regulation 17, 198
RENFREW, 232–237
Richardson, John, 178
RICHMOND HILL, 328–329
Richmond military settlement, 199
Rideau Canal, *59*, 60, 129
Ridgetown, founding of, 114
Ridley College, 181
Robertson, John Ross, 291
"Ripple Rock", 1
Robertson Manufacturing Co., 80
Robinson settlement, 220
Robinson Superior Treaty, 275
Roblin, Rodmond P., 228
ROCKLAND, 225
ROCKWOOD, 81, 324
"Rockwood", 55
Rockwood Academy, 324
Roebuck Indian village site, 141
Rogers, James, 143

INDEX

Rolph, John, 39
RONDEAU PROVINCIAL PARK, 114
Rosamonds in Almonte, 123
Ross, George W., 158
Ross, P.D., 198
ROSSEAU, 210
Rosseau-Nipissing Road, 208, 209, 210
ROSSPORT, 268
Rousseaux, Jean Baptiste, 302
Route of the voyageurs, 151
Rowe, William E., 245
Royal Canadian College of Organists, 8
Royal Canadian Henley Regatta, 181
Royal Canadian Yacht Club, 279
Royal George, escape of, 147
Royal Military College of Canada, 57
Royal Sappers and Miners, 138
Royal Yorkers. *See* King's Royal Regiment, 53
Roybon d'Allonne, Madeleine de, 145
Rush-Bagot Agreement, 59
RUSSELL COUNTY. *See* PRESCOTT & RUSSELL UNITED COUNTIES, 224-225
Russell, Edith Kathleen, 296
RUTHERFORD, 120
Rutherford, Alexander Cameron, 200
Ryerse, Samuel, 71
Ryerson, Adolphus Egerton, *74*, 75
Ryerson Polytechnical Institute, 292

ST. ANDREWS, 253-254
St. Andrew's Anglican Church, Grimsby, 169
St. Andrew's Church, Beaverton, 28
St. Andrew's Church, Colborne, 192
St. Andrew's Church, L'Orignal, 225
St. Andrew's Church, Maple, 326
St. Andrew's Church, Niagara-on-the-Lake, 173
St. Andrew's Church, St. Andrews, 253
St. Andrew's Church, Toronto, 285
St. Andrew's Church, Williamstown, *257*, 258
St. Andrew's Presbyterian Church, Fergus, 318
Sainte-Anne des Pins, Sudbury, 262
St. Anne's Anglican Church, Toronto, 290
ST. CATHARINES, 179-182
St. Clair Tunnel, 121
St. Davids, burning of, 182
ST. GEORGE, 15

St. James' Cathedral, Toronto, *283*, 284
St. James' Church, Maitland, 136
St. James-on-the-Lines, Penetanguishene, 247
St. John Ambulance, 297
St. Johns, 168
St. John's Anglican Parish, Richmond, 199
St. John's Church, Peterborough, 221
St. John's Church, Windsor, 48
ST. JOSEPH, 105
St. Lawrence Hall, 284
St. Lawrence River, submerged communities, 251
St. Luke's Church, Burlington, 79
Sainte-Marie Among the Hurons, 244
St. Mark's Church, Barriefield, 52
St. Mark's Church, Niagara-on-the-Lake, 175
St. Mark's Church, Port Hope, 194
ST. MARYS, 216
St. Mary's Church, Strathroy, 159
St. Mary's Pro-Cathedral, Hamilton, 88
St. Michael's Cathedral, Toronto, 288
St. Michael's College, 297
St. Paul's Cathedral, London, 155
St. Paul's Church, Cardinal, 132
St. Paul's Church, Hamilton, 88
St. Paul's Church, Minden, 77
St. Paul's Church, Woodstock, 205
St. Paul's H.M. Chapel of the Mohawks, Brantford, 9
St. Peter's Anglican Church, Mississauga, 213
St. Peter's Cathedral Basilica, London, 155
St. Peter's Church, Cobourg, 191
St. Peter's Church, Tilbury Township, 115
St. Peter's Church, Tyrconnell, 40
ST. RAPHAELS, 254-255
St. Stephen-in-the-Fields Anglican Church, Toronto, 293
ST. THOMAS, 37-39
St. Thomas' Church, St. Thomas, 38
St. Thomas' Church, Shanty Bay, 248
ST. WILLIAMS, 72
Salter's meridian, 261
Sangster, Charles, 54
SARNIA, 120-121
Saugeen Indian Treaty, 19
Sauk Trail, 43
SAULT STE. MARIE, 4-6
Savanne portage, 268
Scadding, Henry, 288, *289*

INDEX

Scarborough Bluffs, 301
Schneider, Joseph, house, 313
School on wheels, 101
"Schooner Town", 248
SCHREIBER, 270
Schreiber, Charlotte, 214
Schreiber, Collingwood, 270
Schwerdtfeger, Johann S., 252
Scorpion, capture of, 6
SCOTLAND, 15
SCUGOG ISLAND, 33
Scriven, Joseph M., 218
Scotch settlement, 240
Scott's mills, 220
Scugog route, 309
SEAFORTH, 106
Secord, Laura, 177
Seigneury of L'Orignal, 224
Serpent Mounds, 218
Seton, Ernest Thompson, 309
SHAKESPEARE, 217
SHANTY BAY, 248
Sharon Temple, 329
Shaw, Aeneas, 287
Sheaffe, Roger Hale, 179
SHEBANDOWAN, 270
Shelburne, founding of, 27
Sherring, William, 86
Sherwood, Justus, 140
Shickluna, Louis, 180
Shingwauk Hall, 6
Shipyard, first on Lake Superior, 2
Shuniah, founding of, 271
Sifton, Ellis Wellwood, 41
Silver Islet, 267, *269*
SIMCOE (town), 72
SIMCOE COUNTY, 238-249
Simcoe County court house and gaol, 238
Simcoe, Elizabeth, 298
Simcoe, John Graves, 296
Simpson, B. Napier, Jr., 76
SIOUX LOOKOUT, 111
Skirmishes at the Canard River, 42
Slomans and CNR school on wheels, 101
Smellie, Elizabeth, 274
SMITHS FALLS, 129

Somers and *Ohio*, capture of, 167
SOUTH BUXTON, 115
SOUTHAMPTON, 19
Sparta settlement, 40
Speedy, loss of, 190
Spencer, Hazelton, 147
Spencerville, founding of, 141
Springfield, founding of, 40
"Stamford Park", 170
Standard time, birthplace of, 285
STANLEY, 271
Stanley Barracks, 281
Stanton, Ambrose Thomas, 30
Stayner, founding of, 248
Steam train, first in Ontario, 325
Steamboating: Magnetawan River, 207; Muskoka, 163; Upper
    Ottawa River, 236
Steep Rock iron range, 229
Stevens, Abel, 141
Stewart, Thomas and Frances, 220
STIRLING, 98
Stone, Joel, 134
Stone Church, Hastings, 98
Stone Frigate, 58
STONEY CREEK, 90-91
Stoney Point, founding of, 47
Storm (1913), 105
STORMONT, DUNDAS AND GLENGARRY UNITED COUNTIES, 250-
    260
Stouffville, founding of, 331
Stowe, Emily, 202, *203*
Stowe Gullen, Augusta, 12
Strachan, John, 250
STRATFORD, 217
STRATHROY, 159
Streetsville, 214
Strickland, Samuel, 220
Stuart, Charles, 67
Stuart, John, 53
Sturgeon Falls, founding of, 187
Submerged communities of the St. Lawrence, 251
SUDBURY, 261-262
Sudbury basin, 261; discovery of, 262
"Summerhill", 57
Summers, H. George, 86
SUMMERSTOWN, 256

INDEX

Summit House, 127
SUTTON, 329
SWASTIKA, 278
Swiss settlement, 208

Talbot, Thomas, *37*, 38
Talbot Road, 39
Talfourd, Froome and Field, 120
TARA, 19
Tassie's School, 312
Taylor, Frederick "Cyclone", 19
Tecumseh, founding of, 47
Teeswater, founding of, 19
Telephone business office, first in Canada, 10
TEMAGAMI, 188
Temagami post, 185
TERRACE BAY, 271
THAMESVILLE, 115
Thedford, founding of, 122
THESSALON, 6
Thomson, John, 148
Thomson settlement, 301
Thomson, Tom, 63, *64*
THORNBURY, 67
Thornhill, founding of, 330
THORNLOE, 278
THOROLD, 183
Thousand Islands International Bridge, 134
THUNDER BAY, 263-275
Tiffany, Gideon, 153
Tigress and *Scorpion*, capture of, 6
TILBURY, 115
Tillson, George, 204
TILLSONBURG, 204
Timber rafting, Ottawa River, 232
TIMISKAMING DISTRICT, 276-278
Timiskaming mission, 276
TIMMINS, 26
Todmorden Mills, 300
Topham, Frederick G., 303
TOLEDO, 141
Tolpuddle Martyrs, 157
Toronto General Hospital, 293
Toronto, Grey and Bruce Railway, 27, 66
Toronto Horticultural Society, 292
Toronto Island, 279

INDEX

Toronto Normal School, *291*, 292
TORONTO REGIONAL MUNICIPALITY, 279-305
Toronto, Simcoe and Muskoka Junction Railway Co., 163
Toronto-Sydenham Road, 61
Town hall: Dundas, 84; Gananoque, 134; Ingersoll, 201
Town meeting, first in Ontario, 168
Traill, Catharine Parr, 218, *219*
Trans-Canada Highway, 1
Trent University, 223
Trent-Severn waterway, 308
TRENTON, 99
Trinity Church, Port Burwell, 36
de Troyes expedition, 22
Turner, Asa, 98
Turner, Enoch, school, 282
TWEED, 99
Typhus epidemic, 55
TYRCONNELL. *See* WALLACETOWN, 40-41
TYRONE, 33

Umfreville's exploration, 111
Union of North West and Hudson's Bay Companies, 275
UNIONVILLE, 330
Unitarian congregation, 290
University of Ottawa, 198
University of Waterloo, 315
University of Windsor, 50
Upper Canada College, 300
Upper Ottawa River: rapids, 235; steamboating, 236
Uranium, first discovery, 2
UXBRIDGE, 34-35

Van Egmond, Anthony, 101
Van Egmond House, 102
Van Horne, William C., 272
VERNER, 189
Verner, Frederick A., 81
VERNON, 200
Victoria boat disaster, 156
Victoria College, 191
Victoria Cross, Canada's first, 284
VICTORIA COUNTY, 306-310
Victoria Hall, 192
Victoria Railway, 76
Victoria Road, 309
VIENNA, 40

VINELAND, 184
VITTORIA, 73-75
Vollick, Eileen, 90
von Koerber, Elise, 208
Voyageurs' canoe route, 151

Walkerton, founding of, 20
WALLACEBURG, 116
WALLACETOWN, 40-41
Wallis, James, 306
Walsh, James Morrow, 140
WARKWORTH, 195
Warner, Christian, 182
WASAGA BEACH, 248
Wasdell Falls hydro-electric development, 248
WASHAGO, 248
WATERDOWN, 92
Waterford, founding of, 75
WATERLOO, 311-315
Waterloo Lutheran University, 314
Watson's Mill. *See* Long Island Mill, 196
Waubuno, sinking of, 209
WAUPOOS, 228
WAWA, 6
Welland Canal, 180
Welland Mills, 183
Weller, William, 190
WELLINGTON COUNTY, 316-324
Wellington County court house, 319
West Lake Boarding School, 227
West Montrose covered bridge, 315
Western route of the CPR, 272
Weston, founding of, 302
WESTPORT, 142
Wheat, world championship, 80
When You And I Were Young, Maggie, 90
WHITBY, 35
Whitchurch Quaker settlement, 331
WHITCHURCH-STOUFFVILLE, 331
White Chapel, Picton, 228
Whitefish Lake post, 261
"Whitehern", 87
Whitney, James Pliny, 253
Whitton, Charlotte, 197
WIARTON, 20, 68
Wilberforce settlement, 157

Wilkins expedition, 114
WILLIAMSBURG, 256
WILLIAMSTOWN, 256-260
Williamstown Fair, 260
Willison, John S., 107
Willow Creek depot, 245
"Willowbank", 178
Willson, John, 90
Willson, Thomas "Carbide", 206
WILNO, 237
WINDSOR, 47-51
Windsor, battle of, 47
Wingham, founding of, 106
Wintemberg, William J., 313
Wolseley expedition, 108
Wolverton, Asa, house, 15
Wolverton, Newton, 206
Wolverton Hall, 204
Women's Institute, first, 91
Woodbine Race Course, 286
Woodchester Villa, *161*, 162
WOODSTOCK, 204-206
Woodstock College, 205
Woodsworth, James Shaver, 303
Wycliffe College, 297
WYEBRIDGE, 249
Wyle, Florence. *See* Loring-Wyle studio, 299

Yellowhead, Chief William, 245
York, battle of, 280; second invasion of, 280
York Mills, 304
YORK REGIONAL MUNICIPALITY, 325-331
York University, 305
Youmans, Letitia, 227
Young, James, 312

ZEEP reactor, 235
Zion Evangelical Lutheran Church, Maple, 326
ZURICH, 107